THE SANCTITY OF LIFE
AND THE CRIMINAL LAW

THE SANCTITY OF LIFE AND THE CRIMINAL LAW
is an expanded and revised version of a series of
five lectures delivered at the Columbia University School of Law in the James S. Carpentier
Series by Glanville L. Williams in April 1956.
These lectures were the 15th in a series established in 1903 by General Horace W. Carpentier
of the Class of 1848 Law in honor of his brother.
General Carpentier expressed the desire that the
lecturers be "chosen for pre-eminent fitness and
ability" and that "this lectureship will be made
so honorable that nobody, however great or distinguished, will willingly choose to
decline your invitation."

Previous lectures in this series have been
given by

1904–5	JAMES BRYCE, VISCOUNT BRYCE
1907–8	JOHN CHIPMAN GRAY
1910–11	ARTHUR LIONEL SMITH
1910–11	DAVID JAYNE HILL
1911–12	SIR FREDERICK POLLOCK
1913–14	SIR COURTENAY ILBERT
1916–17	HAROLD DEXTER HAZELTINE
1919–20	WILLARD BARBOUR
1923–24	SIR PAUL VINOGRADOFF
1926–27	SIR WILLIAM SEARLE HOLDSWORTH
1927–28	BENJAMIN NATHAN CARDOZO
1940–41	SIR CECIL THOMAS CARR
1955	EDMUND MORRIS MORGAN
1955	THOMAS REED POWELL

The Sanctity of Life

and the Criminal Law

BY

GLANVILLE WILLIAMS

WITH A FOREWORD BY

WILLIAM C. WARREN

ALFRED A. KNOPF: *NEW YORK*

1 9 7 2

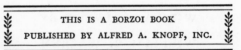

Error of opinion may be tolerated when reason is left free to combat it.

THOMAS JEFFERSON

FOREWORD

BY WILLIAM C. WARREN

IT IS MY GREAT PLEASURE to commend to members of the
Bar—and to other thoughtful readers—this book based on
lectures delivered by Glanville Williams last Spring at
Columbia University and at the Association of the Bar of
the City of New York in the James S. Carpentier Series.

These lectures were unusually well attended and aroused
great interest and discussion in University circles where
audiences are sometimes surfeited by the lavish intellectual
fare so generously and continuously proffered. The author
deals with his subject, "the Sanctity of Life and the Criminal Law," in dimensions at once legal, medical, and
moral, and brings to bear on each aspect uncommon de-
tachment and scholarship. The whole is leavened by that
wit and discernment which we have come to expect of
our British lecturers.

We were aware during the oral presentation of these
lectures that limitations of time had set irksome bounds
upon the full development of the subject so rich in content
that the lecturer had plainly studied profoundly and extensively. It is therefore gratifying that in preparing this
book for publication Professor Williams has been able to
give us a full and satisfying treatment of the difficult and
challenging subject he has chosen.

Since their inauguration in 1904 when James Bryce was
the speaker, the Carpentier lectures have brought to our
Law School numerous distinguished scholars from Great
Britain. This volume bears ample testimony that Glanville
Williams is of this tradition. The issues raised herein
touch upon the very meaning of life and are, therefore,
immediately controversial. It is a particular tribute to
Glanville Williams that he has the courage to discuss all

aspects of his subject and the discretion to deal fairly and
objectively with matters of extreme delicacy.

William C. Warren

Kent Hall,
Columbia University,
November 1956

PREFACE

IT IS CUSTOMARY in a preface to give any necessary explanation of the nature of the work. This, then, is a book of legal argument, of social history, of philosophy and biblical texts. It is a book about the conflict between the ideals of happiness and holiness; about the way in which morals become entangled with semantics; about the humanitarian impulses of medical men, and the anxiety neuroses to which these give rise in the sister professions of theology and law; about the alternate fears of mankind that the human race will dwindle out of existence or fill the planet to bursting point. It treats of monsters and morons, reproduction and repression, eugenics and euthanasia, original sin and the origin of the soul. The connecting thread is the extent to which human life, actual or potential, is or ought to be protected under the criminal law of the English-speaking peoples.

These problems of legal biology and legal ethics involve me in many risky trespasses outside the lawyer's proper sphere, and heavy indebtedness to the specialists in other disciplines from whom I have drawn. My justification, as a lawyer, for extending my discussion to the moral, religious, medical, social, eugenic, demographic, and penological aspects of the subject is that they are important not only in considering the political question of possible changes in the law but also in the approach one makes to its present administration. In some respects the law is doubtful, and the way in which a judge resolves these doubts may depend upon his outlook and understanding of the problems involved. But, for the most part, a new approach to the legal protection of human life would need the aid of the legislature, and here it is essential to secure an informed public opinion.

The main theme of the book may be simply stated. Much of the law of murder rests upon pragmatic con-

siderations of the most obvious kind. Law has been called
the cement of society, and certainly society would fall to
pieces if men could murder with impunity. Yet there are
forms of murder, or near-murder, the prohibition of which
is rather the expression of a philosophical attitude than
the outcome of social necessity. These are infanticide,
abortion, and suicide. Each extends the disapprobation of
murder to particular situations which raise special legal,
moral, religious, and social problems. The prohibition of
killing imposed by these three crimes does not rest upon
considerations of public security. If it can be justified at
all, this must be either on ethico-religious or on racial
grounds. There are related problems, all of them highly
prickly in the present state of opinion. To what extent
should the procreation of children be controlled by law?
What should be the legal attitude to sterilization and artificial insemination? To what extent can the law effectively, and to what extent should it properly, penalize one
who, perhaps from motives of humanity, kills another
with his consent? I have attempted to keep the treatment
objective by dealing fully, and I hope accurately, with the
factual background—the present law, the movement of
thought before and after the law was established, and the
wider issues raised by the law; but being objective does
not mean being impartial, and I have not refrained from
the expression of opinion on issues that are still controversial.

In thanking the Trustees of the Carpentier Lecture
Fund and the Faculty of Law of Columbia University for
giving me the opportunity to deliver the lectures on which
the book is founded, I should like particularly to express
my lively sense of their liberal outlook in allowing me to
broach these matters in public discussion under their auspices. In the exchanges of opinion, both public and private, that followed my lectures, I found that although my
own solutions naturally provoked differences of opinion,
even those members of the audience who belonged to

religious communities holding pronounced views were anxious to discuss the social problems involved with a welcome measure of factual objectivity. They did not— and this gave me much satisfaction—challenge the right of even the most outspoken discussion of these moral questions which concern every one of us so deeply.

Glanville Williams

Kent Hall,
Columbia University,
June 1956

CONTENTS

THE SANCTITY OF LIFE
AND THE CRIMINAL LAW

I

THE PROTECTION OF HUMAN LIFE

The definition of human life

The seemingly simple injunction not to kill, like every other moral, religious, and legal rule, involves us in a problem of interpretation. We may, it is conceded in Christian countries, kill any of the lower animals, at least if this is necessary for human welfare. We may not, generally, kill human beings. But what is a human being is not so simple a question as it may sound.

In common sense, in everyday speech, and in religious thought, man is a discrete entity. The individual man has a body, which we recognize as in some sense continuous and identical even though its chemical constituents are always being replaced. He has a mind and personality, which are demonstrably different from those of his parents. The personality ends dramatically, at least in a terrestrial sense, at death.

Scientific investigation blurs the edges of this sharp picture. To the eye of science, nature is a continuum, and man, like everything else, is part of a process. Man's beginning in the union of two germinal cells, and his development in the body of his mother, is quite evidently a process, and we have lately become aware that death is a process too. The medical difficulty of deciding whether a person is dead has long been known;[1] what

[1] As in the case of the "suspended animation" of the practitioner of Yogi, and sometimes of the new-born infant. There are celebrated and disconcerting instances of mistaken certification, as of the man in Belgium who was found in the mortuary seated on top of his coffin, not only alive but very hungry. See C. T. Polson: *The Essentials of Forensic Medicine* (London, 1955), p. 2.

3

has more recently become appreciated is that the problem lies not merely in the interpretation of symptoms, but in deciding what we mean by death. It is said that an animal begins to die when it begins to live, because its recuperative power dwindles gradually with age. But the problem of drawing a line in "the cold gradations of decay" appears in cruder form when medical means are used to revive the heart. It is not uncommon, when a patient's heart stops in hospital, that it is revived by mechanical means or by the injection of adrenalin. Generally these measures must be undertaken with great promptitude, because a stoppage of the heart for even a few minutes causes extensive damage to the brain— then, even if the patient is kept "alive," he is without brain, having merely an automatic heart-beat and respiration. But if special precautions are taken, this result may be avoided. Not long ago a woman's heart stopped beating on the operating-table for fifty minutes, during which she was given oxygen, blood, adrenalin, atropine, and massage; at the end of the time she was fully revived.[2]

This medical practice obviously raises an entirely novel problem of definition. Its religious aspects were explored in Pirandello's play *Lazzaro,* set in an Italian village, where the population temporarily lost its simple faith because a man who was revived after his heart had stopped beating could not recall having been in paradise. An interesting legal problem can likewise be devised: suppose that when a rich man's heart stops, and as the physician is about to attempt to revive him, his heir plunges a dagger into his breast in order to make sure that he is not restored to life. Is such an act the murder of a living man, or a mere unlawful interference with a corpse? The answer to the question obviously depends upon the legal definition of death. Is it death in law

[2] *Reader's Digest,* May 1955. Cf. J. D. Ratcliff: "The 'Stopped Heart' Operation in Surgery," *Reader's Digest,* July 1956.

when the heart stops beating? If so, there can be life on this earth after death. But perhaps death is only when the heart stops beating beyond the known limit of medical recall. On this view, we cannot tell whether a man is dead or merely in a state of suspended animation, until such time has elapsed as puts revivification out of the question. But such a definition would introduce some indeterminacy into the time of death.

The meaning of "born alive"

The question just posed is at present more of a legal curiosity than an ethical or social problem. However, when we look at the beginning of man's span, problems of greater practical interest appear. The rule of the common law is that the full protection conferred by the law of murder applies only to human beings who are born alive.[3] The fetus is given a lesser degree of protection by the law of abortion. This limitation upon the law of murder involves the law in giving a meaning to birth, and particularly to live birth; and both these matters—birth and life—are capable of giving rise to great difficulties.

The meaning of birth is taken in the English cases to mean complete extrusion from the body of the mother. The umbilical cord need not have been severed, but no part of the child must remain within the parts of the mother if it is to be regarded as born. Thus if the child is deliberately throttled when only its head is protruding,

---

[3] There is, however, a curious rule by which an attempted abortion may turn itself into murder. If a person intending to procure abortion (i.e., to kill the fetus) does an act that causes the child to be born alive in such a state that it is incapable of continuing to live, and it dies, the act is murder.

5

this is not murder according to the English authorities.[4] The consequence seems so absurd that there has been a movement to deny it. Stanley Atkinson, in a learned study published in the *Law Quarterly Review* in 1904, suggested a new definition to cover the case. He thought that "it should be held that a viable child in the process of being born is a human being within the meaning of the homicide statutes, whether or not the process of birth has been fully completed. It should at least be considered a human being where it is a living baby and where in the natural course of events a birth which is already started would naturally be successfully completed." [5] His opinion has been judicially adopted in California and Alabama,[6] but not hitherto in England, so that American law on this point seems now to be different from the English. Even in England, the rule of the common law has been robbed of most of its practical importance by the child-destruction statute, which makes the killing of a viable fetus a special offence. It will be considered in a moment.

The question of live birth is of still greater difficulty than that of birth: there is the difficulty of diagnosis, and the difficulty of deciding what one means by life. In any normal birth, the child must have been alive to start the birth; but it may die naturally in the course of being born, and then it cannot be killed—for the notion of killing involves the assumption that what is killed is at that instant alive. Thus the prosecution must prove that the child was alive at the moment of the act of destruction. The question of life, however, according to the weight of nineteenth-century authority, is rather

[4] Nor is it abortion, for this offence is committed only when the embryo, fetus, or child is induced to miscarry or be prematurely born. Abortion is inapplicable when the child is born in the natural course. See 20 *Law Quarterly Review*, at 157 (1904).

[5] "Life, Birth and Live-Birth," 20 *L.Q. Rev.* 134 (1904).

[6] People v. Chavez, 77 Cal. App. 2d 621, 176 P. 2d 92 (1947); followed in Singleton v. State, 33 Ala. App. 536, 35 S. 2d 375 (1948).

involved with that of birth, because it is laid down that the child, to be accounted as born alive, must have a circulation "independent of the mother." [7] This formula, though it is still heard in the courts and repeated in American and English legal works, may be founded on a mistake of the physical facts, since already within a month of conception the embryonic heart is maintaining the fetal blood-stream, which at no stage is directly communicating with the maternal blood.[8] It seems obvious from this that the phrase "independent of the mother" fails to place any effective qualification upon the word "circulation," unless the phrase is read in some special sense. In practice the tests of postnatal life adopted are the inflation of the lungs with air and the continued action of the heart. The two tests are capable of yielding opposite conclusions, and it is, therefore, of some importance to decide between them. It is generally true to say that before birth, and even perhaps for some short time after, the child does not breathe air, oxygen being obtained instead through the birth-cord, which is connected with the afterbirth. When the afterbirth is detached from the womb the child is compelled to breathe in order to sustain its life. Breathing (that is to say, breathing air) has always been taken as evidence of life, and breathing is itself traditionally evidenced by the uttering of a cry. However, a positive requirement of breathing would leave a sizable gap in the protection of the infant, because it is recorded of some infants that they have not breathed air until after vigorous treatment and great delay. Consequently the rule is that breathing is not necessary. As an English court said in 1834, "if a

[7] The English cases are discussed by Atkinson in 20 *L.Q. Rev.* 134 (1904); D. R. S. Davies in 1 *Modern Law Review,* at 206–8 (1937) (reprinted in *The Modern Approach to Criminal Law* [London, 1948], pp. 304–7); Winfield in 4 *University of Toronto Law Journal* 278 (1942) (reprinted in 8 *Cambridge Law Journal,* at 79 [1942]).

[8] Atkinson: op. cit., at 152–4; Taylor: *Medical Jurisprudence,* 9th ed., II, 173.

child has been wholly born, and is alive, it is not essential that it should have breathed at the time it was killed." [9] This negative rule leaves us to search for some other and more conclusive test of life. It may be thought to be sufficient to show that the child's heart has continued to function after parturition. But this, again, may be regarded as inconsistent with the judicial requirement that the child should have had an "independent circulation." If the child does not breathe, its existence is dependent on the birth-cord, through which its blood-stream is passing in both directions, and so long as the birth-cord is pulsating in this way, the child may be held not to have either an independent circulation or (if that test be rejected) a separate existence.

As if these were not difficulties enough, the question of live birth is usually complicated by deficiencies in the evidence. Since the physician is unlikely to have been present at the time of the alleged live birth and murder, the medical evidence will have to be derived from the autopsy examination. But it will often be impossible to tell with certainty from the autopsy whether such signs of life as are found to have been left in the infant's body show life after birth or only life before birth. It used to be thought that microscopy of the lung afforded reliable evidence of breathing after birth, but it is now accepted that the fetus before birth makes positive respiratory movements which, contrary to previous tenets, expand the lung and create a microscopy very closely similar to that of the newborn who has breathed air.[1] Nor is it conclusive to show that the child has breathed air, because that may have happened during the act of separation (which in England at any rate is regarded as being before birth), or even (in rare cases) while the child is still in the womb. An instance is on record where birth

[9] R. v. Brain, 6 C. & P. 349, 172 Eng. Rep. 1272.
[1] Keith Simpson, ed.: *Modern Trends in Forensic Medicine* (London, 1953), p. 13.

8

was being induced, and after air had passed into the womb the fetus was heard to cry three times in the womb, before being born twelve hours later.[2] It is said by one medical authority that full aeration of the lungs is reliable evidence of live birth [3] (though not the mere fact that they fill the pleural cavity).[4] However, this cannot be taken as authoritative on the legal issue, because the medical definition of live birth differs from the legal one. In medical works, respiratory action of the child whether initiated partly within or wholly without the maternal parts is taken to be indicative of live birth,[5] but this is not the legal view, for as a matter of law what happens before birth cannot indicate the position after birth. What the law requires is life after birth, not life before birth. This difference between legal and medical terminology is capable of giving rise to misunderstanding when medical evidence is given in court.

I have dwelt at this length upon the definition of live birth not in order to suggest a simple solution, nor merely because of the medico-legal interest of the problem, but principally because it illustrates one of the leading themes of this book, the rather arbitrary nature of legal and moral lines. It may be said that in morals the question of the time of birth raises no problem, because the infant is morally a person before birth and should be protected as such. However, this view would merely put the difficulty of drawing a line back a stage. I shall come to this when dealing with the law of abortion.

To return to the present subject, even if live birth is established the pathologist is often under a difficulty in distinguishing between death from natural causes and death from criminal acts. Here, again, medical diagnosis is now thought to have frequently erred in the past:

[2] Simpson: op. cit., p. 15.
[3] Simpson: op. cit., pp. 33–4.
[4] Ibid., p. 36.
[5] John Glaister: *Medical Jurisprudence and Toxicology,* 9th ed. (Edinburgh, 1950), p. 399.

9

"there is little doubt," says Keith Simpson, "that many babies thought to have died from over-lying have really died from some other acute disease such as acute bronchiolitis or bronchopneumonia."[6] The slightest deficiency in the evidence is likely to result in an acquittal, because not only juries but appellate courts are generally reluctant to convict a mother of the murder of her newly born child, and strain to take a view of the evidence favourable to an acquittal. Sometimes a jury will acquit in face of the clearest evidence.

Concealment of birth

An early legislative attempt to deal with this triple difficulty of law, proof, and sentiment was the statutory offence of concealment of birth. The ruling English statute is the Offences against the Person Act, 1861, s. 60, which makes it a crime to endeavour to conceal the birth of a child (whether it is still or live born) by a secret disposition of its dead body. The maximum punishment is the very severe one of imprisonment for life; under the original statute of 1623[7] it was death. The legislation has been adopted in other common-law countries, including some American states, though generally with a much lower maximum punishment—in New

[6] Simpson: op. cit., p. 51. The general point is well illustrated by Table 4 given on pp. 20–1 of Simpson's work. The importance of post-mortem examination by an expert pathologist, and the unreliability of circumstantial evidence in the absence of such a post-mortem, is well brought out by W. H. Davison in (1945) 2 *British Medical Journal* 251; Werne and Garrow in 37 *American Journal of Public Health* 674 (1947); and Orrahood in *Legal Medicine*. Gradwohl, ed., (1954), pp. 350–61. I am indebted for these and many other medical references of which I have made use, and for valuable comments, to Dr. John Havard, of Lowestoft, England.

[7] 21 Jac. 1, c. 27.

York, for example, the maximum for a first conviction is generally one year's imprisonment.[8]

There are two views about the legislation, an English judge condemning it as creating "an imaginary crime,"[9] and an American professor regarding it as "a very practical approach to the problem of child killing."[1] Perhaps the better view lies between these extremes. It is certainly wise to forbid the irregular disposal of human bodies, as, for example, by unauthorized cremation. This, however, is a mere administrative, not a moral, offence. It is juridically objectionable to make the breach of such a regulation an excuse for punishing for the unproved crime of homicide—which is what seems to be envisaged by the severe punishment mentioned in the English Act.

The anomaly of the offence of concealment of birth is heightened by the presence, in the statute books of all jurisdictions, of a minor offence of failing to register the birth, or disposing of a dead body without the proper formalities, such as the authority of the Registrar.[2] The existence of this statutory offence, which is specifically directed to the public notification of births, seems to remove any justification for continuing the misdirected offence of concealment of birth.

The special offence of child destruction

A more satisfactory approach to the problem of evidence is the English statute creating a special offence of feticide, called child destruction. This was proposed in England by bills of 1867 and 1874, and by the Draft

[8] N.Y. Penal Law ss. 492, 1937, 2461; but cf. Correction Law s. 203.
[9] Pollock B., quoted in Kenny: *Outlines of Criminal Law* (Turner, ed., 1952), p. 149.
[1] Perkins in 36 *Journal of Criminal Law and Criminology* 394 (1946).
[2] E.g., New York Public Health Law ss. 4102, 4130, 4144, 4160.

Code of 1879, s. 212, but it did not reach the English statute book until 1929.[3] The legislation penalizes the destruction of unborn infants and infants not completely born. It thus straddles part of the law of abortion and the no man's land between abortion and murder, and obviates some of the difficulties connected with the proof of birth without exempting the prosecution from having to prove an act of killing with the requisite mental state (*mens rea*). The new offence also facilitates conviction by refraining from using the term "murder" and withholding the extreme penalty. The offence is a felony punishable with imprisonment for life. It is committed by "any person who, with intent to destroy the life of a child capable of being born alive, by any wilful act causes a child to die before it has an existence independent of its mother." This definition makes child destruction overlap abortion, the differences being that abortion covers the whole period of gestation, child destruction only the latter part, when the fetus is viable;[4] while, on the other hand, child destruction is possible after birth has started, an event that may make abortion inapplicable. The statute does not assist the prosecution to prove its case where the defence is that the child was already dead before the alleged act of destruction; consequently, it does not help on the difficult matter of defining and ascertaining life. In the United States there is no special legislation of this kind. In New York the wilful killing of an unborn quick child is made manslaughter in the first degree, but only when the killing is accomplished by an injury committed upon the person

[3] Infant Life Preservation Act. The measure had earlier been adopted into the Transkeian (Native Territories') Penal Code by the Cape Act No. 24 of 1886, s. 164.

[4] "Capable of being born alive" in the Act clearly means capable of being born alive if delivered at the time when the act was done. The Act provides that evidence that a woman was pregnant for twenty-eight weeks shall be *prima facie* evidence that she was pregnant of a child capable of being born alive.

of the mother.[5] Consequently, this offence cannot be charged when the act is performed immediately upon the child. Apparently the courts will solve most practical questions by fixing the time of birth earlier than is done in the English cases; this will make the mother guilty of murder, though only if it can be shown that the fetus was alive after birth had started.

It may be added that the incidence of infanticide or neonaticide has been greatly reduced, both in the United States and in Britain, by the general use of maternity hospitals, where the mother is under observation and will be separated from her baby or closely attended if she appears to be suffering from a dangerous neurosis or psychosis. It is probably for this reason that in the state of New York the crime of infanticide has, I am told, become so rare as to be almost unknown.

The legal evaluation of infanticide

Far more important than matters of definition and legal evidence is the problem of treatment when a mother kills her own child. An initial question is our moral reaction to this act. Do we regard it as an ordinary murder, or as something more venial?

Social anthropologists distinguish between infanticide and murder. Infanticide is the killing of a new-born child committed by the parents or with their consent. The killing of another man's child is, according to this definition, simple murder; it is the killing by or on behalf of the parent that raises special problems.[6]

Many primitive peoples practised infanticide (along with contraception and abortion) as a means of popula-

[5] N.Y. Penal Law s. 1050.
[6] See *Encylopaedia of the Social Sciences*, s.v. "Infanticide."

tion control. Infanticide is a more crude and wasteful method of keeping down numbers than contraception. On the other hand, if we put aside ethical considerations for a moment, infanticide has the advantage that it does not endanger the mother, as unskilled abortion does, and as some primitive contraceptive practices are capable of doing.

Non-Christian peoples are frequently found to resort to infanticide not merely from sheer necessity but from considerations of convenience, such as the woman's fear that her husband may be faithless while she is nursing the child. Even such sophisticated folks as the Greeks and Romans of classical times, as well as some of the Germanic tribes, practised infanticide for prudential reasons, where the uncontrolled growth of the family would have left the parents less able to provide for the established children. Among nearly all people who give the parent this *jus vitæ necisque,* the decision has to be made at birth, and is in some cultures rendered easier by not counting the child as a full human being or a member of the tribe until some ceremony has been performed. Thus in Athens the child could be exposed before the Amphidromia, a family ceremony at which the child was carried by its nurse around the hearth and thus received religious consecration and its name.[7]

What seems appalling to the modern mind about the behaviour of the Athenian Greeks of the classical age, and of the Romans, too, is perhaps not so much their custom of getting rid of newly born children for whom they could not provide, as the means they adopted for doing so. The practice of exposing the baby meant that

[7] *Enc. Soc. Sci.,* s.v. "Infanticide"; Westermarck: *The Origin and Development of the Moral Ideas* (London, 1906), I, 393ff.; Lecky: *History of European Morals,* 3rd ed. (London, 1911) 24ff.; W. W. Tarn: *Hellenistic Civilization,* 3rd ed. (London, 1930), pp. 92, 100; Cameron in 46 *Classical Review* 105 (1932); William L. Westermann: *The Slave Systems of Greek and Roman Antiquity* (Philadelphia, 1955), p. 86.

death was the most merciful fate that might befall it; often the child might be picked up by someone, and reared for slavery or prostitution. This appalling callousness and want of parental feeling, as it seems to us, was not condemned by any writer; Plato and Aristotle positively approved of it, at least for weakly and deformed children. "Habit," wrote Sir J. R. Seeley, "dulls the sense and puts the critical faculty to sleep. The fierceness and hardness of ancient manners is apparent to us, but the ancients themselves were not shocked by sights which were familiar to them. To us it is sickening to think of the gladiatorial show, of the massacres common in Roman warfare, of the infanticide practised by grave and respectable citizens, who did not merely condemn their children to death, but often in practice, as they well knew, to what was still worse—a life of prostitution and beggary. The Roman regarded a gladiatorial show as we regard a hunt; the news of the slaughter of two hundred thousand Helvetians by Cæsar or half a million Jews by Titus excited in his mind a thrill of triumph; infanticide committed by a friend appeared to him a prudent measure of household economy."

The change in moral outlook was very largely, if not entirely, the work of the church; it proceeded partly from an interpretation of the Sixth Commandment, and partly from the theological doctrine of the soul. The last needs a word of explanation. The mere supposition that the newly born child had a soul could not have given rise to a prohibition of infanticide, since, even if the child had a soul, and even if it were further supposed that souls after death were divinely punished for sin (either by pain or by annihilation), the soul of a child killed shortly after birth could evidently not be punished for any sin committed during life, because it had had no opportunity of sinning. From this point of view, infanticide might have been regarded as a positive benefit to the child, in excluding the possibility of damnation.

Christian theology countered this argument in advance by adopting the theory of an original sin that could be removed only by baptism. Adam sinned by breaking God's commandment, and this sin vitiated his seed and so was transmitted to his children and his children's children; Christ the Redeemer offered the opportunity of escape from the consequences of sin, both original and acquired; but the ceremony of baptism was the essential cure for original sin. If a child died after baptism he was capable of going to heaven; if before, he was condemned at best to eternal death.

There were, indeed, always some theologians who disputed this opinion, holding that a loving God would punish a person only for his own sin, and not for the sin of Adam; but their opinion was powerfully and effectually combated by St. Augustine of Hippo.[8] According to Augustine, every man who is born, whether in wedlock or even in fornication or adultery, is God's work; but he is born damned, born into the grasp of the devil, unless he is lucky enough to be baptized before death.

The real sin in slaying a newly born child, then, was not so much depriving it of life, as depriving it of the opportunity of baptism, whereby its soul passed without salvation, with all that implied for the life to come. It followed from this opinion that killing a newly born child was a worse sin than killing a baptized adult.[9]

Although St. Augustine is still regarded with great

[8] Augustine's principal writings on the subject were his *On the Baptism of Infants* and *On the Grace of Christ and on Original Sin*. Among the texts that he quoted were Rom. v., 12 ("Wherefore, as by one man sin entered the world, and death by sin; and so death passed upon all men, for that all have sinned"); John iii, 5 ("Except a man be born of water and of the Spirit, he cannot enter into the kingdom of God"). Augustine was, of course, well aware of other texts which he might have used to support the opposite conclusion, e.g., the passages in Jeremiah and Ezekiel asserting that if the fathers have eaten sour grapes, the children's teeth will not be set on edge.

[9] Lecky: *History of European Morals*, 3d ed. (London, 1911), pp. 23–4; Westermarck: op. cit., 411–12.

veneration in the Roman Church, and his doctrine has never been explicitly disavowed, it is not always actively maintained. St. Thomas Aquinas suggested the possibility of salvation for an infant who died before its birth,[1] and it is not a long step from this to admitting salvation for the infant who dies unbaptized. The story of Adam has, since Darwin, come to be recognized as allegorical, and when biologists outside the Soviet sphere are firm against the inheritance of acquired characteristics, the doctrine of original sin might seem to be deprived of its last vestige of rational support. It is true that neither the doctrine of original sin nor the practice of infant baptism has been totally abandoned by those churches that have been accustomed to profess them;[2] but most Protestants now look upon baptism as a traditional way of affirming a religious belief rather than as a necessary step for the receipt of divine grace. At the least it may be said that the ancient ideas are no longer regarded with the assurance that makes them an acceptable support for a rule of the criminal law. Criminal prohibitions cannot, at the present day, be founded upon supernaturalism of any kind. It is true, again, that the idea that the killing of any human being is in some way a sinful interference with the divine purpose persists, but the former religious view of infanticide seems now to be a strange inversion of values. Infanticide appears to our generation to be a crime less heinous than ordinary murder. Even if there is no social justification for the act, the killing of babies who are not old enough to experience fear is different from the murder of adults. This

[1] Lecky: *History of the Rise and Influence of the Spirit of Rationalism in Europe* (London, 1904), I, 360, n. 2.

[2] A survival of the older ideas may be seen in the English Book of Common Prayer, which forbids the burial service to all who die unbaptized—even though infants—as well as to those who die excommunicate or have laid violent hands upon themselves. In the American Book of Common Prayer the first prohibition applies only to unbaptized adults.

opinion was well and courageously expressed by Mercier, an English physician, in 1911.

In comparison with other cases of murder, a minimum of harm is done by it. . . . The victim's mind is not sufficiently developed to enable it to suffer from the contemplation of approaching suffering or death. It is incapable of feeling fear or terror. Nor is its consciousness sufficiently developed to enable it to suffer pain in appreciable degree. Its loss leaves no gap in any family circle, deprives no children of their breadwinner or their mother, no human being of a friend, helper or companion. The crime diffuses no sense of insecurity. No one feels a whit less safe because the crime has been committed. It is a racial crime, purely and solely. Its ill effect is not on society as it is, but in striking at the provision of future citizens, to take the place of those who are growing old; and by whose loss in the course of nature, the community must dwindle and die out, unless it is replenished by the birth and upbringing of children.[3]

In this passage Mercier evidently puts aside religious eschatology and considers infanticide exclusively from a secular or utilitarian point of view. Even granting this assumption, however, not everyone will agree with his concluding remark that infanticide is in fact a racial crime, or, if it is a racial crime, that this is the only secular reason for its place in the law. Whether infanticide is racially an evil depends on the demographic situation at the time—in conditions of overpopulation infanticide is a positive benefit to existing society. But there is another reason for suppressing child-slaying within the utilitarian ethic, namely that the happiness of the child is to be considered. Worldly happiness, after

[3] Mercier: *Crime and Insanity* (London, 1911), pp. 212–13; cf. his *Crime and Criminals* (London, 1918), pp. 193–4. Much the same argument had earlier been propounded by Bentham (*Theory of Legislation,* p. 264).

For an argument that the approach to child-killing should be social, e.g., by assisting the unmarried mother, see J. W. Jeudwine: *Observations on English Criminal Law* (London, 1920), Chap. 10.

The Protection of Human Life

all, is impossible without a life in which to enjoy it. It is worth observing that utilitarianism, though it originated as a secular system of ethics, is not devoid of a metaphysical foundation. As an ethical theory it depends upon an intuited premise, namely that the greatest happiness of the greatest number of human beings is the supreme good. This intuited premise or categorical imperative may be given any one of a number of interpretations, according to the opinion of the particular moralist who puts it forward. For example, the premise may assert that every child, once born, is entitled to its portion of happiness; or the premise may even accord moral rights to unborn children. On the other hand, it may take a restrictive view and make the moral question depend on the prospect of happiness enjoyed by the particular infant. According to the latter interpretation, severely handicapped infants may rightfully be put to death. General opinion is certainly far from taking this opinion at the present time, and all religions with any pretence to an ethical content are firmly against it. Even the modern infidel tends to give his full support to the belief that it is our duty to regard all human life as sacred, however disabled or worthless or even repellent the individual may be. This feeling, among those who do not subscribe to any religious faith, may sometimes be in fact a legacy of their religious heritage. Although morals need not logically depend on a transcendental faith, the system of morals professed in a society with a long religious tradition is likely to be coloured by that religion.

I am not clear in my own mind that this general opinion, whether religious or secular, on the subject of the sanctity of life justifies the punishment of a mother who, finding that she has given birth to a viable monster or an idiot child, kills it. I venture to doubt whether society has the right to stand in judgment upon a mother placed in this terrible predicament. We need to remember that toleration is a virtue, and that even a strictly moral person may be flexible in his morality, exercising his judgment upon the facts of the particular case and not looking exclusively to the rules of a legalistic ethic. Regarded in this spirit, an eugenic killing by a mother, exactly paralleled by the bitch that kills her mis-shapen puppies, cannot confidently be pronounced immoral. And where this certainty is lacking, should not liberty prevail?

However, even if this suggestion is not immediately put aside as impossibly wicked, there are difficulties in providing for the situation by law. Any acceptable scheme for the euthanasia of severely handicapped babies would involve the co-operation of the medical profession, which might not be forthcoming; in any case the proposal would occasion acute religious conflict. The most practicable course is, therefore, to recognize the condition of the child killed by the parent may be the strongest possible mitigation of legal guilt. Courts have now obtained a very wide discretion to discharge without punishment where this appears to be expedient or where there are sufficiently weighty circumstances of mitigation. The general subject of euthanasia will be taken up again in the last chapter.

"Monsters"

There is, indeed, some kind of legal argument that a "monster" is not protected even under the existing law. This argument depends upon the very old legal writers, because the matter has not been considered in any modern work or in any court judgment. Bracton, writing under Henry III, seems to say that a monster is not a human being, *"quia partus monstruosus est cum non nascatur ut homo."* Bracton is, understandably, not precise in his definition of a monster, and makes the utterly fanciful remark that a monster utters a roar, whereas a true child of Eva will cry the note E or A. He is careful to add, however, that a child is not accounted a monster merely because it has the wrong number of fingers or joints, or is crooked or humpbacked or has twisted limbs or otherwise has its members useless.[4] This passage is substantially repeated by Blackstone,[5] who says that a monster, who in any part evidently bears the resemblance of the brute creation, cannot be heir to any land, albeit it be brought forth in marriage; the reason, he says, is too obvious, and too shocking, to bear a minute discussion. Blackstone is here undoubtedly expressing the belief that a monster is the product of an animal paternity. Locke relates that women were known to have conceived by apes, "if history lye not,"[6] and it was an easy inference that monsters were the result of such an unnatural liaison. This error detracts from the legal authority that the passage in Blackstone might otherwise have possessed. Yet the question still remains whether it is not permissible both morally and legally so to define a human being as to exclude the grosser sports of nature. This is only another illustration of the fact that value-judgments have somewhat arbitrary limits, and are frequently hard to separate from questions of meaning. Since the determination of meaning must be made by men, the limits of the value-judgment must be settled by men, too.

Fortunately, the question whether a monster is human has small practical importance for the most extreme cases, because the acephalous, ectocardiac, etc., monster

[4] Bract. f. 438a-b; cf. ibid., ff. 5a, 70a; he is not, however, speaking of homicide, which he does not consider in this connection. See also Coke upon Littleton, f. 7b.

[5] Blackstone: *Commentaries,* II, 246.

[6] Locke: *Essay concerning the Human Understanding,* III, Chap. 6, s. 23.

will usually die quickly after birth. This beneficent tendency of nature is assisted, in Britain at any rate, by the practice of doctors and nurses, who, when an infant is born seriously malformed, do not "strive officiously to keep alive," even though they do nothing positive to kill it. The infant will be left unattended for a number of hours; a normal child will survive for quite a time without attention, but the monster usually dies. On rare occasions such a monster will live. It may belong to the fish stage of development, with vestigial gills, webbed arms and feet, and sightless eyes. The thing is presented to its mother, who struggles to nurture it for a few months, after which she sends it to a home. In one such case of which I was informed, a mother who already possessed a normal child gave birth to a viable monster. Both monster and normal child contracted influenza with a high temperature; the doctor treated the normal child but not the monster. The monster nevertheless survived.[7]

It seems probable that the medical practice is unduly cautious, and that a creature that is clearly a monster in the old-fashioned sense could lawfully be put to a merciful death. This appears to be a reasonable deduction from the rule stated by the Bracton and the other institutional writers that a monster is not a man. It is true that they give or imply the wrong reason for it; but the same rule might be approved for a better reason. The only possible objection, apart from the extreme view that even a monster is the abode of an immortal spirit, is the difficulty of drawing the line; but all moral and legal rules require a line to be drawn somewhere. It may be noticed that even the Catholic religion, which is very strict on these matters, does not suppose that a monster is a man. According to the *Rituale Romanum,* "a monster which does not belong to the human species

[7] Many examples of monsters from medical and general literature are given by Theodrick R. Beck and J. B. Beck: *Elements of Medical Jurisprudence,* 11th ed. (Philadelphia, 1860), pp. 422ff.

should not be baptized; if there is any doubt, it should be baptized with this condition expressed: 'If thou art a man, I baptize thee, etc.' " [8]

Locked ("Siamese") twins present a special case, though they are treated in medical works as a species of monster. Here the recent medical practice is to attempt a severance, notwithstanding the risks involved. Either the twins are successfully unlocked, or they die. [9]

Monsters are sometimes the unintentional result of medical treatment. One instance of this is worth mentioning because it bears also on the subject of abortion, which is to be discussed later in the book. It has been known for some time that folic acid is essential for the embryological development of the fetus, and experiments have therefore been made in using a folic acid antagonist as an agent for therapeutic abortion. The treatment is a simple one, and can be successful, but if it fails to work the child, when born, is likely to be grossly abnormal. [1] In normal medical practice this is perhaps not a grave drawback, because the failure of the drug is a clear indication for surgical evacuation, which will prevent the monster from being born. Such a surgical operation is, of course, justified on the same therapeutic grounds as the original administration of the drug. The

[8] Quoted by William Reany: *The Creation of the Human Soul* (New York, 1932), p. 196. But Gerald Kelly: *Medico-Moral Problems* (Dublin, 1955), p. 80, states that all monsters are to be baptized: the only problem he discusses is the problem that may arise whether a monstrosity is one person or more than one. Here the ambiguity of the English "you" is found to come to the rescue.

For a Protestant opinion that a monster is not human see E. L. Mascall: *Christian Theology and Natural Science* (London, 1956), p. 283.

[9] In February 1955 an operation was performed in London to separate twins joined at the crown of their heads but perfectly healthy. Both children died after the operation.

[1] The original paper on the drug by Thiersch will be found in 63 *American Journal of Obstetrics and Gynecology* 1298 (1952). He notes the danger of the drug not producing abortion if given in too small a dose or at the third month or later of pregnancy.

real danger lies in the risk that the drug may fall into improper hands. This seems already to have happened. It is reported that a woman who had been given the drug, apparently by an illegal abortionist, was admitted to hospital where she gave birth to an infant with a club foot and multiple skull anomalies.[2] It would be horrifying if this drug, in the hands of unscrupulous abortionists, were to bring about an increase in the number of mentally and physically defective children.

Another scientific advance tends even more seriously in the same direction. The use of nuclear energy, by increasing radiation, is probably increasing the number of mutations, which are usually harmful. It may well be that in the future this also will add to the number of malformed and imbecile children brought to birth, and so give greater urgency to the legal and ethical problems involved. A serious increase in the number of degenerate children might well force mankind to a policy of "weeding out" which is at variance with our present humanitarian outlook.

The treatment of the mother

Let us assume that these problems are put aside, and that the act of infanticide is regarded not only as absolutely wrong but as subject in all instances to the control of the criminal law. There remains the question of treatment or punishment. On this matter, the ecclesiastical doctrine had a calamitous result. For many centuries in the countries of Europe the mother who killed

[2] See Meltzer in 161 *Journal of the American Medical Association* 1253 (1956). The dose advocated by Meltzer had been given, and apparently under optimal conditions, i.e., less than two months after pregnancy; yet it failed to produce abortion. I am indebted for this and the last reference to Dr. John Havard.

her child, perhaps when her mind was disturbed or when she was overcome by grief or worry at having given birth to a bastard, was, under the stimulus of the church, put to death. Some countries provided special pains for her: thus in Germany and Switzerland, the criminal code of Charles V provided the almost unimaginable punishment of burying the miserable offender alive with a pale thrust through her body.[3] The Christian church has often been praised for the heightened value that it attached to human life: the debit side of the account—the frightful punishments practised by our professedly Christian ancestors, in gross misinterpretation of the plain teachings of the New Testament—must not be overlooked. Bertrand Russell described moral progress as consisting in the main of widening the bounds of human sympathy. Our forefathers were so solicitous for the dead that they sometimes forgot all decency and humanity to the living.

Even today, in England and in a number of other Commonwealth countries that retain capital punishment, if once the mother is convicted of murder, the court has no problem to consider, because she must be sentenced to death. The law follows the religious view and refuses to regard the killing of an infant, even by the mother, as belonging to a lower legal category than the murder of an adult. However, the attitude proves to be impossible to maintain in practice. Not for many years—not since 1899 in England—has there been any question of the grim sentence being carried out, so that it has become nothing more than a devilish kind of jest, though the unhappy woman herself may not realize that the working of the law is kindlier than its professions. This fact, together with the frequent refusal of juries to convict mothers of the murder of their children, prompted in England a widespread desire for change in the law.

One line of approach is to treat the mother who kills her child at a time when she has not fully recovered

[3] Westermarck: op. cit., p. 412.

from the effects of the birth as not fully responsible for her actions. To some extent the desired result can be achieved if she pleads insanity, but there are various difficulties with this. In the first place, the rejection in most Commonwealth jurisdictions of the defence of "insane impulse" means that the insanity plea is a limited one. It is available where the mother kills her child in a confusional state, for then she may be taken as not knowing what she is doing, or that it is wrong; but a depressive psychosis, which is by far the most usual psychosis during and immediately after pregnancy, may have no legal effect upon responsibility. In the second place, the disturbance in the mother's mind which causes her to kill her child is not necessarily a psychosis (insanity). She may merely have been suffering from the obvious stress of having an illegitimate child; or there may possibly be an endocrine lack. In the third place, the insanity plea is disliked because of the supposed stigma of an insanity verdict, and the fear of committal to a state mental hospital of the security type. A way out of these difficulties was suggested in England by the Criminal Code Bill of 1878, which, as amended, proposed the institution of a new offence to meet the case.[4] This proposal did not reach the statute book till 1922.[5] The Infanticide Act of that year was replaced with amendments by an Act of 1938, which provides that where a woman by any wilful act or omission causes the death of her child being under twelve months, but the balance of her mind was disturbed by reason of her not having fully recovered from the effect of giving birth

[4] See the *Report of the Criminal Code Commission of 1879*, p. 251. See also *Report of the Royal Commission on Capital Punishment, Cmd 8932 of 1953*, pp. 57–9.

[5] It had been anticipated in Natal by Act No. 10 of 1910, s. 9, which created a special offence of infanticide where the child was killed within a week of the birth. Elsewhere in South Africa there is no special legislation because extenuating circumstances can be recognized in any charge of murder.

to the child or by reason of the effect of lactation consequent upon the birth, she shall be guilty of the felony of infanticide, punishable like manslaughter. This means that she can be sentenced to imprisonment for life—a purely theoretical possibility, too fantastic for consideration, when the woman has been found to have been deranged. In practice she is generally treated with leniency. In 1955, for example, thirteen women were charged in England with statutory infanticide and all were convicted, but most were discharged without punishment or merely put on probation; only two were sent to prison, one for a year and the other for three years.[6]

It may be observed at this point that the use of the term "infanticide" in the statute is unfortunate, because the statutory definition is narrower than the meaning adopted by anthropologists, who do not confine "infanticide" to cases of mental unbalance. The offence designated in the English statute might better be called by some such distinguishing name as "puerperal infanticide," but the specification of a whole year as the time during which the child may be deemed to be newly born shows a desire to interpret the puerperal period with the utmost generosity.

The Act, which has been adopted in some other parts of the Commonwealth,[7] has undoubtedly effected a great improvement in practice. On the other hand, from a technical point of view, it may be said to be an illogical compromise between the law of murder and humane feeling. It recognizes the inadequacy of the present law of insanity for the case of infanticide, and has the advantage of sparing the woman the agony of a murder trial when there are strong circumstances of mitigation. Yet it allows the conviction as for crime of a woman

[6] *Criminal Statistics England and Wales, 1955 (Cmd 9884)*, pp. 33, 40.
[7] See *Report of the Royal Commission on Capital Punishment, Cmd 8932 of 1953*, p. 447.

who may in fact have been afflicted by puerperal mania, a real temporary insanity. If the woman was insane, the verdict should be one of insanity, and conviction should be out of the question. Under any rational system it should be better to be acquitted of an offence on the ground of insanity than convicted of another offence of slightly lesser degree.[8]

When the outcome of an infanticide trial is merely probation or discharge, this is perhaps not a serious criticism. But a severe judge may send the woman to prison, and there are instances of this happening. This is a grave matter, because many a jury that would acquit of murder will convict of infanticide, not expecting that punishment will follow from their conviction. Again, the Act does not save the woman, who may already be in great mental distress, the humiliation, disgrace, and agony of a formal trial before judge and jury. Although the charge will in England be heard in the first instance by examining magistrates, they have no power to deal with it summarily with the consent of the accused, even though the facts are such that it is certain that she will receive a nominal sentence only. This is a legacy of the ancient and discredited doctrine that the criminal law must look to the abstract nature of the crime rather than to the circumstances in which it was committed and the treatment needed by the offender. Another criticism is that the Act leaves it optional to the prosecution to charge either murder or infanticide as it thinks fit. Generally, in circumstances covered by the Act, the

[8] The offence of infanticide presents, indeed, one particular legal difficulty. Sometimes when a woman is charged with infanticide the facts may show that she is exempt from responsibility under the McNaghten rules, as when she acts in a state of automatism. For an instance, see William C. Sullivan: *Crime and Insanity* (London, 1924), pp. 96–7. In such cases it seems that the verdict should be one of insanity—that is to say, in England, a verdict of guilty of the act of infanticide, but insane at the time. Such a verdict is one that all parties to the case wish to avoid, and it was perhaps the intention of Parliament to enable it to be avoided.

charge will be of infanticide. But sometimes the prosecution frustrates the whole object of the Act by charging murder. An instance occurred in England during the last war, when a woman killed her newly born child and her own mother connived at the act. But for the participation of the older woman, the mother would probably have been charged with infanticide. As it was, the prosecutor imagined that he would be met with legal difficulty if he brought in a secondary party to a charge of infanticide;[9] so he indicted both women for murder. The defendants were convicted, and, despite a strong recommendation to mercy by the jury, lay in the condemned cell for nine weeks before being reprieved.[1]

Although the Infanticide Act applies to the killing of children up to the age of one year, it is still in some respects a limited measure. One may regret that the Act was not extended to cover the mother who, deranged by the birth of a child, thereupon kills an older child. Also, the Act takes no account of circumstances of mitigation other than disturbance of mind resulting from giving birth or lactation, and for this reason it applies only for a year after the birth. It sometimes happens that a mother, loving her children, kills them to save them from the menace of insanity, disease, or desperate poverty, perhaps after trying in vain to have them taken off her hands by a children's home. Such a woman must, under present English law, be charged with murder, and, on conviction, sentenced to death, even though the sentence is certain to be commuted. But the law works capriciously, because the actual outcome of the

[9] There was in fact nothing to prevent the mother of the child being convicted of infanticide, and her own mother being convicted of murder, acting through a semi-innocent agent. See my *Criminal Law: The General Part* (London, 1954), § 62.

[1] 6 *Howard Journal* 184 (1944–5). An Australian judge ruled, on legislation similar to the English, that the Crown should not indict for murder where a woman kills her newly born infant and the facts reveal an absence of premeditation, but should confine the charge to infanticide: Barry J. in Rex v. Hutty [1953] V.L.R. 338.

case depends on the leniency of the jury and the temper of the judge. In 1949 a charge of murder against a young married woman ended with a probation order. Her husband falling out of work, she had got into arrears with hire-purchase instalments; this preyed on her mind, and she was found unconscious with her child in a gas-filled room. The mother recovered, but the child did not. The mother was charged with murder of the child, pleaded guilty to manslaughter, and was placed on probation. This was a sensible solution, because it enabled the probation officer to help the unfortunate woman with her difficulties.[2] Contrast the outcome when, in 1953, a Scotswoman was charged with the murder of her child. In just over seven years of married life she had had six children. Her own upbringing was bad, both parents being heavy drinkers. The birth of the fifth child, Thomas, was very difficult, and the mother was thenceforward liable to violent fits of temper. Thomas was delicate and sickly, often crying and moaning, and one day his mother, finding that he had woken up the baby, beat him to death with a broken chair-leg. Thomas was then a little over two years old. The mother's record as to the other children, in care and treatment, was good beyond the average. She was convicted of manslaughter, and received the terrible sentence of six years' imprisonment. Her husband, who had presented the overburdened woman with the six children, was exonerated from complicity![3]

To sum up, it may be said that the special feature of infanticide from a social point of view is that the mother is killing her own child; but instead of avowing that this feature removes the crime from ordinary conceptions of murder, the legislature in the Infanticide Act confines its attention to diminished mental responsibility.

[2] 113 *Justice of the Peace Journal* 337.
[3] A brief account of the case (Regina v. Hampton) appears in *The Times* (London), July 22, 1953.

From a political point of view the compromise was a reasonable one, because otherwise it might not have been possible to overcome the opposition of religious groups. But this does not mean that we have reached finality in this part of the law.

No legislation like the Infanticide Act is found in the United States, but the problem is somewhat alleviated by the possibility of finding second-degree murder, which does not carry the death penalty, and by the discretion given to the jury in most states to decide or recommend against the death penalty even where they convict of murder in the first degree. These provisions do not entirely dispose of the problem, because there are frequently minimum periods of imprisonment of some severity, which can, however, be evaded by the use of probation. The experts in criminal law at Columbia University tell me that no full studies have been made of the way in which infanticide is actually treated by the American courts, and much depends upon the degree of enlightenment of the judge and jury. In an Alabama case of 1948, a mother who was convicted of murdering her newly born child received a sentence of twenty years' imprisonment; happily, the conviction was reversed on appeal for lack of evidence, but there was no animadversion upon the terrible sentence that the trial court had thought fit to impose.[4] Severe sentences naturally lead to a refusal on the part of juries to convict, and this has in turn led law enforcement officers to consider the desirability of something like the English infanticide legislation.[5]

[4] Singleton v. State, 33 Ala. App. 536, 35 S. 2d 375.

[5] The *Annual Report* of the Attorney General for Massachusetts for the year ending January 17, 1894, p. 12, contains the following passage: "One of the capital cases tried during the year illustrates anew the difficulty of securing the conviction of a woman charged with the murder of her infant child. Under the existing law the Grand Jury and the prosecuting officer, though having the power to indict for manslaughter, are logically and morally bound to indict and try such cases, if appearing to be malicious, as for murder, which leads upon conviction to the penalty of death or imprisonment for

Where a woman is charged with murder and not in-fanticide (either because there is no infanticide statute in the particular jurisdiction or because it is inapplicable on the facts of the case), she may be forced to plead insanity as a defence. On that plea being upheld, she may be sent to a hospital for the criminal insane—in England, Broadmoor or a Broadmoor institution. Nearly all women in Broadmoor are there because they have killed one of their children. Such a woman will—according to the present English practice, which seems to be a settled one although it is not officially avowed—be detained in Broadmoor for three years and then released. In official theory she is kept there for her own good and the safety of society; but the real unavowed reason appears to be that Broadmoor is a punishment for sin and a warning to other mothers. Many will think this to be a perversion of the idea of treatment for which a mental hospital stands. To remove a woman temporarily from her home surroundings, when she has killed her child, is for her benefit; but surely it is cruelty to send her to Broadmoor, when her home and loved ones are perhaps at the other end of the country; and to keep her there

---

life. This is liable to result in a failure of justice which might be avoided if the penalty were less severe. Some of these cases are of great hardship and appeal strongly to the sympathies of the jury, as, for example, when the mother has been seduced and abandoned by the father of the child; and in many of them, even in the absence of extenuating circumstances, the evidence is not of such a character as to procure a conviction of murder, though there may be no substantial doubt of the guilt of the accused. There is also high medical authority for the belief that some of these homicides are due to the mental disturbance which sometimes accompanies childbirth, rendering the mother more or less irresponsible for her conduct. For these and other reasons, both of justice and humanity, I suggest the expediency of providing that such homicide, even if appearing to be done with legal malice, may in the discretion of the Grand Jury and the prosecuting officer, be indicted as manslaughter instead of murder." I am indebted to Professor Joseph Goldstein, who is working on the treatment of the criminal insane, for bringing this Report to my notice and allowing me to use it.

for as long as three years may spell the end of her marriage. The pretence that there is any medical or social reason for three years' quarantine will not stand a moment's examination. A woman who kills her child under the stress of adverse circumstances is almost certainly not dangerous to anyone but her other children, if any, and not necessarily to them. The problem of the mother who is dangerous to her own children can be met otherwise than by keeping the mother locked up.

In conclusion, a plea may be made for a greater exercise of the discretion of prosecuting authorities to refrain from prosecuting. The law makes a number of simplified moral judgments and enforces them on the ground of the public interest in social conduct. To a large extent these rules of conduct can be fitted to the individual case by adjustment of the punishment or treatment, or discharge without punishment. But one element in the legal process is ineluctable—the distress of mind caused to the offender by being summoned before a court, particularly where this involves much publicity in the press. This reinforces the argument that a legal inquisition into conduct is not justified on moral or religious grounds if no sufficient social purpose is to be served.

II

THE CONTROL OF CONCEPTION

The propaganda for contraception

The revolution in the attitude towards contraception that has taken place during the last century, and particularly during the last fifty years, has, in Britain, after an initial defeat, succeeded in keeping the criminal law out of this department of conduct. In the United States success has been less complete, and in many states the sale of contraceptives is possible only by subterfuge or plain illegality. Moreover, the Governments of the two countries still maintain what Lord Simon of Wythenshawe called a "conspiracy of silence" on the subject of birth control and its relation to population problems of world importance.

For England, and America, too, the story can best be started in 1798, when a Surrey curate and Fellow of Jesus College, Cambridge, by name Thomas Malthus, published his famous *Essay on the Principle of Population*. Malthus lived at a time when improved midwifery and hygiene were greatly reducing child mortality, and so increasing the size of the family. In London, which was notorious for high child-mortality, it was estimated in 1836 that deaths of children under five had fallen from about 745 per 1,000 in 1730–49 to 318 in 1810–29.[1] It is perhaps not surprising, in these conditions, that a voice should have been raised to proclaim the bitter theory that since human fertility must outrun the power of the earth to produce sustenance, the human race is doomed to misery. Pre-

[1] *Population Policy in Great Britain* (P.E.P.: London, 1948), p. 69, quoting M. C. Buer: *Health, Wealth and Population in the Early Days of the Industrial Revolution* (London, 1926).

mature death must in some shape or other visit a large part of mankind. "The vices of mankind," wrote Malthus, "are active and able ministers of depopulation. They are the precursors in the great army of destruction; and often finish the dreadful work themselves. But should they fail in this war of extermination, sickly seasons, epidemics, pestilence, and plague, advance in terrific array, and sweep off their thousands and ten thousands. Should success be still incomplete, gigantic inevitable famine stalks in the rear, and with one mighty blow, levels the population with the food of the world." [2] In short, there must always be a large body of mankind whose increase will be checked in the last resort by lack of food.

From this premise, which he regarded almost as self-evident, and indeed as embodying the divine law, Malthus deduced the conclusion that it was impossible to found a society upon benevolence. The poverty of the working class was to be accepted as a necessary part of the social order, thus justifying the biblical utterance that the poor always we have with us. Poverty, being inherent in the order of things, could not be relieved, so that legal provisions for alleviating the distress of the poor, and all proposals for statutory minimum wages, were unjustifiable.

The only means of escape that Malthus could himself see from the logic of his own arguments was by the widespread adoption of "moral restraint," by which he meant the celibacy or late marriage of those who could not afford a normal family. He admitted, however, that the undue postponement of marriage was likely in fact to result in prostitution and other sexual irregularities which ill became the title of "moral restraint." Thus Malthus himself did not set much store by his own solution. [3] He

[2] *An Essay on the Principle of Population* (London, 1798) (Bonar's edition, London, 1926), pp. 139–40.

[3] Malthus's solution has succeeded in Catholic Ireland, though at what cost in misery and frustration cannot be estimated. Memory

did not contemplate any form of restraint within marriage, and in particular he rejected what he called "improper arts."

The widespread acceptance of Malthus's doctrine, which was in effect an argument for the perpetuation of existing oppressions and inequalities, was a sore blow to the radicals and socialists. As Godwin wrote: "Every generous attempt for any important melioration of the condition of mankind, is here at stake. The advocates of old establishments and old abuses, could not have found a doctrine, more to their heart's content, more effectual to shut out all reform and improvement for ever." [4]

It was imperative to find some answer to all this—to suggest some means, other than the Malthusian devils of disease and famine, by which the increase of population could be kept within bounds. Godwin suggested that even a practice of child exposure would be preferable to the misery of death in later years; but he thought that there would be no need to have recourse to such an expedient, because the population—he was speaking of England—was adequately kept in check by a high infant-mortality, monogamy, celibacy, and late marriages. [5]

This was evidently too complacent, for the most important of the checks enumerated by Godwin, the natural mortality of infants, was, at its ancient high level, the result solely of poverty and ignorance, and it was already being brought under control in Godwin's day. Moreover,

---

of the potato famine of 1846 lies behind the severe restraint placed by the population upon its own reproduction, without assistance from modern contraceptive technique. "Moral restraint" coupled with emigration has replaced the poverty-stricken eight million Irish of the last century with the relatively prosperous four million of the present day. See A. M. Carr-Saunders: *World Population* (Oxford, 1938), p. 114.

[4] *Thoughts Occasioned by the Perusal of Dr. Parr's Spital Sermon* (London, 1801), p. 63, quoted by Kenneth Smith: *The Malthusian Controversy* (London, 1951), p. 39.

[5] Kenneth Smith: op. cit., pp. 39–40.

could it not be said that infant mortality, celibacy, and late marriage enforced by poverty were themselves part of the misery comprehended in Malthus's theory? The hedonists had to find some way of limiting population that would free men from the empire of suffering.

The solution obviously lay in the control of conception. Various preventive devices were already known and practised in the England of the eighteenth century, but rather among rakes and prostitutes than among respectable married people. Malthus himself was aware of them, and considered them as a possible answer to his problem; but he seems to have thought them "unnatural" and, therefore, irreligious; and on the secular side he feared that if it were possible for married people to limit by a wish the number of their children, there would be removed a necessary stimulus to industry, and the population would not reach its "natural and normal" extent.[6] This unconvincing pessimism, which has been falsified by events, gives the impression of being produced by a psychological "block" resulting from Malthus's religious training. Undoubtedly, however, it would have required very considerable courage for a parson to have advocated contraception at a time when there was a powerful taboo on the public discussion of all sexual matters.

So far as is known, the first public argument for contraception came from that daring reformer Jeremy Bentham. As early as 1797 Bentham had advocated the use of the sponge as a method of reducing the burden on the poor rate.[7] But the first person to make family limitation the subject of a crusade among the masses was Francis Place. In his *Illustrations and Proofs of the Principle of Population,* published in 1822, Place advocated that the poor should be taught to postpone their marriages, but went on to suggest that even marriage it-

[6] See Himes, in his edition of *Place on Population* (London, 1930), pp. 283–98.
[7] Himes: *Medical History of Contraception* (London, 1936), p. 141.

self did not necessarily imply uninhibited procreation. "If it were once clearly understood, that it was not disreputable for married persons to avail themselves of such precautionary means as would, without being injurious to health, or destructive of female delicacy, prevent conception, a sufficient check might at once be given to the increase of population beyond the means of subsistence; vice and misery, to a prodigious extent, might be removed from society, and the object of Mr. Malthus, Mr. Godwin, and of every philanthropic person, be promoted, by the increase of comfort, of intelligence, and of moral conduct, in the mass of the population."

Place was not content with a mere pronouncement in favour of birth control. Himself the father of fifteen children, five of whom had died in childhood, and with bitter personal experience of poverty and starvation, he had the best reason to know the vital importance of his message. His most important propaganda consisted of handbills, addressed to "The Married of Both Sexes," which set out practicable methods of contraception by the use of the sponge. Place's "diabolical handbills" naturally aroused strong opposition, not only because of the sexual prudery of the time, but because they were thought to be fraught with danger. The desire not only to reproduce oneself but to see the human race continuing is part of our genetic endowment, and there was a natural and persistent fear that the widespread adoption of contraceptive practices would lead to racial suicide. On top of this, long religious conditioning had led men to regard birth control as tantamount to infanticide. John Stuart Mill became aware of the difference when he witnessed the discovery of the dead bodies of unwanted infants; this made such an impression on him that he took to distributing birth control handbills in slum tenements, an activity which earned him a number of days in prison.[8]

Notwithstanding all opposition, Place's handbills evi-

[8] Karl Britton: *John Stuart Mill* (Pelican ed., 1953), pp. 17–18.

dently enjoyed a considerable circulation, and were re-printed in America, where they led indirectly to the publication of Robert Dale Owen's *Moral Physiology* (1830), the first American tract on birth control, which was reprinted in England two years later. This in turn influenced Knowlton, a Massachusetts physician, to pub-lish in New York in 1832 a pamphlet entitled *Fruits of Philosophy,* for which he served three months' hard labour. This work, also, speedily crossed the Atlantic, and later became the occasion of a signal victory of the birth control or neo-Malthusian movement. The English pub-lisher of *Fruits of Philosophy* was prosecuted for publish-ing an obscene book, and was induced to plead guilty, so that the merits of the case were not tried. At this time, Charles Bradlaugh and Mrs. Besant, both militant Freethinkers, were the leaders of the birth control move-ment in England, and although they did not approve of Knowlton's pamphlet in all its details, they were anxious to vindicate the legality of its publication. Accordingly they took a shop and notified the police that at a certain time they would be present in person to sell the pam-phlet. Detectives came, bought, and arrested. In the pros-ecution that followed, in the year 1877, the jury convicted, notwithstanding a direction favourable to the defendants by Lord Chief Justice Cockburn; but this conviction was reversed on appeal on a technical point.[9] The outcome might seem to be a moral defeat, but in fact the great public interest aroused by the trial was the best advertise-ment that the movement for voluntary parenthood could have had. The effect is well summarized in a modern study.

[9] L.R. 2 Q.B.D. 569; on appeal, L.R. 3 Q.B.D. 607. The reversal was because the words alleged to be obscene had not been set out in the indictment. Annie Besant, in her *Autobiography,* alleged that the conviction by the jury was due not to the merits of the case but to their dislike of the defendants' atheist beliefs. Cf. Norman St. John-Stevas: *Obscenity and the Law* (London, 1956), p. 73.

Up and down the country the idea of family limitation became a subject for public discussion. It was made clear to all that many important respected personages did not regard family limitation necessarily as a set of "indecent, obscene, unnatural, and immoral practices." The spell was broken above all by the spectacle of a woman willing to risk ostracism and imprisonment in her outspoken defence of birth control, pleading before the chief magistrate of the land, who did not hide his interest. The trials fulfilled that function of catalysis which was needed for a large-scale change in marital habits.[1]

About 185,000 copies of Knowlton's pamphlet were sold after the trial, and the sale of other similar tracts enormously stimulated. It is well known that a rapid decline in the birth rate commenced in western Europe towards the end of the nineteenth century, and in England the drop commences shortly after the year 1870.[2] There seems to be no doubt that the birth control propaganda and particularly the Bradlaugh-Besant trial accelerated and extended the practice of family limitation, at any rate among the lower middle-class and the skilled artisans. It was not, however, the only factor at work: the fall in child mortality had been succeeded by legislation which forbade the employment of children, and by the Act of 1880 which established compulsory education: this meant that the large family was a greatly increased financial burden for the working-class man. Coupled with this, also, was the increased sense of parental responsibility resulting from the medical and administrative improvements of the nineteenth century, and the new aspirations that parents had conceived for their children and for themselves.

It must be said that the trial of 1877 did not immediately end the attempt to defeat the crusade for sexual enlightenment in England. The next year one Edward

---

[1] *Population Policy in Great Britain* (P.E.P.: London, 1948), p. 67.
[2] Ibid., p. 42.

Truelove was convicted of endangering the morals of youth by republishing Owen's *Moral Philosophy;* and other prosecutions for selling birth control literature took place in the twentieth century.[3] They have now been wholly discontinued.

The English propaganda by the advocates of birth control had a readership in other countries, such as Holland, where it was translated and gave rise to Continental offshoots of the Neo-Malthusian League. The overseas dominions of Britain were also affected. France, however, followed her own history. Contraception seems to have been common among the French upper classes for several centuries, and by the beginning of the nineteenth century the practice had spread to the peasantry, religious prohibition notwithstanding. To this practice was attributed the marked decline in the birth rate which occurred after 1830, leading to a falling population. Instead of taking active measures to remove obstacles to marriage and parenthood, France has adopted the reactionary policy of forbidding all public discussion of birth control and the sale of contraceptives. Notwithstanding this, family limitation is still a fact in France.[4]

Developments in Britain and the United States in the twentieth century

Odd as it may seem, until the year 1913 the Neo-Malthusian League confined itself to propaganda in fa-

[3] D. V. Glass: *Population Policies and Movements* (Oxford, 1940), p. 35.
[4] For the history of the birth control movement, upon which the account in the text is based, see James Alfred Field: *Essays on Population* (Chicago, 1931); Norman E. Himes: *Introduction to Place on Population* (London, 1930); *Enc. Soc. Sci.,* s.v. "Birth Control"; *Population Policy in Great Britain* (P.E.P.: London, 1948), Chap. 3.

vour of birth control, leaving the supply of devices to commercial enterprise, which charged a high price. Only in 1913 did the League issue any specific material on contraceptive methods. After the First World War Marie Stopes identified herself with the cause, founding a new Society for Constructive Birth Control which emphasized the importance of the subject for maternal health and marital relations. Under her guidance a chain of clinics was established, thus bringing reliable methods for the first time within the reach of the poor. The opening of each and every clinic was violently opposed by an Anglican and Roman Catholic minority. In 1934 it was made the duty of local authorities to give contraceptive advice in maternal and child welfare clinics, but only to married women and only "if it is found medically that pregnancy would be detrimental to their health." [5] Even this limited instruction was slow in being adopted, and the way in which it is interpreted in practice depends very much upon the religious opinion of the local Medical Officer of Health. No official step has been taken in England to extend state advice in regular clinics to unmarried women—even those contemplating matrimony for whom a pregnancy would be dangerous—or to healthy married women who wish to space their families, or to obtain advice for economic or eugenic reasons.

The refusal of advice to unmarried women is a typical instance of the unimaginative moral outlook which fears that the giving of contraceptive advice will encourage immorality. In fact, if an unmarried woman comes for such advice without reference to marriage, the only probable consequence of refusal is that a child will be born with all the disadvantages of illegitimacy. This view was well expressed by an investigator in North Carolina,

[5] *Ministry of Health Circular 1408,* based on the recommendations of the Departmental Committee on Maternal Mortality and Morbidity, 1932.

where there is a state service of contraceptive advice and supplies.

One public health officer, concerned more with facts than with moral issues, said that everyone who came to his pregnancy spacing service was advised, irrespective of marital status. The woman is asked if she is married, but no follow-up inquiries are made. Dr. X's attitude is to prevent illegitimacy with its inevitable bad effects on child health and, therefore, he thinks, if a woman comes for birth control you should give her the information. He takes a realistic point of view, knowing that if a single woman makes this request she is going to be exposed to pregnancy risk anyway, and at least you may save a handicapped child from being born.[6]

Progress has been made in Britain, but in a typically indirect way, namely by co-operation between state and private enterprise. Local authority clinics increasingly tend to refer cases to the voluntary clinics; and the Family Planning Association now conducts more than three quarters of its two hundred clinics on the premises of a local health authority or of a regional hospital board. Recently, the Minister of Health paid an official visit to the Association on the occasion of its twenty-fifth birthday.[7] Also, doctors under the National Health Service are free to advise their patients upon contraception, and to provide appliances, for such reasons of health as they may think sufficient.

A recent survey conducted with the aid of family physicians showed that of women married between 1935 and 1939, 66 per cent replied that they had used some form of birth control during marriage, as compared with only 15 per cent of women married before 1910 who gave this reply. Both figures are likely to be minimal. The study also showed a steady growth in the use of appliance methods of birth control as opposed to non-appliance

[6] Moya Woodside: *Sterilization in North Carolina* (Chapel Hill, N.C., 1950), pp. 108–9.
[7] Dr. Joan Malleson in *The Observer* (London), April 1, 1956.

methods (the latter meaning chiefly *coitus inter-ruptus*).[8]

In the United States the tale of prosecutions is a longer one. Knowlton's pamphlet survived prosecution and enjoyed a large circulation, but that remarkable crusader Mrs. Margaret Sanger was prosecuted in 1916 on a charge of public nuisance for opening a contraceptive clinic in Brooklyn, and served a sentence in prison. A Federal statute known as the Comstock Law of 1873 (section 211 of the Penal Code) declares information on contraception and contraceptive devices to be non-mailable, along with "every obscene, lewd, or lascivious, and every filthy book"; the penalty for infringement may be a fine or imprisonment for five years. This ban on the acquisition of scientific knowledge, which makes no express exception even for medical grounds (though such exception has since been read in by the judges[9]), seems to the foreign lawyer who meets it for the first time to be scarcely credible in the legislation of a liberal and predominantly Protestant country. To add to the mystery, a majority of the states also have repressive legislation, contraception again being classed for legislative purposes with obscenity, indecent exposure, bawdy-houses, and so on; but for the most part the states' prohibition of contraception is drawn in such a way as to permit some instruction in technique to be given, e.g., by physicians, and some sales of appliances to be made. In a few states, including New York,[1] contraceptives are banned except for the cure or prevention of disease, which means that a sale is lawful if it professes to be for V.D. prophylaxis, but not if it professes to be for birth control—a quite astonishing distinction, which expresses neither the

[8] E. Lewis Faning: *Report on an Enquiry into Family Limitation and its Influence on Human Fertility during the Last Fifty Years* (*Papers of the Royal Commission on Population*, Vol. I; London, 1949), pp. 7–9.
[9] United States v. One Package, 86 F. 2d 737 (2d Cir., 1936).
[1] N.Y. Penal Law s. 1142, enacted in 1881–7; but cf. s. 1145.

ancient Christian attitude towards sexual intercourse nor the humanist one, but is apparently motivated by the fear of a declining population. Partly because of the width of the exceptions, and partly because of the condition of public opinion, this legislation is little enforced and does not prevent a vast traffic in contraceptives or the operation of many clinics. Some states have established birth control clinics as part of their public health programs, and there are also private ventures: the Planned Parenthood Federation operates or sponsors some 165 clinics. Even so, this number is quite inadequate for the needs of the population. In Connecticut the governing statute forbids all use of contraceptives; and both in this state and in Massachusetts birth control clinics are strictly forbidden, even when attended by physicians who give advice on health grounds, though contraceptives remain purchasable for real or fictitious prophylaxis.[2]

Legislators are inhibited from repealing these outmoded laws for reasons that are not altogether explicable, but seem to include distaste for the whole subject, fear of immorality among the young, and fear of the Puritan and Catholic vote. The latter fear certainly has much substance, and world Catholicism in particular thinks that it has a moral duty to act frankly as a political force, one of the objects of which is to oppose appliance methods of contraception. But that the fear of this opposition can be exaggerated seems to be shown by a survey of American opinion conducted in 1943, when 85 per

[2] This astonishing interpretation of the law of Massachusetts is confirmed by two decisions: Commonwealth v. Gardner, 15 N.E. (2d) 223 (1938), where it was held that a physician may not prescribe a contraceptive for a patient even though pregnancy would mean certain death for her, and Commonwealth v. Corbett, 29 N.E. (2d) 151 (1940), where it was held that contraceptives could be sold to prevent disease among those who engaged in sexual intercourse (even illicit). The constitutionality of legislation of this type is open to question in the Supreme Court of the United States: see Note, 7 *Wyoming Law Journal* 138 (1953).

cent of women questioned were found to favour contraceptive advice for married women, and more than two thirds of the Catholic women questioned favoured it.[3]

The practice of contraception, which has persisted despite religious and governmental hostility or apathy, has been found to have other beneficial effects than that of raising economic standards. Not only can the children in a small or medium-sized family be better educated and looked after, resulting in great physical, social, and cultural improvement, but the status of the mother, emancipated from the burden of over-fecundity, is vastly improved. The practice of contraception, too, greatly reduces the crude and wasteful methods of family limitation—abortion and infanticide—that tend otherwise to be resorted to. (In England at the time of the Industrial Revolution, infanticide by smothering was of common occurrence.) As so often happens in moral and religious issues, opponents of contraception have sometimes sought to support their objection, which is fundamentally on the plane of values, by saying that the practice is physically harmful. Medical opinion is now decisively the other way, and is indeed almost unanimous that the harm, if any, is done not by contraception but by continued repression, and by the practice of the so-called "natural" method of family limitation which is veiled in the decent obscurity of the Latin phrase *coitus interruptus*. One may also point out that it is the religious objections that have done so much to retard medical exploration of this field of knowledge. When religious opinions are embodied in the law, the cramping effect upon free scientific inquiry is even more disastrous.[4]

[3] Elmo Roper in *Fortune* magazine, March 1943, quoted by Joseph Fletcher: *Morals and Medicine* (Princeton, N.J., 1954), p. 74. For a history of the American legislation and the repeal movement see Mary W. Dennett: *Birth Control Laws* (New York, 1926).

[4] See J. Rock: "The Scientific Case Against Rigid Legal Restrictions on Medical Birth-Control Advice," in *Clinics,* April 1943.

Such is the history to date of the movement for preventive measures of birth control in Western civilization. We have still to consider the subject as a topic in applied religion; but before doing this, the contributions made to the discussion by anthropologists are worth recording.

Birth control among primitive peoples

Until Dr. Norman E. Himes published his important *Medical History of Contraception* in 1936, the fact had largely been lost sight of that primitive peoples all over the world adopt positive measures to prevent human births exercising an undue pressure upon resources. These measures include not only infanticide, abortion, and various customary ways of controlling fertility (such as the prohibition of intercourse for a certain period after the woman has given birth), but also mechanical, chemical, surgical, and magical devices intended to prevent conception. One of the best is reported of the Negro women of Guiana or Martinique (the author of the account does not make it clear which), who were found to use diluted lemon juice as a douche solution; it turns out that this is medically approved as an effective spermicide. Many kinds of pessaries, suppositories, and even condoms are recorded from the ancient civilizations and primitive peoples of the present day, of varying degrees of efficacy and harmfulness. Himes concludes that "the human race has in all ages and in all geographical locations desired to control its own fertility; that while women have always wanted babies, they have wanted them when they wanted them. And they have wanted neither too few nor too many."

All this does not prove that birth control is right, because savages do many wrong things. But it does tend to show that the demand for birth control cannot be characterized as "unnatural," except in a very peculiar sense of that word.

Religious objections: the Old Testament

To one innocent of knowledge of the history of religions, the preoccupation of ecclesiastics, many of them celibate, with sexual matters may seem inexplicable. "Religions," said Remy de Gourmont, "revolve madly around sexual questions"; and a contemporary observer, commenting upon certain beliefs expressed in the Church of England, remarked that "there seems to be something about the human reproductive system which throws the ecclesiastical mind off its balance." [5] This is not true of Islam, which has kept itself relatively free from the strong emotions attached to sex, and has made no difficulty about accepting the control of human fertility; but it is largely the case with the Jewish and Christian religions, for historical reasons that go back ultimately to the scriptural texts on which they are founded.

In the Old Testament, there is, in the first place, the peremptory "Be fruitful, and multiply" of Gen. i, 28; ix, 1. Dr. Ganz [6] expresses the opinion that this was originally pronounced as a blessing, though later interpreted by the Rabbis as imposing a duty upon the male partner. According to the majority opinion of the Rabbis, it did not bind the woman, and the duty of reproduction was in any event satisfied by the birth of two children. The freedom of the woman meant that she could use a sponge as a contraceptive. This practice is mentioned in the *To-*

[5] Sir L. E. Jones: *Beyond Belief* (London, 1949), p. 58.
[6] In a chapter contributed to Himes: *Medical History of Contraception* (Baltimore, 1936), p. 69.

48

sephta as early as A.D. 230. However, the question is still not finally settled in Judaism, the Chief Rabbi in London expressing the opinion in 1933 that the moral obligation of propagating the race continues to rest on the man even after he has had two children, and that contraceptives are permitted to the woman only where considerations of health make them necessary.[7] Pronouncements of this kind do not necessarily put an end to divergent opinions, since the Jewish religion, possessing no central authority, has not the monolithic character of Catholicism. In the United States, a strong body of rabbinical opinion is in favor of the control of parenthood as one of the methods of coping with social problems.[8]

The second text, also from Genesis, relates to the sin of Onan, who spilled his seed upon the ground in order to avoid the duty of the levirate.[9] This spilling of seed appears from the text to have taken place by way of *coitus interruptus* (Onan "went in unto his brother's wife" before he spilled his seed), and Onan's sin was evidently regarded as residing in the deceitful evasion of his duty to procreate children on behalf of his deceased brother.[1] Refusal to procreate was not, as such, a sin according to the Bible. The matter is of some importance outside the Jewish religion, because Catholic theologians even at the present day quote the case of Onan as establishing that *coitus interruptus* is wicked in itself, disregarding the whole sense of the text which is concerned with the levirate, an institution rejected by Christian custom as well as by Jewish custom since the tenth century.

The Jewish insistence upon the duty of reproduction obviously has an advantage for racial survival, particu-

[7] See Halliday Sutherland: *Control of Life* (London, 1944), p. 188.
[8] See *Therapeutic Abortion,* Harold Rosen, ed. (New York, 1954), pp. 169, 173, 174; *Medical Aspects of Human Fertility* (National Committee on Maternal Health, Inc.: New York, 1932), p. 11.
[9] Gen. xxxviii, 7–10; see Himes: op. cit., p. 70, and below, p. 137, n. 4.
[1] See Deut. xxv, 5–6.

larly when combined with the belief in the virtue of racial inbreeding. Such a belief is not, however, incompatible with acceptance of family limitation, and the religious principles of Judaism have not been pressed to excess.

One may perhaps add, without giving serious offence, that it is only by careful selection of texts that a work as primitive as the Old Testament can be made to yield standards of civilized morality. The Mosaic injunction "Thou shalt not suffer a witch to live" (Exod. xxii, 18), which was interpreted literally even by men of such intellectual stature as Sir Thomas Browne, Hale, Blackstone, and John Wesley, was partly responsible for many thousands of women being put to death in Europe.[2] The sacred books abound with authority for the practice of persecuting heretics and for religious wars, and they were in fact used to support these abuses over a long period of European history. In a less mischievous way, Hebraism was still strongly affecting the English Parliament in the nineteenth century. Thus the text "Six days shalt thou labour" was a favourite answer to proposals for a shorter working-week, and the controversy over marriage with a deceased wife's sister was conducted in terms of quotations from Deuteronomy and Leviticus. Fortunately, the literal words of the Old Testament are no longer a dialectical source of strength on political issues, though

[2] "The witchcraft laws were only repealed in 1736, and as late as 1768 John Wesley protested against the tendency to treat stories of witches as 'mere old wives' fables.' It is believed that 70,000 persons were killed as witches between 1600 and 1700. Hale, alas, presided at the trial of two widows, Rose Cullender and Amy Duny, for bewitching seven persons, at Bury St Edmunds in March, 1665. He said to the jury, 'That there are such creatures as witches I make no doubt at all. The Scriptures have affirmed so much.' The women were convicted and hanged." Sir Gerald Hurst in 70 *Law Quarterly Review* 348 (1954). The trial referred to is reported in 6 Howell's (Cobbett's) State Trials 687. At the trial, Sir Thomas Browne, the noted physician, gave his expert opinion that the persons were bewitched, and said that in Denmark there had lately been a great discovery of witches, "who used the very same way of afflicting persons, by conveying pins into them, and crooked as these pins were, with needles and nails."

they still have political importance to the extent that they have been embodied in fundamentalist creeds.

The New Testament and its later interpretations

The traditional Christian opposition to birth control may appear to one who does not sympathize with it to be irrational and obscurantist, as perhaps it is; but examination of the history of Christian thought will at least show the way in which this kind of thinking has arisen.

The explanation of the specifically Christian objection to contraceptive practices is that it is a legacy of the ascetic ideal, persisting in the modern world after the ideal itself has deceased.

The early Christian attitude towards marriage was largely negative, or at least one of indifference, as befitted a religion that concentrated upon the hereafter; and celibacy was long regarded as a peculiar virtue—as, indeed, it still is in Catholic circles. Religion rather easily runs to a form of masochism, and the great advantage of celibacy was supposed to be its denial of the desires of the flesh.

The text relied on to support the ascetic and antisexual interpretation of the Christian's duty was a passage in the First Epistle to the Corinthians (vii, 1–9). St. Paul thought that it would be best of all if a man did not touch a woman, but remained celibate as he himself was. The obvious difficulty about this course of conduct did not strike St. Paul, because he expected the Second Coming in his own lifetime,[8] so that there was no need to think of continuing the human race. What St. Paul was concerned with was to prevent the dread sin of fornica-

[8] Cf. verse 29.

tion. To avoid fornication it was permissible to marry, not because marriage had any positive value in human relationships, but because it was better to marry than to burn (the word "burn," used in the Authorized Version, is translated in the Revised Standard Version as "to be aflame with passion").

When the Kingdom was longer delayed than had at first been thought, questions naturally arose as to the validity of St. Paul's views. Since children had evidently to be procreated if the human race was to continue, was there any special virtue in virginity, or any intrinsic sin in the sexual act? These questions were answered by St. Augustine, in his work entitled *On the Grace of Christ and on Original Sin* (A.D. 418). Continuing the ascetic philosophy of St. Paul, St. Augustine propounded the opinion that all carnal lust was sinful. This opinion was derived in part from the story of Adam, since the "original sin" that Adam was supposed mystically to have transmitted to his descendants was taken to refer to concupiscence.[4] On the face of it this doctrine might seem to make marriage sinful, and render impossible the virtuous propagation of the race. Augustine, however, drew a distinction between lust and procreation. Before the Fall, procreation was accomplished as a virtuous act of will and without lust, but as a punishment for his disobedience against God, Adam found that his procreative members no longer responded to the mere beck of his will, but emulated against himself the disobedience that he had practised against God, "moving at their own arbitrary choice as it were, and instigated by lust." The ideal would still be for the nuptial act to be quietly discharged, without lustful passion and indelicacy of mo-

---

[4] Although this may seem a natural interpretation of the biblical narrative, it was only slowly developed in early Christian thought, and hardly at all in Judaism. On the whole subject see the scholarly study by N. P. Williams: *The Ideas of the Fall and of Original Sin* (London, 1927).

tion; this is impossible, and, therefore, there is evil in marriage, though evil that is turned to a good use, namely the procreation of children.

This morbid, guilt-ridden attitude towards sex, which persisted in Christian thinking until our own generation, necessarily meant that any venereal pleasure not prompted by the object of producing children was not only sinful in itself (as such pleasure in Augustinian thought always was), but not even redeemed by its purpose. For the believer, whose sins had been remitted by his baptism and belief, it was safe to indulge in sexual union for the procreation of children, but radical ruin would follow from indulgence for any other purpose. This is so, says Augustine, "even in the marriage state itself, whenever husband and wife toil at procreation, not from the desire of natural propagation of their species, but as mere slaves to the gratification of their lust out of very wantonness." Further reflection brought about a modification of this view, for in his work *On Marriage and Concupiscence,* written in the next year, A.D. 419, Augustine, basing himself upon a somewhat obscure passage in the text of Paul (I Cor. vii, 3–6), allowed that such embraces of husband and wife as have not procreation for their object, but are nothing more than concessions to an overbearing concupiscence, are permitted, so as to be within the range of forgiveness; in other words, they are merely a venial sin. This modification, however, applies only if the pair, though not acting from a motive of propagating offspring, do not attempt to prevent such propagation. If they use an "evil appliance" to prevent propagation, though called by the name of man and wife they are really not such; they retain no vestige of true matrimony, and are consequently, it appears, in mortal sin. Augustine did not explain the reason for his objection to "evil appliances." He was not a believer in the duty to reproduce; on the contrary, he thought, like Paul, that Christians needed to make little effort in this direction, because there was a plentiful supply of heathen children to be won over to the faith.

The indifference of the early Christians to the sexual urge was one aspect of their desire to mortify the flesh, to thwart natural impulses merely for the sake of thwarting them, an aim that they regarded as the highest form of holiness. It was expressed, also, in their repudiation of personal cleanliness. "The cleanliness of the body," says Lecky, "was regarded as a pollution of the soul, and the saints who were most admired had become one hideous mass of clotted filth."[5] Lecky devotes a number of pages to the nauseating foulness and almost incredible self-tortures of these anchorites; they throw much light on the mentality of a form of religion that attempted to erect self-denial and suffering into ends in themselves and to abrogate all sane and normal living.

The immediate effect of the Christian attitude towards sexual life was to frustrate and embitter marital relations. To quote Lecky again:

> Whenever any strong religious fervour fell upon a husband or a wife, its first effect was to make a happy union impossible. The more religious partner immediately desired to live a life of solitary asceticism or at least, if no ostensible separation took place, an unnatural life of separation in marriage. The immense place this order of ideas occupies in the exhortatory writings of the Fathers, and in the legends of the saints, must be familiar to all who have any knowledge of this department of literature. Thus—to give but a very few examples— St. Nilus, when he had already two children, was seized with a longing for the prevailing asceticism, and his wife was persuaded, after many tears, to consent to their separation. St. Ammon, on the night of his marriage, proceeded to greet his bride with a harangue upon the evils of the married state, and they agreed, in consequence, at once to separate. St. Melania laboured long and earnestly to induce her husband to allow her to desert his bed, before he would consent.[6]

[5] *History of European Morals,* 3rd ed. (London, 1911), II, 109.
[6] Ibid., p. 322.

Apart from sex-phobia and masochism, the mystical view of "nature" contributed powerfully to the clerical attitude towards contraception. This appears in the writings of St. Thomas Aquinas (1225-1274), who ranks, with Augustine, among the chief architects of Catholic ethics. Aquinas expressed the opinion that every carnal act deliberately done in such a way that generation cannot follow is a vice against nature, and a sin ranking next in gravity to homicide, since the generation of offspring is impeded.[7] Of course, the generation of offspring is impeded by every person who chooses to remain celibate, but Aquinas did not discuss this aspect of the question.

It is unlikely that Aquinas intended his words to be taken as expressing a general moral duty not to deny life to the unborn. Such a duty would be too extravagant for contemplation. Moral value cannot be attached to the billions of spermatozoa that are necessarily wasted even in a fruitful mating, nor to unfertilized ova. If there were a moral duty upon everyone to reproduce to the limit of his capacity, and if this duty were observed, the human race would indeed fulfil Malthus's gloomiest predictions. Aquinas's argument was, in fact, an argument not for unlimited procreation but for the strict limitation of sexual expression, and it thus followed in the same line as Augustine.

It is only slowly and with strong rear-guard opposition that the religions of the West have given up the doctrine that suffering and self-mortification are worthy in themselves. At the present day the majority of people regard these ancient notions, if they know about them at all, as a perversion of Christianity, which is essentially an ethical religion—a religion regulating man's conduct towards his fellow as well as his conduct towards God. Partly because of the attacks of the utilitarians, but still more because of the increased freedoms provided by

[7] *Summa Theologica,* Part II, Second Part, Question 154, Art. I; *Summa contra Gentiles,* Bk. III, Chap. 122.

modern civilization, men have renounced the sour doctrine that all indulgence of the sexual impulses is libidinous sin. Clerical notions have followed in the wake of this change in outlook, and the ancient formulas have been reinterpreted to keep pace with the evolution of ideas. The shift of ground is particularly easy for the Protestant varieties of the Christian religion, most of which are liberal in the sense that they hold themselves free to understand the ancient text in accordance with contemporary common sense.

However, the change was rather long delayed in the sexual field, because here prudery tended to support the old beliefs. It was only in 1930 that the Church of England gave guarded and limited approval to contraception at the Lambeth Conference: the resolution said that there may be justification for family limitation, recommended total abstinence as the "primary and most obvious way," but added that "if conception would clearly be wrong, and if there is a good moral reason why the way of abstinence should not be followed, we cannot condemn the use of scientific methods to prevent conception." Although this very cautiously worded resolution went too far for some of the bishops, there has since been little active opposition to the spread of contraceptive practices from the Church of England in its corporate capacity. Thus Hilaire Belloc, from the Catholic camp, was able to signalize the defeat of the old guard of Anglican bishops by saying that the majority were "agreed upon the whole on sodomy and birth control."

The Protestant sects of the United States have followed the same path. The Methodist Church, largest single Protestant denomination, unanimously endorsed birth control at its General Conference in 1956.[8] Similarly, to give one other illustration, the Synod of the Augustana Lutheran Church unanimously adopted broad guiding

[8] *Planned Parenthood News,* Summer 1956.

principles of family planning at its meeting in Los Angeles in 1954.

The Roman Church, it is scarcely necessary to say, continues unbending opposition to the use of appliances to prevent conception. In a statement criticizing the report of the Royal Commission on Population, the Roman Catholic hierarchy of England and Wales said:

We must proclaim again that artificial contraception is intrinsically evil, contrary to the law of God, and a mutilation of the purpose and process of the sexual act. That the practice is already widespread, that it is accepted by a large part of public opinion, in no way invalidates the truth of the above statement or diminishes our duty to publish it.[9]

The utmost Catholic concession to the demand for birth control, won after much hesitation and difference of opinion, is the use of the rhythm method or so-called "safe period." It may be noticed that recourse to this had been explicitly denounced by St. Augustine, as indeed his general philosophy demanded.[1] The concession was, however, made by Pope Pius XI, who, in an encyclical of 1930, allowed not only continence when practised by mutual consent, but also the use of the "safe period." *Coitus reservatus* is also permitted, but not (an astonishing distinction) *coitus interruptus,* the reason given being that the latter involves deliberate frustration of the act. Apparently there is no such deliberate frustration either in *coitus reservatus* or in the calculation of the safe period,[2] with the latter, said the Pope, "the intrinsic

[9] *The Times* (London), April 14, 1951.
[1] *On the Morals of the Manichæans,* XVIII, 65.
[2] For Catholic views see D. V. Glass: *Population Policies and Movements* (Oxford, 1940), pp. 165, 430. Professor Glass adds: "Presumably there would be no sin if, although *coitus reservatus* was intended, subsequent withdrawal was followed by emission." Some Catholic writers permit the use of a douche after intercourse to prevent conception. For a discussion see Joseph Fletcher: op. cit., p. 91. See also Rev. William J. Gibbons, S.J.: "Fertility Control in the Light of Some Recent Catholic Statements," 3 *Eugenics Quarterly* 9 (1956).

nature of the act is preserved." Since the "safe period" is supposed to last about half the month, according to tables furnished for the use of Catholics,[3] it provides, if reliable, a fairly good solution of the problem. The general medical opinion, however, is that the rhythm method is not a dependable method of control, because of the menstrual irregularity of many women, the risk of the woman making an error of calculation, and the uncertainty of the time of ovulation.

From the logical point of view, the permission to use the rhythm method seems to make any further resistance to birth control on the part of the Catholic community difficult to defend. Catholics now concede that the object of family limitation is capable of being rightful, and that it may be accomplished otherwise than by abstinence. Since sexual intercourse may rightfully take place without the aim of procreation, the old tendency to find something unclean and sinful in the sexual instinct seems to have been given up. Thus the whole controversy is narrowed to the means used to obtain family limitation. One would think that this question is merely one of efficiency, and that priestly dictation of methods is unscientific and absurd. The Catholic objection to contraceptives nevertheless continues to be rigorously maintained, and is rested on two grounds: the extremely subtle doctrine of the "intrinsic nature of the act" (which may mean that preventive measures are lawful provided that they are unreliable[4]), and the argument from "nature."

[3] See the table in Halliday Sutherland: *Control of Life* (London, 1944), App.; Leo T. Latz: *The Rhythm of Sterility and Fertility in Women* (Chicago, 1944); Frederick L. Good and Otis F. Kelly: *Marriage, Morals and Medical Ethics* (New York, 1951), p. 129.

[4] Catholics have freely admitted in conversation that the "safe period" is not safe, and this seems to be the very reason why in their view it is permissible. But if unreliability sanctifies, quite a number of appliance methods should be approved for the same reason.

Notwithstanding the unqualified words of the Pope allowing this method, Catholic physicians will generally refuse to instruct in its use unless with the permission of the priest who has seen the patient,

The argument from "nature"

One of the surest ways of running off the rails in a moral discussion is to introduce the words "natural" and "unnatural." This is what opponents of contraception persistently do. They assert that mechanical or chemical preventives are against nature, and, therefore, wrong. Place's short and offensive reply to this was that nature was a "blind and dirty old toad." The more academic reply is that the supposed connection between nature and morals (a connection that underlies the terminologyy of natural law in its Catholic currency) is completely mistaken. It is hardly necessary to point out that men do many things that are unnatural (in the sense of being a merely acquired skill or habit). Miscellaneous examples are washing, shaving, driving automobiles, building cathedrals, and giving blood transfusions, to which may be added all the rest of the intricate routine that has prolonged men's lives upon this planet; such acts all go without opposition on ethical grounds. The Trappist monk takes a vow of perpetual silence, and the Carthusian has his meals (except once a week) pushed to him through

and this permission is given only on grounds of health or for serious economic reasons; see Good and Kelly: op. cit., pp. 128–9; Gerald Kelly, S.J.: *Medico-Moral Problems* (Dublin, 1955), pp. 130ff., 270ff.; Joseph B. McAllister: *Ethics with Special Application to the Nursing and Medical Professions,* 2nd ed. (Philadelphia, 1955), pp. 344–5. The latter, a Catholic professor, justifies the use of the safe period for "just cause" on the ground that "if conception does not follow it is not because of anything they do." To some readers this way of escaping from an asserted moral obligation may seem to be casuistry in the worst sense; and the reason, if valid, does not explain the limitation to cases of "just cause." The limitation is perhaps due to the desire for religious aggrandizement; at any rate, Catholic writers frequently exult in the superior fertility of the Catholic family. Professor McAllister says: "The good of the family, the welfare of the state and the church requires children" (op. cit., p. 346).

bars in his solitary cell; these modes of existence are thought in certain quarters to be natural and admirable.

Such instances seem to show that the statement that an act is unnatural, coming from a moralist, means little more than that he does not like it. The term "unnatural" has been applied at different times to vaccination, anæsthetics, male gynæcologists, the emancipation of women, and the use of steam engines. In each of these applications the word was used of something that was new and, therefore, strange; although given an ethical content, it really expressed nothing more than conservatism, conformism, the exaggerated fear of the unfamiliar.

Just as an act may be both "unnatural" and permissible, so it may be both natural and wrong. This, perhaps, is not so likely a situation as the first. If an act is in accord with the ordinary nature of men, it may still be pronounced wrong for good reason, but only a puritanical moral code would attempt to thwart normal tendencies at every point. However, a simple example of the instincts leading one astray is this: when a particle is felt in the eye, the natural thing is to rub it—this is what children always do, and they have to be corrected. Here the natural act is only medically wrong, but it is not difficult to think of natural acts that are morally wrong. Jealousy and vengeance are quite natural, but have to be checked. The fact that it is natural to hate a criminal does not prove that retributive punishment is justified. Colour and racial prejudices may be natural, but that does not make them right.

Arguments of the type here considered, from the natural to the moral and from the unnatural to the immoral, are, in fact, only examples of the ancient confusion between "is" and "ought." As applied to contraception, the argument has not even its usual small measure of plausibility, because contraception is now a common practice, and is, therefore, as "natural" as any other aspect of civilization.

Catholic moralists sometimes try to put their case more specifically by saying that contraception is not merely artificial but against nature, because it prevents the natural consequence of the sexual act. They personify nature, and attribute an intention to nature which man frustrates by contraception. This extremely primitive if not blasphemous theology can perhaps be sufficiently answered by pointing out that nature evidently intends males to have beards, which intention they steadily frustrate by the use of the razor.

A slightly different form of the same reasoning is the argument, deriving from Aquinas, that contraception is wrong because it violates the primary end of a natural function.[5] Here what may be called the biological purpose of the sexual function is fallaciously identified with an assumed ethical purpose, and the use of the function for a different purpose is pronounced to be a violation. It might perhaps be shown that man's reasoning powers were developed in order to enable him to foresee and avoid danger from wild beasts; on the above argument, indulgence in pure mathematics then becomes wrong because it is a violation of the primary end of the mental function.

The argument from nature might have some relevance to ethics if it started from the common human needs— food, clothing, health, and so on. Sexual expression is certainly a deep psycho-physical need, which most people find it impossible permanently to frustrate without adverse effects upon their personality. Yet uncontrolled fertility will certainly thwart still more basic needs. The conclusion from these premises would be in favour of contraception.

A peculiar offshoot of the clerical outlook on marriage, which is worth mentioning here, was its attitude to analgesia in childbirth. St. Augustine thought that pain in labour was a consequence of the Fall, a divine punish-

[5] 6 *The Catholic Medical Quarterly* 39 (1953).

ment imposed upon all women for Eve's disobedience. The mother's agony expiated a sin in which both parents had participated. Hence Sir James Simpson, the pioneer of anæsthesia, was told that it was sinful, and particularly so in childbirth: not only was it unnatural, but it was a direct violation of the text of Genesis: "In sorrow thou shalt bring forth children." [6] Sir James retorted by pointing out that God put Adam into a deep sleep before extracting his rib—the first example of surgical anæsthesia on record. [7] Another story, perhaps apocryphal, is told of Queen Victoria, who, when asked why she accepted chloroform in her later confinements, in face of the text in Genesis, replied that she saw the men around her equally avoiding the Curse imposed on them —"In the sweat of thy face shalt thou eat bread." The controversy had a dying echo in January 1956, when the Pope announced that there was nothing sinful in the new techniques of painless childbirth without anæsthetics, even though they had been developed by scholars professing an ideology belonging to a materialistic culture. As to the quotation from Genesis, the words of Holy Scripture remained "true in the sense intended and expressed by the Creator—namely, motherhood will give the mother much suffering to bear." Nevertheless, said the Pope, Christianity does not interpret suffering and the cross in a merely negative fashion, so that mothers can accept the new techniques without any scruple of conscience. [8]

A chance visitor from Mars who happened to read this report in the morning paper might marvel that the leader of a world religion in a civilized age should think it necessary to make so obvious a pronouncement on a medical matter. He would not realize that it represented a hard-

[6] Gen. iii, 16.

[7] E. S. Turner: *Roads to Ruin* (London, 1950), p. 11; Joseph Fletcher: *Morals and Medicine* (Princeton, N.J., 1954), p. 30.

[8] *The Times* (London), January 9, 1956.

won victory against fundamentalism in religion, and a partial renunciation of the mischievous dogma of original sin.

"Increase and multiply"

The issue in the English-speaking countries now is not whether intelligent and prudent people should be allowed to practise contraception, but whether knowledge of contraception should be brought by government action to the backward and depressed classes and peoples. Here we are in a paradoxical position. Many persons who control their own fertility by scientific means have been opposed to the spread of these facilities, perhaps because they fear an uncontrolled decline in population. When to this is added powerful clerical opposition, it is not surprising that governments all over the world have been slow to adopt positive policies.

In Britain the question has been largely settled by private enterprise, so that population growth is not a major social problem. The opposite fear, that population will fall catastrophically, has now been exorcised. An alarm note was sounded in 1936, and continued through the war years; but a measure of reassurance was supplied by the Royal Commission on Population in 1948, and fears are no longer expressed of any catastrophic fall. Indeed, for the ordinary English citizen who is not a professional demographer, and who is, perhaps, too prone to take a superficial view, nothing would seem to be more welcome than a reduction of numbers in that tight little island. In the United States, after alarms of a diminishing population in the 1940's, the reproduction rate is now one of the highest in the world, and continually increasing; but expanding prosperity has hitherto succeeded in matching it.

That Malthus's fears proved premature for Britain was largely due to the rise of the movement for the birth control that he refused to contemplate, and also partly due to the opening up of the New World and increased efficiency in food production and transport. "The theories of Malthus," says Vogt "were buried beneath the bounty from the New World cornucopia.[9] But that they were fundamentally well-grounded is shown not only, it may be, by the difficult economic position in which Britain now finds herself—a position that may be aggravated as the newer continents fill up and find themselves with smaller exportable surpluses—but, far more immediately and dramatically, by what is happening in many other parts of the world—China, Egypt, India, Italy, Jamaica, Japan, Java, and elsewhere. The story is everywhere the same: advancing civilization brings death control in backward areas, but ignorance, poverty, and the scruples of a narrow morality and antiquated sexual outlook prevent this from being accompanied by adequate birth control. The consequence is, to quote Vogt again, that "more millions live more years in increasing misery."

Puerto Rico may well be taken as a near perfect illustration of Malthus's theories. This small Caribbean island, only twice the size of Long Island, and with less than half its area arable, had a population of about a million when in 1898 it became a dependency of the United States. This population was maintained by the balance of a high death rate with a high birth rate. With the introduction of modern medicine and sanitation the death rate was progressively reduced, while with improved economic opportunities the birth rate progressively increased.

The spiral of interacting forces grew tighter. By 1928 the population had grown to a million and a half; by 1943 it had

[9] William Vogt: *Road to Survival* (New York, 1948), p. 63.

passed two million. The 1950 census total was 2.2 million, giving a density of 645 people per square mile. Slightly more than one-third of an acre of farm land, much of it deteriorating from overuse, must provide food, clothing and shelter for each Puerto Rican.

By 1948 the Puerto Rican people reached an all-time high in rate of increase—and one of the highest recorded in human history. The present population of 2.2 million will at this rate double in about twenty-four years. The good intentions of 1898 have proved their inevitable consequences. By 1948, just fifty years after the battle of San Juan Hill, the symbol of American success in good works was 200,000 families—each averaging five members—many of which were in desperate need of even the most primitive shelter. Today, the slums and hovels in which they live bring tears to the eyes of those who have seen them.[1]

The failure of governmental agencies to foresee and forestall this problem was not due entirely to ignorance or inattention. Partly it was the result of what Dr. Robert Cook well calls the "instinctive obsession with fertility which is as old as man himself." Partly it was the result of a fear of political reactions through meddling in a sphere that religion tends to regard as its own prerogative. In Occupied Japan, with its endemic problem of fecundity, the Catholic Women's Clubs had a succession of remarkably easy victories in their campaign to prevent the United States Government from accompanying its medical and food relief measures with measures to reduce the phenomenal rise in population that was being recorded. However, the Japanese were allowed themselves to organize the provision of contraceptives, and even to enact a sterilization and abortion law. In Puerto Rico, a beginning has been made with spreading contraceptive knowledge through the clinics of the Bureau of Maternal

[1] Robert C. Cook: *Human Fertility: The Modern Dilemma* (New York, 1951), pp. 25-6. Copyright 1951 by William Sloane Associates, Inc. This and other passages are quoted by permission of the publishers, William Sloane Associates.

and Infant Hygiene, but much remains to be done before even the present rate of increase of births in the island can be reduced.

The case of Puerto Rico illustrates on a comparatively small scale what is happening, or beginning to happen, over a large part of the earth. Lord Boyd Orr recently stated that eight years ago it was estimated that the population of the world would be doubled by the end of the century. But, he added, this estimate has had to be revised, and the latest figures show that the doubling will occur in 1980.[2] It seems obvious that accelerating increases of this magnitude cannot be accommodated by better agricultural or fishing methods, which can at best alleviate the situation.[3] So far as I am aware, no non-Catholic food expert who has made a study of the situation has expressed the opinion that scientific or economic advances would be sufficient to solve the population problem without the control of fertility. Scientists look forward to the possibility of the chemical manufacture of

[2] The latest estimates of population growth by the Population Division of the United Nations are higher than ever before, and the medium estimate gives a world population of 3,628 million by 1980. See *World Population and Resources* (P.E.P.: London, 1955), an able and alarming survey of the situation. The human race, now totaling 2,600 million, is increasing by more than 80,000 a day (ibid.).

[3] Among works suggesting tempered optimism in the improvement of food supplies may be mentioned Sir E. John Russell's authoritative *World Population and World Food Supplies* (London, 1954) (he, however, advocates birth control); F. Le Gros Clark, ed., *Four Thousand Million Mouths* (London, 1951); Sir George Thomson: *The Foreseeable Future* (Cambridge, 1955), Chap. 6; Jacob Oser: *Must Men Starve?* (London, 1956). But the authors of *World Population and Resources* (P.E.P.: London, 1955), pp. 42–3, point out that in general those areas having greatest expectation of population increase are those which already have the most deficient diets. They conclude that "inequalities in population density, in health and happiness, in food and material supplies, and in much else besides are likely to be greater thirty years hence than at the present time, unless the growth of population in the overcrowded countries can be restrained. The whole problem is one of urgency and unparalleled importance."

food without the aid of living vegetation; [4] but it would be unwise to renounce population policies in reliance upon such a promise. Already two thirds of the world's population are living pitifully on or below the margin of subsistence.

India and Pakistan provide another example of the population problem that arises when medical science is brought to a technically backward country. Until 1919 the growth of population was sporadic—sometimes negative, sometimes positive, but never so fast as in the period since 1919. It was calculated a few years ago that the sub-continent's population was growing at the rate of about 1.2 per cent a year; if this is continued, the already swollen population will double in 58 years. Not only has this rate continued, but it has risen to 1.3. The special difficulty of the situation is that the increase of population is not matched by a proportionate increase in prosperity. Britain had for a time an even greater rate of increase during the nineteenth century, but that could be accommodated because, as already said, it coincided with great industrial advance and with the opening of new parts of the world which were able to supply food in exchange for manufactures. In India, as in Puerto Rico, the rise in population has resulted from improved medical measures without an adequate industrial or agricultural improvement to correspond. The Indian Finance Minister, Sir C. D. Deshmukh, said recently that four million new jobs had been created during the first four years of India's Five-Year Plan. But he proceeded to say that the natural growth of population had at the same time forced seven million new seekers after jobs on to the labour market. To give some idea of the pressure already exerted upon the resources of the country, calculations have been made of the number of persons dependent on agriculture per square mile of cultivated land

[4] Rosin, Jacob, and Eastman: *The Road to Abundance* (New York, 1953).

in various parts of the world. In the United States, in 1930, the number was 48 per square mile; in British India (in 1931) it was 422. In Puerto Rico it was 533.[5]

Recent scientific advance has accelerated the general tendency. In Ceylon, when malaria was eliminated by DDT, the death rate fell from 22 to 12 a thousand between 1945 and 1952—a fall in the death rate that took 70 years in Britain. Fecundity that was tolerable with the former death rate becomes an impossible burden with the new. Figures like these show the practical impossibility of maintaining the religious theory that although everything done by science to reduce the cruel and horrible natural checks on the increase of population is right, scientific methods to replace these natural checks are wrong.

The most encouraging feature of the situation is that Asiatic countries are spontaneously adopting measures to relieve the pressure of their teeming millions. Japan has an official policy of restricting population growth, and so now have India and China. India accepted a World Health Organization consultant on family planning, and under his advice set up a number of pilot projects to try the rhythm method of birth control. Calendar cards were used, with beads to count the days; but the method had only moderate success, notwithstanding that when incredulity was overcome the people received the clinical workers eagerly.[6] In Malaya the World Bank Organization urged Government support for family planning "in the long-run interest of Malayan people and of their welfare";[7] this has actually been done in Singapore,

[5] Kingsley Davis: *The Population of India and Pakistan* (Princeton, 1951), pp. 22–3. For other calculations, see Sir E. John Russell: *Science and Modern Life* (London, 1955); Horace Relshaw: *Population Growth and Levels of Consumption* (London, 1956).

[6] *New Statesman and Nation,* January 15, 1955, p. 59; C. P. Blacker: "The Rhythm Method: Two Indian Experiments," 47 *Eugenics Review* 93, 163 (1955).

[7] *The Times* (London), October 1, 1955.

as well as Barbados and Bermuda, but in no other part of the British Commonwealth. In China the subject has had to meet with resistance from Communist ideology, which is reluctant to admit that the economic system cannot cope with an unlimited addition to the number of mouths to be fed; but the facts of population growth have forced the widespread propagation of birth control methods.

Attempts to use the United Nations to promote education in family limitation on a world scale have been blocked by Catholic opposition: when Norway, in 1952, made this proposal in the World Health Organization, delegates from Roman Catholic countries threatened to leave the meeting, so that the matter was not even discussed. It is not easy to reconcile this attitude with the papal concession of some kinds of anti-conceptional measures. The explanation seems to be that many Catholics have not reconciled themselves even to this measure of indulgence. But, as Professor Julian Huxley commented, "it is surely the height of immorality to condemn hundreds of millions of human beings, existing and yet unborn, to a sub-standard existence on the strength of religious convictions or doctrines, when family limitation holds out the only hope of lesser misery and greater possibilities of human fulfillment."

These facts are relevant to the moral discussion because they show that moral ideas cannot be conceived and maintained in complete disregard of their actual effects upon human happiness. There is still no evidence in the policies either of the United States or of Great Britain that the terrible urgency of the conflict between numbers and resources is appreciated. Large sums are given, particularly by the United States, to assist the economic development of backward countries, but no attention seems to be paid to the impressive evidence that such aid may not prevent the average standard of nutrition from falling if it is not accompanied by the stabilization of population. The Colombo Plan, for example, made no provision for the reduction of fertility in the countries of south-east Asia, and the proposal in Britain and the United States (afterward withdrawn) to help finance the High Aswan Dam in Egypt was another example of a plan for this one-sided kind of material assistance to an overcrowded area.

Contraception and eugenics

The problem does not only concern the limits of subsistence, though this in itself is one of sufficient magnitude. There is, in addition, the problem of eugenic quality. We now have a large body of evidence that, since industrialization, the upper stratum of society fails to replace itself, while the population as a whole is increased by excess births among the lower and uneducated classes. There is, in short, an inverse ratio between fecundity and education or success. Dr. Robert C. Cook, the director of the Population Reference Bureau and editor of the *Journal of Heredity,* sums up the situation in the following arresting words:

Economic and educational success works eugenic miracles in reverse in an industrial society. The price for success is a slow, steady, remorseless biological extinction. Those who move up the ladder are, in effect, fractionally sterilized, in direct ratio to the degree of success they achieve. In terms of maximum fertility, graduation from high school is followed in the United States by a process equivalent to a 50 per cent reproductive sterilization. Graduation from college has the effect of removing, as though with laboratory precision, 75 per cent of the fertility present when the education process began.

Ever since the Republic was founded, Americans have recognized that the stability of a democratic government rests on an intelligent, literate, and informed citizenry. Today, in the United States, the intelligent get degrees, and the diligent and competent get houses and bank accounts and stomach ulcers. But it is the poor and unschooled who beget.[8]

This differential fertility between different classes is largely, if not entirely, due to the fact that the well-off and the intelligent make use of contraception, while those of low socio-economic status do not do so on the same scale, doubtless largely owing to the fact that contraceptives are not so readily available to them. There is evidence that the position would be radically altered if the number of birth control clinics in the country were made adequate to serve all classes of people.[9]

While the fact of "recruitment from the bottom" in present society is beyond question, its interpretation is a matter of some controversy. Owing to the extremely intricate way in which genes determine physical and mental qualities, differential class fertility has not the immediately catastrophic results that might be naïvely expected. Geniuses can come from poor families, and morons from university graduates. What is in issue, as Dr. Cook expresses it, is whether the national stock of fa-

[8] *Human Fertility: The Modern Dilemma* (New York, 1951), p. 222. Some of the statistical evidence is summarized on pp. 220–1 of Cook's work. It shows that, taking the number of children born to American white women of "old American" stock aged 45–9 years in 1940, the gain in replacement for those with no schooling was 80 per cent; for those with 1 to 4 years grade school it was 97 per cent; with increased schooling the rate fell steadily, becoming a loss of 20 per cent for those with 4 years in high school, and finally a loss of 44 per cent for those with 4 years in college. The figures became even more striking when an economic instead of educational standard was taken. For the negative correlation between family size and intelligence test score, see *Social Implications of the 1947 Scottish Mental Survey* (Publications of the Scottish Council for Research in Education XXXV) (London, 1953).

[9] See Frederick Osborn: *Preface to Eugenics* (New York, 1940), p. 132, Table 32, showing that among university graduates, belonging to a fairly homogeneous social and intellectual group, the most successful had substantially larger families than the least successful.

vourable genes is being built up or running down. It has not yet been possible to answer this question by statistical demonstration, because of the difficulty of measuring intelligence within close limits, but the probabilities seem to point strongly to a decline. Such British experts as Sir Cyril Burt and Sir Godfrey Thomson fear that the national decline in intelligence may be as high as 1 or 1.5 points per generation. Anything like this figure would be extremely serious: the figure of 1.5 decline would mean that the percentage of pupils of "scholarship" ability would be halved in little over 50 years, and the percentage of feeble-minded children almost doubled.[1] The weight of this evidence was recognized by the British Royal Commission on Population, which also remarked that unless steps were taken to correct fertility differentials, advances towards equality of opportunity could only make matters worse, since a growing proportion of the intelligent members of society would move up into the social group whose fertility was too low for replacement. It may be added that even if there is no ground for saying that intelligence or the lack of it is inherited, this does not justify complacency. It is impossible to be satisfied with a state of affairs in which tomorrow's citizens are produced and brought up, in disproportionate numbers, by the under-educated and poverty-stricken groups.

One might have thought that the warning of the Royal Commission, which was obviously of the greatest social concern, would have been immediately attended to by the British Government. Instead, that Government has ignored the Commission's suggestions for giving parents financial incentives commensurate with their social status.[2] Arrangements have been intensified for se-

[1] See the calculations of Professor Haldane and Sir Cyril Burt in a report prepared for the Royal Commission on Population (*Papers of the Commission,* Vol. 5, H.M.S.O., 1950).

[2] *Cmd 7695 of 1949,* p. 228. For the evidence in favour of these differences see *Population Policy in Great Britain* (P.E.P.: London,

lecting the brightest children of all classes for university education. At the same time, Britain operates a family allowance scheme which gives an incentive to produce children only to the poorest orders of society. This failure to produce a rational policy to correct dysgenic tendencies can perhaps be attributed partly to ignorance and failure to realize the social importance of the question, but it seems most of all to be due to the pressure of democratic opinion which refuses to see any genetic differences, even in terms of the broadest tendencies, between the different social classes. As Bertrand Russell puts it:

> The ideas of eugenics are based on the assumption that men are unequal, while democracy is based on the assumption that they are equal. It is, therefore, politically very difficult to carry out eugenic ideas in a democratic community when those ideas take the form, not of suggesting that there is a minority of *inferior* people such as imbeciles, but of admitting that there is a minority of *superior* people. The former is pleasing to the majority, the latter unpleasing. Measures embodying the former fact can therefore win the support of a majority, while measures embodying the latter cannot.[3]

This philosophy of eugenic egalitarianism is current also in the United States, and added to it is the pressure of powerful religious groups.

Few questions are more intimately connected with public health than those arising from organized efforts to inculcate birth control among low-income families: yet this is a field into which responsible heads of the United States Public Health Service hardly dare to look. The subject is scarcely mentioned, much less explored, at staff conferences, for it is considered "political dynamite."[4]

1948), pp. 140–1; *Papers of the Royal Commission on Population* (H.M.S.O., 1950), V, 55.

[3] *Marriage and Morals* (London, 1929), p. 206.

[4] Barrow Lyons: *Tomorrow's Birthright* (New York, 1955), p. 38.

III

STERILIZATION

The nature of sterilization

So deeply is the sexual instinct implanted within us that the word "sterilization," until one gets used to it, gives an unpleasant emotion. It may be well to begin by pointing out that sterilization is not the same as castration: it is not a desexing operation, and in no way interferes with sexual activity from the physiological point of view. This matter cannot be too strongly insisted upon, because it is not generally understood, and a grasp of the physiological facts is necessary if the social and personal importance of sterilization is to be appreciated. The point may be restated, then, in simple language by saying that the effect of the operation is completely unobservable by the patient; all that it does is to prevent sexual activities from bearing their normal fruit. In this it has the same effect as the use of efficient contraceptives.[1] Also, the risk to life in the performance of the operation is negligible.

Various surgical techniques may be used. For females,

[1] Sterilization of women sometimes increases libido because it removes the inhibitions resulting from fear of pregnancy; in any case the removal of this fear is in itself a source of satisfaction. A minority of women report a decrease of libido, but it seems that this is not to be connected with the operation and can be explained by reasons of health: see Moya Woodside: *Sterilization in North Carolina* (Chapel Hill, N.C., 1950), pp. 117-18, 132-4. For similar results in California, see E. S. Gosney and Paul Popenoe: *Sterilization for Human Betterment* (New York, 1929), and for England see *Cmd 4485 of 1934*, p. 29, and C. P. Blacker: *Voluntary Sterilization* (London, 1934), p. 22. Untoward psychological complications of vasectomy are mentioned later.

the ordinary method where sterilization is performed by itself is to make a break in the Fallopian tubes by tying or cutting (tubal ligation; salpingectomy). This blocks the passage between ovary and uterus. It can be done with a small incision, even under a local anæsthesia; and there is a method that does not require an abdominal incision at all. For males, vasectomy, tying the *vas* above the testis, is a still simpler procedure which takes five minutes; it can be done under local anæsthesia and without entering the abdominal cavity. The effect is merely to shut off a vital but very small portion of the bulk of the seminal fluid. It has no ill effects on the production of testicular hormones; the prostate gland and seminal vesicles continue to perform their function; and finally the operation preserves the theoretical possibility of fertility being re-established by operative correction of the condition, if this becomes desirable at a later date.[2] It seems, however, that the reversal operation is at present successful in only 35–40 per cent of cases.[3] The importance of reversal is largely a matter of psychology, for if the reversal of vasectomy and tubal ligation were to become a perfectly reliable operation, a powerful disincentive to submission to sterilization would be removed. The possibility of reversal also has some importance on the legality of sterilization, as will be shown later.

Although far more reliable in its effect than the use of contraceptives, the operation in its simple form is not 100 per cent successful, for an occasional pregnancy has followed, due to the reopening of the channel which was supposed to be closed. In California there were only four known pregnancies after 2,500 operations on women, and only three after 3,500 operations on men. There are techniques of testing whether the operation has been

[2] Frederick H. Falls in *Symposium on Medicolegal Problems,* Samuel A. Levinson, ed. (Philadelphia, 1948), p. 134; Gosney and Popenoe: op. cit., Chap. 9 and p. 150.

[3] V. J. O'Connor in 136 *Journal of the American Medical Association* 162 (1948).

successful.[4] Also, there are more drastic forms of the operation (as, by removing the uterus) which are infallible.

The close conceptual connection between surgical sterilization and appliance methods of birth control is shown by the fact that efforts are now being made to find a form of chemical or bio-chemical birth control that can be taken by the mouth or by way of injection. If such medicinal birth control, inducing temporary sterility by chemical means, were to be perfected, would it be "sterilization" or "birth control"? The obvious answer is that sterilization is a form of birth control, and birth control means at least *ad hoc* sterilization.

Therapeutic sterilization

In practice, sterilization is performed for one or other of three reasons: therapeutic, eugenic, and simple convenience.

Both in the United States and in England women are frequently sterilized for therapeutic reasons, that is to say for reasons of health, of course with their consent. It may be done either as a separate operation or when they undergo therapeutic abortion. There is a growing tendency on both sides of the Atlantic for surgeons to combine sterilization with therapeutic abortion in suitable cases, because the same condition that indicates the abortion may indicate that the woman should not become pregnant again.[5] Among therapeutic indications

[4] Gosney and Popenoe: op. cit., pp. 72–4, 79–80.

[5] It is reported that at the Chicago Lying-in Hospital, almost 70 per cent of patients undergoing a therapeutic abortion were sterilized at the same time. See Myrna F. Loth and H. Close Hesseltine: "Therapeutic Abortion at the Chicago Lying-in Hospital," 72 *American Journal of Obstetrics and Gynecology* 304 at 306 (1956). The authors

are malignant tumors, severe diseases of the heart or kidneys, recurrent toxæmia of pregnancy, and repeated Cæsarean section.

The strictly medical indication shades into a medico-social one where the circumstances of the woman are such that it would be unduly onerous for her to bear another child. How far sterilization can lawfully be performed on the medico-social indication apart from statute will be considered later. Partly because of the obscurity of the legal position, and partly because of a lack of interest on the part of some practitioners in the subject of preventive medicine, it is sometimes made a matter of complaint that the medical profession does not make enough use of sterilization to benefit the health of over-burdened mothers.

It may be mentioned that in Sweden, by an act of 1941, a woman may be sterilized on eugenic, social, medical, and medico-social indication. The results of this operation have generally been favourable, when carried out at the request of the woman, because it frees her from the fear of future pregnancies while not adversely affecting her capacity for sexual satisfaction. Of the cases studied by Professor Ekblad in Sweden, 86 per cent of the women sterilized had been grateful for the steriliza-

---

say: "Instances where sterilization may not be indicated would include such maternal disorders as severe hyperemesis gravidarum, certain cases of pulmonary tuberculosis, active rheumatic fever, rubella during the first trimester, and other conditions from which the patient may recover or improve medically to the extent that the present hazard would be likely not to recur. On the other hand, there are instances in which sterilization is indicated but is deferred as an unjustifiable surgical risk. . . . There has been a marked increase in recent years in the number of hysterectomies performed for this purpose, since hysterectomy affords the surest method of sterilization, and since modern medical advances have sharply decreased the risks of this procedure to the patient. An additional advantage of removal of the uterus and cervix is the elimination of existent or future disease of these organs. With the increase in hysterectomies has come a corresponding decrease in the number of abdominal hysterotomies and the associated tubal ligations."

tion ever since its performance. Of the rest, only four women (5 per cent) were wholly dissatisfied with the operation, which had been performed against their wishes as a condition for legal abortion, either on eugenic or on social grounds. No woman who had herself desired to be sterilized was afterward dissatisfied with the operation.[6] Studies in the United States reach similar conclusions.[7]

It need hardly be pointed out that there are often indications for therapeutic abortion that are not also indications for sterilization. Some writers allege that obstetric surgeons who perform abortions may sterilize the woman unnecessarily by way of expressing their resentment at having to perform the abortion.

Therapeutic sterilization of males is uncommon except as an incident of some other operation.[8] However, a husband may be sterilized where it would be dangerous for his wife to bear another child.

The advantage of sterilization over contraception

It may be asked why surgical sterilization should be preferred to advice on contraceptive techniques. One reason is that no contraceptive is infallible, and a single failure may mean grave danger to the mother. Even where the circumstances have not quite this urgency, there may be special difficulties in advising upon a satisfactory method of contraception. The husband may refuse to co-operate, and a multipara is difficult to fit with a satisfactory diaphragm. Or, as very commonly happens,

---

[6] Martin Ekblad: *Induced Abortion on Psychiatric Grounds* (*Acta Psychiatrica et Neurologica Scandinavica,* Stockholm, 1955), Chap. 15.
[7] See particularly Woodside: op. cit., pp. 143ff.
[8] Blacker: op. cit., pp. 26–7.

the woman may be too lacking in intelligence, foresight, or dexterity to be relied upon to follow instructions.
Although some persons experience no difficulty in learning and practising contraceptive technique, others find
it repugnant, difficult, or impossible. In the previous
chapter an opinion of Dr. Himes was quoted to the effect that women want children only when they want
them. The assumption of the birth control movement
is that if people are given the opportunity of planned
parenthood they will use it in their own interest and
that of their children. That this assumption is not entirely
justified by the facts is shown by Mrs. Moya Woodside,
whose first-hand and objective study of the sterilization
practice in North Carolina deserves to be regarded as one
of the important social documents of this century.

Even when every facility is provided, indifference and inertia
are shown by a large proportion of those whom it is wished
to help; while on the other hand, competent individuals with
expressed desire for restriction of parenthood, able to carry
out the necessary techniques, often display a high percentage
of unexplained contraceptive failure. As a general rule, efficient practice is directly related to intelligence and intensity
of motivation, and therefore no great success would be expected from the introduction of birth control knowledge to
the unintelligent and socially irresponsible persons who make
up the social problem or subnormal group.

For a decade now, the material conditions for achievement
of a neo-Malthusian utopia have existed in North Carolina.
Incorporated as part of the public health service, contraceptive advice and supplies are provided free of charge at almost
all the city and county health departments throughout the
State, and public health nurses are encouraged to inform
their patients about the advantage of planned pregnancy. Yet
the program fails to reach many women of normal intelligence or seriously to affect their reproductive behavior, and
has had practically no success with women of borderline or
subnormal mentality. Workers in the contraceptive service
are unanimous about the difficulty of persuading such per-

sons to attend clinics, of instructing them in procedures, and ensuring that advice is carried out.[9]

It is this limitation upon the effectiveness of contraception that creates the need for both sterilization and abortion as subsidiary means of family planning and of eugenic and population control. Abortion, though sometimes the only possible solution, is a costly and wasteful form of birth control; and besides, some women will not accept abortion, either because they fear the operation or because they are indifferent to the quantity and quality of the children they produce and the surroundings in which they will be brought up. Sterilization settles the problem once and for all.

Eugenic sterilization

The obvious social importance of preventing the birth of children who are congenitally deaf, blind, paralyzed, deformed, feeble-minded, mentally diseased, or subject to other serious hereditary afflictions, and the inadequacy of contraception for this purpose, has naturally given rise to the proposal to use sterilization of the unfit as a means of racial improvement.

Religious principles, which still give a certain support to reproductive laissez-faire, were conceived at a time when the mechanism of life was an almost impenetrable mystery. A man was mad or blind not because his father had contracted syphilis or carried a dominant or recessive gene of that character, but because he himself was

[9] Moya Woodside: *Sterilization in North Carolina* (Chapel Hill, N.C., 1950), p. 105; cf. ibid., pp. 123–5. This and other quotations are by permission of the publishers, the University of North Carolina Press.

possessed of a devil or visited by God. Even such an elementary biological fact as the equality of male and female contributions to heredity was the subject of hot argument as late as the seventeenth century. The discovery of the units of heredity—chromosomes, genes, and plasmagenes—has certainly not made the inquiry seem to be a simple one; but great advances have been made and an enormous vista of inquiry opened up. Inevitably, as new knowledge is won, there arises the demand to turn it to use. Genetic knowledge can only be utilized by interfering with the process of reproduction.

One argument for surgical sterilization is that it is a necessary corollary of medical and social advances in other fields. We have evolved by natural selection, but, by keeping alive mentally and physically ill-equipped children, we are opposing natural selection. The logical deduction seems to be that, unless steps are taken to counteract the tendency, we shall as a race become progressively less fit. Indeed, evidence of genetic deterioration is already found by some observers. Others disagree and point to the difficulty of statistical proof of deterioration. The mere fact that more and more people are admitted to mental hospitals is not a proof, because this may well reflect improvements in diagnosis, in the possibilities of treatment, and in the public acceptance of the mental hospital as a fit place for the care of the insane.

Whether or not a genetic decline has set in, the fact remains that the community is burdened with an enormous number of unfit members, and that every humane person must concur with the eugenist in wishing to see an improvement. Acceptance of the logic of the eugenist's argument by the adoption of practical programs would, however, involve a considerable change in traditional ideas. The common view is that every man and every woman has a right to the fulfillment of parental instincts, and to the kind of substitute immortality conferred by reproduction. Romantic marriage, also, is contracted with almost complete disregard of genetic aspects, and if the results are not generally calamitous, this is not due to any foresight of the parties. The propagation of poor stock is regarded by public opinion as neither a sin nor a crime against humanity. It is outside the range of morals, social action, and individual responsibility. There is a striking contrast between human fecklessness in our own reproduction and the careful scientific improvement of other forms of life under man's control. No rose-grower, pigeon-fancier or cattle-breeder would behave as men do in their own breeding habits. "Imagine," says Bertrand Russell "the feelings of a farmer who was told that he must give all his bull calves an equal opportunity!" [1]

For close on a hundred years, ever since the writings of Sir Francis Galton, the popular attitude has been under attack from a eugenist movement which has sought to make men take thought for posterity. The sterilization laws found in some parts of the world represent the first social acknowledgment of this new approach. The United States was the pioneer. After unsuccessful efforts in Michigan and Pennsylvania, the first sterilization act was passed by Indiana in 1907. This was later declared unconstitutional, as were all other similar statutes (with one anomalous exception) that came before the courts before 1925. The earlier statutes tended to confuse sterilization as a measure of negative eugenics with sterilization as a punishment or defense measure for rape and other crimes; but the tendency of the later legislation has been to eliminate reference to criminality, and this has strengthened the constitutional position of the measures. That sterilization statutes are capable of being constitutional was finally decided in

[1] *Marriage and Morals* (London, 1929), p. 206.

the United States Supreme Court in 1927,[2] Justice Holmes uttering his famous remark that "three generations of imbeciles are enough."

The progress of the sterilization movement to the present date may be summed up in a few facts and figures. Twenty-eight of the United States now have laws of this character. All designate feeble-minded persons as subject to sterilization, and all but one cover the insane. Most laws specifically include epileptics. There is hardly any reference to hereditary physical defects.

Most of the laws are confined to persons in institutions. Some are voluntary in that they require the consent of the patient or his relative or guardian; others are compulsory. The task of making an order for sterilization is conferred upon an administrative board or court, and there are various provisions as to appeals, surgical procedure, and so on, which vary from one state to another.

A total of roughly 50,000 sterilizations had been performed in the United States by 1949, to which California alone contributed about 20,000. Although sterilization has found favour in a few states as a branch of social medicine, most states having sterilization laws have never put them into serious effect. Sometimes this is due to uncertainty as to the constitutionality of the law, but the most important factors are cessation of interest and divided public opinion.

Laws similar to those in the United States are in force in the Canadian provinces of Alberta and British Columbia. In Europe, sterilization laws have been passed in Scandinavia[3] and in the cantons of Vaud and Berne in Switzerland. Contraception and sterilization were legalized in Japan in 1948, along with abortion, notwith-

[2] Buck v. Bell, 274 U.S. 200. See also, on the history and constitutionality of the legislation, 35 *Iowa Law Review* 253 (1950); J. H. Landman: *Human Sterilization* (New York, 1932).

[3] For a summary see Hermann Mannheim: *Criminal Justice and Social Reconstruction* (London, 1946), pp. 24ff.

standing that the majority religion, Buddhism, disapproves of birth control. In 1954, 38,056 sterilizations were carried out under this law.[4]

The cause of eugenics suffered a set-back through its unwelcome espousal by the Nazi government of Germany in the law of 1933. This introduced both sterilization and castration on a compulsory basis, and was immediately put into effect on a large scale. The authoritarian character of the measure, and strong suspicions that it was used as a racial and political instrument rather than as a scientific one—suspicions intensified by the way in which this legislation was followed closely by mass-killing on racial grounds—brought the whole cause of eugenics into a disrepute among freedom-loving peoples that is only slowly being dissipated.

This brief history might seem to indicate substantial if chequered progress for the eugenic idea. However, concurrently with the movement for eugenic sterilization, geneticists began to have serious doubts as to the scientific praticability of substantial racial improvement through this means. The reason is that almost all the common serious hereditary ills—including the genetic types of insanity, feeble-mindedness, deafness, and blindness—are carried by recessive or multiple genes, and so may be transmitted by an individual who himself shows no sign of the disease; conversely, an individual who is himself affected may have a normal child. For example, it has been estimated that 89 per cent of all feeble-minded children come from normal parentage;[5] while feeble-minded parents may have children who are normal

[4] C. P. Blacker: "Japan's Population Problem," 48 *Eugenics Review* 30 (1956). Good results are claimed in Japan for the method of tubal cautery, which is far simpler than tubal ligation.

[5] Fisher: "Elimination of Mental Defect," 18 *Journal of Heredity* 529 (1927). Calculations of this kind are subject to much difference of opinion, partly because the psychological testing of the parents varies in efficiency. Some estimates of the proportions are lower than that quoted: see C. P. Blacker: *Voluntary Sterilization* (London, 1934), Chap. 4.

in their hereditary characteristics. It follows that to pre-vent the birth of substantially all defectives would re-quire the sterilization of a vast number of carriers who do not show mental defect, and indeed who cannot in the present state of knowledge be certainly identified as carriers until they have had children. Merely to sterilize all actual sufferers would have a comparatively small effect on the total incidence of inherited mental defect in the community.

This new genetic knowledge is a serious set-back for eugenic proposals, and makes the task of racial improve-ment immensely more difficult and protracted than was thought to be the case at the beginning of the century. At first sight it may seem to destroy the argument in favour of the sterilization laws. This, however, is not so. However deep the gloom of the geneticists, the steriliza-tion laws have gained support from two important dis-coveries.

The first is that there is a reason for not allowing defectives to reproduce themselves, distinct from the genetic reason. The undesirability of allowing defectives or near defectives to bear children does not rest solely upon the possibility of their transmitting the defect by genetic means. This is because the child, even if of nor-mal intelligence, will be gravely handicapped by the mere fact of being reared by a feeble-minded parent. As the English Board of Control expressed it, in a report which contemplated favourably the sterilization of de-fectives:

Though it does not necessarily follow that the children of defective parents will themselves be defective, they are liable to be exposed to the miseries and hardships of being brought up by a mother or father incapable of self-control who will almost certainly neglect them, and who may, by reason of mental instability and ungovernable temper, aggravate by cruelty the results of ignorance and neglect.[6]

[6] *Annual Report* for 1928, quoted by Blacker: op. cit., p. 11.

It is partly for this reason that the sterilization laws have found public acceptance in those states, such as California and North Carolina, that still make them an active part of their health programs. In other words, although the historical aim of the legislation is eugenic, its actual administration tends to be on social and economic grounds relating to the individual concerned, and this greatly reduces the difficulty of the philosophical problem involved in compulsory sterilization. Mrs. Woodside says:

In the light of North Carolina experience, theoretical concepts of individual liberty are often remote from the sort of practical situation in which sterilization is usually proposed. . . . Feeble-minded parents . . . many of them public charges, by reason of their deficient mentality are often socially irresponsible, incapable of the proper care of children, and in no sense fitted for parenthood. In practice, sterilization is most vigorously supported by those who see its immediate social and economic advantages; the more abstract considerations of Mendelian inheritance are rarely the moving force.[7]

The second discovery was made by the sterilization states, and is of a distinctly encouraging character. This is that sterilization is to the advantage of the person sterilized, and, at least in the case of females, is actually welcomed.

Among the therapeutic or personal benefits of sterilization which happen to concur with the eugenic one are the following. Female epileptics are protected by sterilization, since convulsions are worse during pregnancy and care of children a heavy responsibility even when the patient is married.[8] Where the patient suffers from puerperal psychosis, the main therapeutic advantage is that the fear of pregnancy—as well as its actual

[7] Moya Woodside: op. cit., pp. 24–5.
[8] Ibid., p. 28.

occurrence—is removed.[9] Again, all defectives are helped by not having the burden of a family.

The last point deserves to be amplified. It is often said that the need for surgical sterilization is obviated where a feeble-minded or other handicapped person is in institutional care. Segregation is *de facto* sterilization, and is, therefore, a substitute for surgery. However, the new conception of the institutional treatment of mental defectives is that it should fit them, so far as possible, for returning to live in the general community under supervision; and a "flowing lake" policy of this kind may need, from the human as well as the eugenic point of view, that the individual should submit himself to be sterilized before leaving the institution. One important reason, particularly in the case of the female defective, is that while it may be very much to her advantage to be allowed to marry and so have the comfort and security of her own home, the burden of having children may nullify the efforts to stabilize her in society.[1] Even if these arguments apply only to a small proportion of institutionalized defectives, they are valid for that proportion.

Sterilization in these circumstances is sometimes made a ground of complaint by opponents, on the ground that the operation is not really a voluntary one. Thus the Rev. Joseph B. Lehane, in his book on the subject written from the Catholic point of view, says that "the word 'voluntary' frequently becomes a mere subterfuge, for it is often a condition of discharge from an institution that the patient be sterilized. . . . Such a condition can scarcely be held to make the decision free and equal, and for practical purposes nullifies the meaning of the word 'voluntary.' " [2] This remark may be true in one

[9] Ibid., p. 30.

[1] See the findings of the Wood Committee in England summarized in C. P. Blacker: *Voluntary Sterilization* (London, 1934), pp. 8–11.

[2] Joseph B. Lehane: *The Morality of American Civil Legislation Concerning Eugenical Sterilization* (Washington, D.C., 1944), p. 14.

meaning of the word "voluntary," but then, in the same meaning of the word, few if any choices in life are voluntary, for every choice involves the acceptance of a course that is more preferred in place of one that is less preferred. The fact is that circumstances do sometimes impose upon the authorities of an institution the unhappy necessity of saying to an inmate that she must either be refused discharge or be sterilized. The third alternative, that she be allowed to run the risk of producing a family, may contain possibilities too tragic for enlightened opinion to tolerate, either for her own sake or for that of her children. It seems unfair to say that giving the defective woman this choice, which is the best that the authorities can do for her benefit, involves a "subterfuge." Surely it is better to offer the opportunity of freedom upon a condition than not to offer it at all.

Nor is the condition attached to the offer necessarily distasteful to the patient. That feeble-minded women welcome sterilization when they have sufficient intelligence to realize its implications is one of the very important findings of Mrs. Woodside's North Carolina study. The author says:

However retarded she may be, no woman welcomes a sequence of unwanted pregnancies and the misery which they entail. The sample of sterilized women interviewed contained several individuals of dull mentality and very poor economic circumstances, and their attitude to the operation was no less appreciative than was that of those of higher intelligence.[3]

Similarly, when a married man who is a patient in a mental hospital is allowed to go home on parole, perhaps

[3] Woodside: op. cit., p. 113.

It is sometimes made a ground of fear that the sterilized female defective will be likely to become promiscuous and spread V.D. But the opinion of those with experience of these people is that sterilization does not increase the risk of promiscuity, because the fear of child-bearing has no deterrent effect on the mentally deficient (ibid., p. 80; Gosney and Popenoe: op. cit., 39).

on a short visit, it is not only eugenically but socially undesirable that he should be allowed to take the opportunity to procreate children. Consequently, such a patient is, in the sterilization states, occasionally operated upon before he goes on parole, often at his wife's insistence.[4] Here, again, the operation may be said to be to the patient's advantage because it facilitates parole.

To sum up, states that have given their sterilization laws a fair trial regard them as beyond the experimental stage and as a proven means of social betterment. The four considerable advantages found to result from the operation are the prevention of the birth of handicapped children, the promotion of family welfare through the limitation of size, the improvement of maternal health, and last and least, the saving of public funds.[5]

The happy concurrence of public and private interest, in the case of mental deficiency or mental disease, has meant that the administration of the law of sterilization has not needed to rely on compulsion. Even in states where the law appears to have a compulsory character, it is found in practice that the compulsory power is rarely exercised, and then only in mental institutions. The nature of the proposed operation is carefully explained to the patient and his or her spouse, guardian, or relatives, and since selection is limited to the urgent and obvious cases, consent is generally forthcoming. Often requests from relatives have already been made.[6]

This means that one of the major theoretical objections to a policy of sterilization disappears. It is objected, *a priori,* that sterilization must either be voluntary and, therefore, ineffective, or compulsory and, therefore, an

[4] Woodside: op. cit., p. 30.

[5] Woodside: op. cit., pp. 151ff. Detailed surveys of the working of the California law will be found in *Collected Papers on Eugenic Sterilization in California*, E. S. Gosney, ed., published by the Human Betterment Foundation, California, 1930.

[6] Woodside: op. cit., pp. 19, 71, and *passim;* Gosney and Popenoe: op. cit., pp. 35–8.

invasion of human rights. We now know that, given the assistance of devoted workers, a voluntary system is adequate. Mrs. Woodside expresses the requirement of good human relations in her usual felicitous way.

The success of voluntary eugenic sterilization depends on a tremendous amount of good case work. Convincing a person of low intelligence and usually little education to have this operation requires endless patience and an understanding from the social worker of feeling as well as fact, of emotional reactions as well as statutory formality. It is not a process which can be carried out routinely, in haste, or by those unskilled in the handling of human relationships.[7]

The result of all this is that no one with experience of sterilization laws now advocates a compulsory system, in the sense that the patient is to be taken to the operating-table by force or fraud. Sterilization laws are workable and can do much good even though the full consent of the patient is required, where the patient has the mental ability to appreciate the issue. If the patient is such a low-grade defective that he or she is totally incapable of understanding what the operation means, there is no need for the operation because the patient needs permanent care in an institution. It may be said that even in the case of higher-grade defectives the notion of consent has a certain unreality, because such persons are highly suggestible, so that their consent is readily obtained. Consequently, for their protection, the consent of relatives is and should be sought in addition to their own consent. With this safeguard, the law is as voluntary as a law dealing with persons of limited mental capacity can ever be.

The American experience is of great interest because it shows how remote from reality in a democratic community is the fear—frequently voiced by Americans themselves—that voluntary sterilization may be the "thin end of the wedge," leading to a large-scale violation of

[7] Ibid., p. 91.

human rights as happened in Nazi Germany. In fact, the American experience is the precise opposite—starting with compulsory sterilization, administrative practice has come to put the operation on a voluntary footing.

These remarks may help to remove some of the misconceptions of the working of these laws, entertained not only in England but in parts of the United States that have not adopted them. Critics of the American laws often point to the fact that some of them include categories of persons (e.g., habitual criminals and homosexuals) which are open to objection, because there is insufficient evidence of hereditary transmission, or else the likelihood of such transmission is small. Also, the inclusion of criminals is psychologically wrong because it fosters the mischievous impression that sterilization is a punitive measure.[8] In fact, however, little use has been made of the powers in respect of these categories, and the actual use has been restrained and cautious.

There is another occasion of mistaken or at least exaggerated criticism. Some of the American laws permit not merely sterilization but asexualization (castration, ovariectomy) where circumstances require it. Recourse to this operation is relatively infrequent in practice, and is being decreasingly authorized under the sterilization laws, but it has been urged from time to time for such persons as very low-grade idiots who manifest unsuitable sexual traits, males permanently institutionalized whose behaviour presents a problem in the hospital, and persons convicted of attempted rape.[9] There would evidently be little loss if these powers of asexualization were given up, and this would probably have a beneficial effect on the public attitude towards sterilization.

[8] Cf. Gosney and Popenoe: op. cit., p. 68.

[9] See Woodside: op. cit., pp. 27–8, 33; Gosney and Popenoe: op. cit., pp. 96–8. According to the latter, castration after puberty often does not take away sexual power. The Committee of the American Neurological Association, in the report cited at n. 1 immediately below, states, at p. 9, that California has abandoned asexualization in practice.

In this discussion we have got away from the eugenic considerations with which we started. To return to them for a moment, if the sterilization laws can be justified on medical and social grounds other than eugenic, does anything remain of the eugenic argument?

The answer is that, notwithstanding the deep divisions among geneticists on some issues, there is still solid scientific support for continuing the policy of sterilization on eugenic grounds. Even in the case of mental deficiency or feeble-mindedness, the sterilization of actual sufferers will tend to reduce the incidence of the affliction, and this is true also of other transmissible diseases. If sterilization can only reduce hereditary ills by a small proportion each year, the result may still be to benefit tens of thousands of persons in each generation, as well as to save the community the cost of their care.

It may be counted a fortunate coincidence, then, that in the case of defectives and others an operation desirable for eugenic reasons in the long view can often be shown to be desirable for social and humanitarian reasons in the short view, and moreover that an operation to benefit posterity can be shown also to benefit the patient. These coincidences make it much more readily acceptable both to the patient and his relatives and to general public opinion, which is apt to be little impressed by the birthright of posterity.

That the weight of opinion among geneticists is still in favour of sterilization, notwithstanding the new understanding of the complexity of heredity, is shown by two reports, one American and one English. In 1936, a committee of the American Neurological Association for the investigation of eugenical sterilization concluded that certain of the mental diseases rest on a hereditary basis, and named these as schizophrenia, manic-depressive psychosis, most of the forms of feeble-mindedness, and possibly epilepsy, together with the very rare neurologic disorders. The committee advocated the passage of voluntary sterilization laws to apply to certified cases of these diseases within private or public hospitals or cared for in the community.[1]

In England, in 1934, a strong committee in what is known as the Brock Report[2] went further, and, while condemning compulsory sterilization, recommended that voluntary sterilization should be declared lawful, under safeguards, not only for mental defectives and persons who have suffered from mental disorder, but for persons who suffer from or are believed to be carriers of grave physical disabilities that have been shown to be transmissible, and also persons believed to be likely to transmit mental disorder or defect. In presenting the recommendations, which were unanimous, the committee said: "We believe that few who approached the question with an open mind and listened week by week to the evidence we have heard could have failed to be struck by the overwhelming preponderance of evidence in favour of some measure of sterilization." The words of the committee on the subject of mental defect are also worth quoting:

In the first place we were impressed by the dead weight of social inefficiency and individual misery which is entailed by the existence in our midst of over a quarter of a million mental defectives and of a far larger number of persons who without being certifiably defective are mentally subnormal. This mass of defectives and subnormals is being steadily recruited and is probably growing. Certainly nothing is being done to diminish it beyond the segregation of a portion of those more obviously unfitted for community life. In the second place, we were increasingly impressed by the injustice of refusing to those who have good grounds for believing they may transmit mental defect or disorder and who are in every way unfitted for parenthood the only effective means of escaping from a burden which they have every reason to dread. Con-

[1] Abraham Myerson and others: *Eugenical Sterilization* (New York, 1936); cf. Myerson in 52 *Yale Law Journal,* at 628–31 (1943).
[2] *Departmental Committee on Sterilization, Cmd 4485 of 1934.*

93

traception is no remedy, since we are dealing with people the majority of whom cannot be expected to exercise the care without which contraceptive measures are bound to fail. Nor is voluntary abstinence any remedy. Facts must be faced. It is idle to expect that the section of the community least capable of self control will succeed in restraining one of the strongest impulses of mankind. The mere suggestion is so fantastic that it carries its own refutation. Without some measure of sterilization these unhappy people will continue to bring into the world unwanted children, many of whom will be doomed from birth to misery and defect. We can see neither logic nor justice in denying these people what is in effect a therapeutic measure.

The proposals of the committee were afterwards supported by a number of public bodies including the Royal College of Physicians, but have not been implemented. The general English public has relapsed into a condition of ignorance and indifference.[3]

It may be mentioned that there are a few afflictions the transmission of which is so simple that they could be stamped out or greatly reduced by sterilization. Examples are Huntington's chorea and some forms of epilepsy. They have been brought within the purview of the Canadian sterilization laws, and it might well be provided that no individual suffering from these diseases shall marry unless he or she has first been sterilized. Even in the case of mental deficiency, as has already been observed, the sterilization of actual defectives would in the long run reduce the total incidence of the disease. The most important matter in any community is to make a start, no matter on how limited a scale. Experience in the actual working of sterilization is

[3] Dr. Barnes, Bishop of Birmingham, advocated sterilization of the unfit in a speech on November 28, 1949, and letters of protest followed in the press. Mr. Chuter Ede, then Home Secretary, said on March 16, 1950 that he was not prepared to introduce legislation on sterilization because "the matter is highly controversial and involves very serious infringement of the liberty of the subject." (*Parliamentary Debates,* [*House of Commons*], vol. 472, col. 1226.)

likely to give confidence for an extension. Moreover, genetics is in its infancy, and the future holds unlimited promise for this most complex of all the natural sciences. There is every reason to expect the day when a man's genetic constitution will be able to be determined otherwise than by the trial-and-error method of waiting for him to sire children and grandchildren. When genes can be docketed under the microscope the prospect of a vast improvement in the human race will, given the willingness to work for it, become a reality.

It should be pointed out by way of postscript to this discussion of eugenics that there is in any event no case for compulsory sterilization unless milder methods are inadequate; and some milder methods have hardly been tried. No special facilities have been provided, either in the United States or in England, for young men and women to obtain expert advice before marriage on their sexual problems and eugenic prospects. Most of the United States, however, require a blood test for freedom from communicable syphilis before marriage, and a few of these states require a medical certificate of freedom from tuberculosis in the infectious state. These provisions have been found valuable and effective in reducing disease. Some states go, in theory, even further: Michigan, Nebraska, and South Dakota forbid the marriage of insane and feeble-minded persons who may transmit their condition to their offspring, and North Carolina requires in the pre-marital health certificate a statement that the applicant for a marriage license is not epileptic, feeble-minded, or of unsound mind. These provisions are of little effect in practice because of the lack of any system of registration of the insane and feeble-minded, lack of time and specialized knowledge on the part of the practitioner who examines, and the ease with which couples can evade restrictions by going into neighbouring states.[4] Finally, no restriction on marriage is effective

[4] Woodside: op. cit., p. 46.

against the feeble-minded and other persons who reproduce themselves outside marriage.

Sterilization of convenience

Since sterilization has become a safe operation—and a particularly simple one for the male—and since it does not result, from a physiological point of view, in sexual impotence, the view may be taken that it is capable of being a reasonable form of birth control, provided, of course, that the individual is quite certain, taking account of all the vicissitudes of life, that he or she will never want another child. Too great importance need not be attached to the fact that the operation is, at least for the female, practically irreversible—provided that sufficient reasons for its performance exist. A mother of three or four children may well decide with finality that she does not want a larger family. After all, if tubal ligation is irrevocable, so is the birth of an unwanted child.

The experience in states possessing sterilization laws is that women are relatively easy to convince of the advantage of the operation. Mrs. Woodside's observations upon the attitude of the women of North Carolina, where sterilization under the local eugenic law has become part of the people's thinking, are worth quoting.

It is a fact of considerable sociological importance that women of all classes in the community are aware that sterilization is available. They know it assures them of permanent protection free from the drawbacks and uncertainties of birth control (which tends in any case to be inconsistently practised among groups who need it most), and they have before them the example of those already operated on who are enthusiastic in their praises. Revolutionary though it may seem in contrast with the folkways and beliefs of a religiously-minded culture, it is fast becoming an accepted pattern of the contemporary social scheme. . . .

There is no doubt as to the popularity of the operation. "I'm proud of mine" was common vernacular approval. "People envy me," said a butcher's wife. "It's really something to be able to plan and know where you are." Many wished they could have been sterilized years sooner, and one woman with a record of 12 pregnancies summed up her view in the spontaneous remark: "I think it's a great thing for poor folks to have." Relief from worry and anxiety was everywhere expressed, not only among the poor but among those better-off women who had obtained what are known to the medical profession as sterilizations of convenience.[5]

This does not mean that there is any immediate likelihood of such sterilizing operations becoming a common practice in the United States, for several limiting factors are at work. Catholic doctors and hospitals, of course, will not perform them. Among Protestant doctors and hospitals much depends on individual attitudes; some hospitals dislike doing too many such operations because "it makes their records look bad."[6] It seems that the American College of Surgeons has adopted a policy of bringing pressure to stop sterilizations of convenience.[7] In pursuance of this restrictive policy, some hospitals require sterilizations to be authorized by special boards. In addition, the uncertainty of the law is sometimes a restraint.

In the Territory of Hawaii and the Commonwealth of Puerto Rico, extreme population pressure has stimulated recourse to this form of birth control, and post-partum sterilization has been undertaken on a considerable scale.[8]

Vasectomy as a form of birth control for males is slow of acceptance. The reason for this reluctance is, in part, a confusion between sterilization and castration

[5] Woodside: op. cit., pp. 50–1.   [7] Ibid., pp. 55–6.
[6] Ibid., p. 55   [8] Ibid., pp. 113–14.

which cannot be wholly eradicated even by explanation. Mrs. Woodside puts the position succinctly:

This expectation of eunuchoid effects is difficult to reverse, nor does intellectual comprehension of its fallacy suffice to overcome doubts and fears which may be largely unconscious. To man, any operation involving the genitalia appears as a threat to his physical integrity and his capacity to perform (and enjoy) what is after all his basic biological function. Psychoanalytic research has demonstrated the strength of these castration fears and the many anxieties to which they give rise; and it was pointed out by two surgeons that performance of vasectomy on a neurotically-disposed individual might well result in functional impotence. This is not the place to embark on extended discussion of the concepts of male sexual psychology, but it is being increasingly recognized that psychic factors, little considered in earlier studies of vasectomy, are of very great importance when an operation is being contemplated.[9]

On the other hand, the same author reports that in some parts of North Carolina, where the rural health department has been successful in persuading a number of husbands to be sterilized instead of their wives, the men so treated have afterward been pleased, and have recommended the operation to their friends.[1]

In California, where sterilization has also become part of ordinary experience through the vigorous use of the local law, one doctor reported that he had sterilized nearly 150 married men, merely at their wish to prevent procreation.[2] It seems from this that male resistance may disappear when the results of the operation give general satisfaction. Of 65 men who had been sterilized at their own request, and who were asked the direct question: "Knowing what you now do, if you had it to do over again, would you have the operation performed?" 62 unhesitatingly answered "Yes." One failed to answer

[9] Woodside: op. cit., p. 67. [2] Gosney and Popenoe: op. cit., p. 52.
[1] Ibid., pp. 68–9.

98

this question, but said he was well pleased with the operation. The other two, who expressed displeasure, had certain abnormalities.[3]

According to an opinion formerly current, vasectomy has a "rejuvenating" effect upon the male; this is probably without physiological basis, but may take effect by suggestion.[4] The conclusion expressed by Gosney and Popenoe in their study of the subject is that "there is no evidence that society has been harmed, but, in the majority of instances, there is also no particular evidence that society has benefited from the operation" upon the 65 men mentioned above.[5] At the same time, these authors express themselves as opposed to sterilization of convenience on population grounds.[6]

A more recent study, by a psychiatrist, emphasizes the danger that "a self-determined vasectomy may, on the one hand, be symptomatic of a serious personality distortion, and, on the other hand, in turn lead to serious personality difficulties, even years later."[7] The experience of this writer, which he recounts in detail, seems to suggest that there are serious psychological risks in the operation, at least for the male. For women, his opinion is that "sterilization deriving from factors beyond the control of the patient is accepted primarily as a regrettable or painful actuality, to which adjustment can be made."

The religious attitude towards sterilization

The most pronounced opinion on the morality of the operation comes from Catholics. They do not object

[3] Ibid., p. 26.   [5] Ibid., p. 66.
[4] Ibid., pp. 88–9.   [6] Ibid., pp. 83–6.
[7] Milton H. Erickson in *Therapeutic Abortion,* Harold Rosen, ed. (New York, 1952), pp. 57ff.

to sterilization where this is the incidental result of an operation performed on therapeutic grounds, as in the removal of a cancerous uterus or of cancerous ovaries. Here the immediate object of the operation is to remove diseased tissue; it is only an incidental result that the patient is rendered sterile. Such a procedure is justified on the Catholic doctrine of "double effect," which will be studied more closely in connection with abortion. Where, however, the whole object of the operation is to produce sterility, it is illicit in Catholic thought. Hence, astonishing as this may appear, the sterilization of a woman is regarded as sinful where it is performed to prevent her from becoming pregnant, even though she is so diseased that pregnancy would directly endanger her life.

Since I am myself unable to comprehend the reasoning underlying this conclusion, I cannot enlighten the reader upon it otherwise than by quoting from a Catholic authority.

Catholic theologians . . . hold firmly to the principle that God has given to private individuals "no other power over the members of their bodies than that which pertains to their natural ends." The reproductive function, as such, is not subordinated to the individual's well-being; hence an operation or treatment which is immediately directed to a suppression of this function is contrary to the purpose of the faculty, and is therefore not in accord with sound moral principles.[8]

In regard to eugenic sterilization, the consensus of opinion among Catholic theologians is that it is illicit—certainly if compulsory, but also if voluntary. Various reasons are offered: eugenic sterilization, because it enables sexual intercourse to take place without the aim of procreating children, is either an inducement to adultery

[8] Gerald Kelly, S.J.: *Medico-Moral Problems* (Dublin, 1955), p. 37. See, for a general statement of the Catholic position, ibid., pp. 21, 34ff., 318.

or a violation of the end of matrimony; it is a "mutilation" and a "partial death sentence" upon the patient, and his consent is no excuse because "man is not the complete master of the members of his own body any more than he is of his own life." [9]

Disregarding the question-begging elements in the argument, the Catholic objection to eugenic sterilization seems to derive from two processes of thought. The first is the Augustinian notion that venereal pleasure without the accompanying risk of procreation is sinful. This idea, if standing alone, would find no objection in a desexualizing operation.[1] There is, however, the second notion, which like the first is no longer openly expressed, but which seems to underlie the arguments used, that any forethought with regard to sexual functions is an interference with Providence, which has apparently planned that deformed and moronic children shall be born.

The only comprehensive Protestant work on the medico-religious problems discussed in this work, to balance against the great output of literature from the Church of Rome, is Joseph Fletcher's *Morals and Medicine*. This points out that the Bible abounds in references to eunuchs, and that Jesus himself refers to them (Matt. xix, 12). It is evident from the general tenor of the book that Dr. Fletcher does not use this argument because it is of a kind that carries conviction to himself; he mentions it because it is always worth reminding the fundamentalist of the texts that he chooses to overlook for the purpose of his dialectic. The fact remains, as Dr. Fletcher points out, that there is no prohibition of sterilization (or of castration) in the Bible, in the creeds,

[9] These opinions were, in essence, endorsed by Pope Pius XI in his encyclical *Casti Conubii* in 1930.

[1] Joseph Fletcher: *Morals and Medicine* (Princeton, N.J., 1954), p. 171, mentions the ecclesiastical practice, current from the fourth century till the year 1884, of having boys castrated in order to provide *soprani falsetti* voices for the Sistine choirs of Rome.

or in the findings of the œcumenical councils. The author also remarks on the peculiar nature of a position which accepts curative medicine in therapeutic sterilization, at least in some of its aspects, but rejects preventive medicine in the form of eugenic sterilization.[2]

The legality of sterilization apart from statute: the question of public policy

Sterilization is frequently performed, and is certainly legal, even apart from statute, where the patient is of sound mind and consents to the operation, which is undertaken to preserve the patient's life or to benefit his physical or mental health. It is probable that the courts would make little difficulty in extending the purely medical indication to a medico-social one, as where it may be foreseen that the exhausted mother of a large family will suffer a mental breakdown if she undergoes a pregnancy. The Supreme Court of Minnesota held that there was nothing against public policy in a husband being vasectomized for the sake of his wife's health.[3]

This common-law sterilization on therapeutic grounds is important even in states possessing sterilization laws, where, as frequently happens, these laws contain no general provision for therapeutic operations, except perhaps by way of a saving clause. In such states therapeutic operations are outside the purview of the local Eugenics Board, but may be performed at the discretion of the physician as an ordinary medical operation.

It is sometimes found that the medical profession is

[2] For another agrument in favor of sterilization on Protestant premises see Rev. J. P. Hinton and Josephine E. Calcutt: *Sterilization: A Christian Approach* (London, 1935).

[3] Christensen v. Thornby, 255 N.W. 620 (1934).

reluctant to act under this general power, except in clear and urgent cases, because of the absence of the defined legal protection to which they are accustomed under the eugenic law.[4] But, contrariwise, the sterilization law may so accustom the medical profession and the general public to the operation that it is more readily resorted to in cases not specifically provided for.[5]

The legality of sterilization at common law is problematical where there are no clinical indications and the operation is performed merely for eugenic reasons or as a form of birth control. Even in states possessing measures for eugenic sterilization, the legality of (other) contraceptive sterilization is generally left to be determined by the common law, though, in two, such voluntary sterilization is expressly disallowed by statute.[6] One state that formerly prohibited sterilization except for therapeutic or eugenic reasons has since abandoned the prohibition, thus restoring the question to the common law.[7]

The issue at common law is whether the patient can validly consent to the operation for non-therapeutic reasons. If he cannot, the operation is a criminal battery upon him by the surgeon, perhaps an aggravated form of battery such as a battery with intent to do grievous bodily harm; the patient himself may also be held guilty of a misdemeanour. Whether consent can validly be given to a surgical operation is generally said to rest upon public policy. The only decided case of anything approaching relevancy in any common-law jurisdiction is a case of the first year of James I, mentioned by Chief Justice Coke, where "a young strong and lustie rogue, to make himself impotent, thereby to have the more colour to begge or to be relieved without putting himself

[4] Moya Woodside: *Sterilization in North Carolina* (Chapel Hill, N.C., 1950), pp. 13–14, 57.

[5] Ibid., pp. 49–50.

[6] Kan. Rev. Stat. c. 76, s. 155 (1935); Utah Rev. Stat. tit. 89, c.O. ss. 11, 12 (1943).

[7] Iowa: see 35 *Iowa Law Review* 266 (1950).

to any labour, caused his companion to strike off his left hand; and both of them were indicted, fined and ransomed therefor." [8] There is obviously a good deal of difference between the amputation of a member like a hand, when the individual becomes less able to work and may be a charge on the public funds, and an operation that is of interest only from the point of view of the production of another generation.

It is sometimes said that a person cannot effectively consent to the commission of a maim (mayhem) upon himself, and the question then resolves itself into whether sterilization is a maim. In principle, a maim was some injury that lessened a person's ability to fight and defend himself, such as cutting off a hand or even knocking out a tooth (which would impair his power to bite an adversary); [9] and castration was also held to be a maim, because it was thought to diminish bodily vigour [1] or courage. Sterilization has no effect upon mental or muscular vigour and so should not be held to be a maim. [2] Also, vasectomy is not a maim because the legal meaning of a maim (as contrasted with a wound) is that it is permanent; the possibility of a reversal operation means that the prosecution cannot prove that vasectomy is permanent. Again, the law of maim seems historically to have no application to women. Even if all these difficulties are surmounted, it may be questioned whether the antiquated law of maim affords a satisfactory basis for a conclusion as to the defence of consent. It seems unlikely that a person would today commit a criminal

[8] Coke upon Littleton, f. 127a-b (R. v. Wright).
[9] Russell: *Crimes,* 10th ed., I, 688. Another definition would make a maim an injury that prevents a person from getting his living: Bishop: *Criminal Law,* 9th ed., Sec. 1001.
[1] Russell: loc. cit.
[2] Some of the United States, such as Pennsylvania (Penal Code, 1939, s. 715), have redefined "maim" in such a way as to exclude sterilization. See generally Justin Millar and Gordon Dean in 16 *American Bar Association Journal* 158 (1930).

offence by having his teeth extracted without adequate reason.

However, to decide that sterilization is not a maiming does not, perhaps, end the question. In *Rex v. Donovan,*[3] where a sex pervert had caned a girl for the purpose of sexual gratification, the English Court of Criminal Appeal held that the girl's consent was not necessarily a defence, even though the injury to her did not amount to a maim. Mr. Justice Swift, speaking for the court, said that if an act is *malum in se,* so that it is in itself unlawful, consent cannot convert it into an innocent act. The question, therefore, said the judge, was whether the blows were likely or intended to do bodily harm. "Bodily harm" was defined for this purpose to include any hurt or injury calculated to interfere with the health or comfort of the victim. The result is that, according to the English court, a person cannot effectively consent to any blow, or presumably to any incision or puncture, that is likely to diminish his comfort.

It used to be said that hard cases make bad law—a proposition that our less pedantic age regards as doubtful. What is certain is that cases in which the moral indignation of the judge is aroused frequently make bad law. Donovan's case is an example. An obvious objection to the reasoning in the judgment is that it seems to be founded in part upon the logical fallacy of begging the question. The court said:

If an act is unlawful in the sense of being in itself a criminal act, it is plain that it cannot be rendered lawful because the person to whose detriment it is done consents to it. No person can license another to commit a crime. . . . There are, however, many acts in themselves harmless and lawful which become unlawful only if they are done without the consent of the persons affected.

These propositions are tautologous; yet they are used to support the introduction into the question of the the-

[3] [1943] 2 K.B. 489, at 507.

ory of *mala in se*. The distinction between acts wrong in themselves and acts wrong only because prohibited (*mala prohibita*) had generally been thought to have been ousted from the law, and there was no previous authority for using this distinction to determine the validity of consent. Moreover, it seems to be much too wide to say that a person cannot effectively consent to any hurt calculated to interfere with his comfort. For one thing, this proposition wrongly omits reference to the question of countervailing advantage. Every surgical operation temporarily interferes with comfort, but is not for that reason illegal. Even if the hurt is consented to for some reason that a court does not regard as adequate, this does not mean that it is illegal. Human beings are usually the best judges of their own interest, and if they consent to damage, there is generally no reason why the law should protect them further. Ritual circumcisions, for example, or skin-grafting or face-lifting operations may be undertaken for reasons of tradition or superstition or vanity, as the case may be, and they undoubtedly produce discomfort; yet it would be absurd to hold them unlawful.

Returning to the specific matter of sterilization, it may be taken as reasonably certain that the courts would uphold a voluntary sterilization submitted to on eugenic grounds. The single difficulty here is in respect of the reality of consent when a feeble-minded person is sterilized. This is discussed later.

The troublesome area is the "sterilization of convenience." The only possible evil that can be discerned even in these sterilizations (there is no evil, but only good, in eugenic sterilizations) is that the power of procreation is removed. Some writers argue that this is against public policy because it imperils the future of the race.[4] This appears to be an unrealistic attitude, neglecting the

[4] Lord Riddell in 19 *Transactions of the Medico-Legal Society* 83 (1924–5).

strength of the reproductive instinct. Moreover, since the mere decision of an individual not to procreate cannot be regarded as against public policy, it should follow that the undergoing of an operation to give effect to this decision is legal. On the particular decision in *Rex v. Donovan,* it may be said that this decision that consent cannot be given to a sadistic act is unsupported by previous authority and of doubtful wisdom and policy. The question whether sadistic and masochistic practice should be penalized is a legislative one on which the opinion of medical experts, among others, would be important; it is not proper to be settled by pretended deduction from the theory of things *mala in se.*

These arguments are advanced in full consciousness that they are quite likely to be rejected by some judges, who may decide, when the question arises, that "sterilization for convenience," at least if the medical evidence is that it is irremediable, is a criminal offence. It may be of some importance, in this connection, that judges belong to the male sex, since, as has been shown, males have a stronger instinctive reaction against sterilization than females. (The tendency to accumulate irrational arguments against sterilization is observable even in purported scientific literature.) A psychologist might predict that a male judge would tend to look with a kindlier eye upon female sterilization than upon male vasectomy; he does not feel the former as such an immediate threat to his own security. Legally, however, it seems impossible to differentiate between the sexes, except possibly by confining the theory of maim to the fighting sex. Another governing factor may be the religious affiliation of the judge, who may be influenced by the traditional view that any divergence from sexual custom is sinful. This is more likely to happen in England than in the United States, where experience has been obtained of the working of legal sterilization.

In an English divorce case, Lord Justice Denning took

occasion to say, though it was in no way necessary for the decision, that sterilization was an offence when done to enable a man to have the pleasure of sexual intercourse without shouldering the responsibilities attached to it.[5] However, this old-fashioned view, which overlooked the change of opinion that had occurred with respect to contraception, was not concurred in by the other two judges, who expressly left the question open. Lord Justice Denning himself agreed that sterilization was lawful when done with consent for just cause, and he gave the example of preventing the transmission of hereditary disease. It may be pointed out that even in this case, where the operation is admitted to be lawful, vasectomy allows a man to have the pleasure of sexual intercourse without its responsibilities. Any attempt to assign "just causes" for sterilization would involve the courts in a somewhat intricate inquiry into the health of each marital partner, their eugenic endowment and economic circumstances, their capacity to make use of contraceptives, and the prospect of unfavourable psychological reactions to sterilization. These matters seem to be unsuitable for decision as incident to an inquiry whether a common-law crime has been committed. On an issue of this character, where there are strong religious and other differences of opinion, it seems only right that the legal question should be decided in favor of liberty, unless the legislature intervenes to answer it otherwise.

The doubt as to the law is unfortunate, because it probably inhibits some surgeons from operating even for eugenic reasons. The advice given to the medical profession in one English medical work is that sterilization is legal

[5] Bravery v. Bravery [1954] 1 W.L.R. 1169 (C.A.), discussed by Minty in 24 *Medico-Legal Journal* 54 (1956). Cf. the unqualified statement in Wharton: *Criminal Law*, 12th ed., Sec. 182: "Consent cannot cure such operations on women as prevent them from having children." No relevant authority is cited.

only where undertaken to preserve the life of the patient or to avert serious injury to physical or mental health.[6] The rule is probably stated too narrowly, but the medical reader will not know that, and in any event will probably be inclined to play for safety. It is said that English medical defence organizations refuse to indemnify any practitioner undertaking eugenic sterilization.[7] Even in those parts of the United States where tubal ligation has become a common operation, and one freely bought as an "operation of convenience" by comfortably-off women who prefer this to contraception, there is still no judicial ruling on the question of legality. Although many surgeons would be glad to see the law clarified, none has yet offered himself as the subject of a legal experiment in a test case. The result of this uncertainty in the law is discrimination against women who cannot make it worth the surgeon's while to take the legal risks involved.[8] Apart from the possibility of being prosecuted, a surgeon who performs non-therapeutic sterilization without the consent of the spouse of the person sterilized runs the risk of being sued for damages by that spouse, because it may be held to be an actionable interference with marital rights.[9] So far the case has not fallen for decision: the legal position seems to depend principally on whether an action lies for loss of the reproductive

[6] Stallworthy in Sir Eardley Holland, ed.: *Obstetrics* (London, 1955), p. 361.

[7] Brock Report, *Cmd* 4485 *of* 1934, p. 6.

[8] "The vagueness of the law means that there is considerable social injustice between one class of women and another. A contraceptive sterilization can usually be obtained by the better-off patient, if she searches diligently enough among the gynæcologists of her acquaintance; whereas the patient who is unable to pay and who comes from a different social class than the doctor has much less chance of assistance, although on every ground her need is likely to be greater." Moya Woodside: op. cit., p. 58.

[9] See 35 *Iowa Law Review* 268 (1950); and for the whole question of civil liberty, see Miller and Dean: op. cit.

capacity of a spouse. In the United States, some courts allow this, while others hold it to be too remote.[1]

As a rule of prudence, most gynæcologists require the spouse's consent. This means that they will sometimes feel unable to act in the patient's best interests merely because of the opposition of the spouse. To quote Mrs. Woodside again:

> Where the client is married, the requirement of the husband's or wife's consent presents the spouse with a right of veto which may be—and in practice often is—unfairly exercised. It happened that of the 48 sterilized women who were interviewed, 9 of them reported that their husbands had at first completely refused to agree to the operation or had required a great deal of persuasion and pleading before they would give consent. Many people feel that such control by one individual over another is hardly to be thought desirable, however orthodox it may appear to the legal mind; and it is frequently criticized by health and social workers who are thus prevented from giving a constructive service to mentally or physically handicapped clients.[2]

The question of reality of consent

Even if the courts should eventually decide that there is nothing against public policy in voluntary non-therapeutic sterilization, the performance of this opera-

[1] Sterilization raises problems in the law of marriage. The principle generally adopted is that a marriage can be annulled for impotence (inability to copulate), but not for the use of contraceptives or for sterility (inability to procreate). However, concealment of a pre-marital sterilization from the prospective spouse was held a ground of annulment in Twiner v. Avery, 113 Atl. 710 (1921), and post-marital sterilization without the consent of the other may be a ground for divorce as a form of desertion (cf. Kreyling v. Kreyling, 23 Atl. 2d 800 [1942]) or cruelty (cf. Cackett [orse. Trice] v. Cackett [1950] P. 253).

[2] Moya Woodside: op. cit., p. 73.

tion upon persons under disability involves legal problems. In particular, there is the difficulty of knowing whether a person who is insane or mentally defective or near defective can give an effective consent. A low-grade defective may be quite incapable of appreciating the nature of the operation; a higher-grade defective may be brought to understand it, but be so subject to the influence of others that his consent can readily be obtained in circumstances in which it might not be forthcoming from a normal adult. The probability is that the courts would not regard as lawful any operation upon a mental defective unless it is for his benefit and with the consent of his parent or guardian. A merely eugenic operation would, therefore, be ruled out. As already shown, an operation which has in part a eugenic purpose may also be to the advantage of the patient; but there are so many doubts about the attitude of the courts that a voluntary sterilization statute is highly desirable. In England the Brock Committee recommended a statute of this scope. The committee, which gave attention to this problem of consent, expressed itself as convinced that when the higher-grade defectives ask for sterilization, perhaps to assist themselves in obtaining a discharge, or in some cases to be allowed to marry, they understand what they ask for. "The essence of a voluntary system," said the committee, "is that those who object should be free to do so. What matters is that there should be no compulsion. So long as there is no unfair pressure and no patient is forced or bribed to consent, it seems to us mere casuistry to discuss how far the patient fully appreciates all the implications of consent."[8]

[8] *Cmd 4485 of 1934*, p. 42.

IV

ARTIFICIAL INSEMINATION

The medical practice

Human beings can alter the "natural" modes of reproduction not only by preventing pregnancies that would otherwise take place but by stimulating them. When the means used are purely medical, as by hormone treatment, no legal or moral problem arises; but the case is far otherwise with the final attack upon the problem of sterility known as artificial insemination.

Artificial insemination is used when the woman is fertile but for one reason or other it is not possible for her to have children by her husband in the normal way. There are two forms, artificial insemination from the husband (A.I.H.), and artificial insemination with the fluid of an anonymous third-party donor (A.I.D.).[1] Insemination from the husband is possible in some cases of impotence. When the husband is sterile—when he has no sperm at all—he and his wife may buy some. This simple transaction has provoked strong objections, with demands for its suppression through the agency of the criminal law. It scarcely needs to be pointed out that forbidding artificial insemination would not eradicate it but merely drive it underground. However, before discussing the ethical controversy, we should say more about the social, medical, and legal aspects.

A.I.H. appears first to have been performed by John

---

[1] Given the misleading "scientific" names of homologous and heterologous A.I. respectively—misleading because the distinction is only legal and emotional, not scientific.

Hunter in London about 1785. A.I.D. is practically a development of the present century, and it is only in our own time that artificial husband- and donor-insemination has become at all common. Exact figures are impossible to obtain, but the practice is much commoner in the United States than in England, and many thousands of barren marriages have already been rendered fertile in this way. There are a few regular bureaus or clinics in which semen is supplied, and procedures have been devised to protect the gynæcologist, the husband, and the donor.[2] Even so, the practice is in its infancy: few doctors will perform it, and those who do are very selective in the patients they accept. So far as is known, artificial insemination has not yet been performed under the British National Health Service.

The great human and social potentialities of artificial insemination can be seen from the calculation that, both in the United States and in Britain, at least one out of every ten married couples is involuntarily sterile. Artificial insemination has already brought much happiness to people in this predicament, and numerous pronouncements have been made in its favour by medical men who are in the best position to judge its results. The American Society for the Study of Fertility, having a membership of medical specialists, approved the following statement by a vote of 79 to 8 at a meeting held in Atlantic City on June 4, 1955.

If it is in harmony with the beliefs of the couple and the doctor, donor artificial insemination is a completely ethical, moral and desirable form of medical therapy. . . .

Those physicians who have carried out donor insemination

[2] For various discussions of the medical aspects see Hermann Rohleder: *Test Tube Babies* (New York, 1934); Mary Barton in *Artificial Human Insemination* (London: Wm. Heinemann; 1947); Edmond J. Farris: *Human Fertility and Problems of the Male* (New York, 1950), pp. 163ff.; Barton, Walker, and Wiesner in (1945) 1 *British Medical Journal* 40; Guttmacher in 3 *Transactions of the American Society for the Study of Sterility* 15 (1947).

for several decades can attest that in many cases it is a more desirable procedure for acquiring a family than adoption. One great advantage of donor insemination is that it provides the opportunity for the husband to share the months of his wife's pregnancy and her childbirth. From observation over many years the membership is impressed by the almost universal good results achieved in respect to children and the entire family unit. The fact that, in some instances, patients have returned for as many as four children by donor insemination is further proof of the happiness it bestows.

Dr. Alan F. Guttmacher, head of the department of gynæcology and obstetrics in the Mount Sinai Hospital in New York, said:

These children mean more to families than children conceived in a normal manner. But for artificial insemination, motherhood would be denied the wife. Babies conceived in this manner are wanted children, often desperately wanted. I know of not a single case in my practice where things have worked out badly.[3]

A child that is the result of donor insemination at least belongs naturally to the wife, and if the husband loves her he will value it on that account. The adopted child is the natural child of neither. Some couples fear that an adopted child may show a bad heredity: an A.I.D. child is less likely to do so. Moreover, there is a great shortage of children who are suitable and available for adoption.

Donor insemination has hitherto been used almost exclusively as a last resort to provide a couple with a child, where the husband is sterile or where there is Rh incompatibility between him and his wife, and not for eugenic purposes. Usually, if a couple can breed at all, they are not too concerned about the eugenic quality of what they produce. People beget and conceive in order to satisfy their own reproductive instincts, not in order

[3] Quoted by J. D. Ratcliff in *Reader's Digest,* June 1955.

to rear children who have the best genetic constitution. Also, there is nothing to stir the emotions, except antipathetically, in the clinical procedure of artificial insemination, which usually has to be repeated several times (perhaps as many as twenty) before it is successful; frequently it fails altogether. Strong motives are required to compel resort to it in the first place, and a fixed determination to carry it through successfully. With these reservations, it may be said that artificial insemination does offer some slight hope of improving human strains. It opens the way for separating the procreative from the companionate and sexual elements in marriage. A woman can now choose one man as the biological father of her children, and another as her lover and companion, and as the father of her children by adoption. It offers the possibility, too, of immensely increasing the number of women whom it is practicable for one man, regarded as of good stock, to fertilize. The exploitation of the invention to its full effect would certainly involve a revolution in our social and moral ideas, which is unlikely but not totally impossible. Bertrand Russell, writing without explicit reference to artificial human insemination, made the following prophecy.

The idea of allowing science to interfere with our intimate personal impulses is undoubtedly repugnant. But the interference involved would be much less than that which has been tolerated for ages on the part of religion. . . . The welfare of posterity is, it is true, a motive by no means sufficient to control the average man in his passionate moments, but if it became part of recognized positive morality, with the sanction not only of praise and blame but of economic rewards and penalties, it will soon come to be accepted as a consideration which no well-conducted person could afford to ignore. Religion has existed since the dawn of history, while science has existed for at most four centuries; but when science has become old and venerable, it will control our lives as much as religion has ever done. I foresee the time when all who care for the freedom of the human spirit will have to rebel against a scientific tyranny. Nevertheless, if there is to be a tyranny, it is better that it should be scientific.[4]

Even where donor insemination is used only for the purpose of providing children, as is practically always the case, it has a eugenic tendency because the donor is carefully selected by the physician for good genetic constitution, as well as for transmissible physical characteristics that will match those of the husband. On the other hand, insemination from the husband may be thought to be dysgenic if the lack of virility of the husband is hereditary. To this the medical reply is made that there is no evidence that infecundity is inherited. Dr. Kenneth Walker, a specialist in the subject of fertility, said: "I used to make inquiries of the infertile male about his family but found there was no relationship between the fertility of the parents and that of the children and I have given up taking family history into account."[5] The reasoning is not conclusive because it neglects the possibility of mutation. Before the invention of artificial insemination there was an obvious impossibility in absolute male impotence being inherited, but that is not so now. Artificial insemination may also have a dysgenic tendency if it is used where the woman herself has some reproductive defect, such as intractable vaginismus (spasm of the vagina), assuming this to have a genetic and inheritable character. These doubts must await further scientific inquiry.

One medical development is too recent to have passed into general use. Animal breeders have discovered that by the addition of glycerol, spermatozoa can be successfully preserved in a frozen state for long periods. Doctors associated with Iowa State University have now used frozen human semen to produce pregnancies that result

[4] *Marriage and Morals* (London, 1929), pp. 213–14.
[5] In *Artificial Human Insemination* (London: Wm. Heinemann; 1947), p. 20.

in normal babies. The way is open for semen banks to be built up, supplying semen methodically classified as to the characteristics of the donor. Such semen would, of course, be used years after the donor is dead.

Yet another technique, distinct from artificial insemination, to which medical science has advanced in experiments with cattle and dogs, is the transplantation of fertilized ova from one female to another, or even of complete ovaries.[6] The foster-mother is thus enabled to bear a child which is biologically the child of the donor and has no characteristics of the foster-mother. Hence the opportunity may be given for women to have children without bearing them. One use that might be made of this is to benefit a woman with healthy ovaries who cannot produce children for some other reason (e.g., heart disease); such a woman might produce her children by proxy. There would, however, be eugenic objections to this course. A more laudable use of the new technique would be to give a barren woman the emotional satisfaction of bearing a child, thus enabling her to have a family that she has nourished in her own body from the start.

It is not proposed to discuss this transfer of ova any further, though when it becomes an established practice it will assuredly set the legal profession by the ears. It will raise the profound and (in terms of established concepts) almost insoluble problem whether a child born from the ovum of A in the womb of B is legally A's or B's. In a blood transfusion we certainly think of the transfused blood as becoming the property of—or part of the body of—the patient, and so it is at least arguable that the ovum or ovary, though emanating from A, becomes B's by the legal process of *accessio*. But this problem may be left to care for itself, since we shall have enough trouble in the discussion of artificial insemination.

[6] 57 *Science News Letter* 202 (1950); 66 ibid. 325.

Legal problems of artificial insemination

It is fortunate that artificial insemination was not much practised in the nineteenth century, or else Anthony Comstock might have got to hear of it, and then America might have been prevented from taking the lead in an interesting medico-social experiment. As things stand, the question is not specially dealt with either in American or in English law, but is left to be decided on general principles. This is not, however, a happy situation, because it is found that these general principles seem to give several wrong results, applied as they are to facts that the lawgivers of past ages did not contemplate.

A.I.H., it is true, raises few legal problems: the child is obviously legitimate, and the only awkwardness arises when the marriage breaks down and a divorce or decree of nullity is sought on the ground of non-consummation. It was held in an English case that the decree can be granted.[7] In most jurisdictions there are statutes which prevent the child of the marriage being bastardized by the decree.[8]

A.I.D. is much more troublesome. Is the child conceived from the donor's semen illegitimate? Most lawyers agree that he is. The only thing to protect him from this consequence is the presumption of legitimacy, which can be rebutted only by clear evidence that the husband could not have been the father.[9] Evidence of the husband's

[7] R.E.L. v. E.L. [1949] P. 211 (held that marriage could still be annulled). The Royal Commission on Marriage and Divorce has proposed that this rule should be altered: *Cmd 9678 of 1956*, paras. 286–7.

[8] In England now by the Matrimonial Causes Act, 1950, S. 9. For the United States see 28 *Indiana Law Journal* 623 (1953), which also discusses the difficulty under divorce laws of the effect of A.I.H. in severing impotency from sterility.

[9] Russell v. Russell, [1924] A.C., at 705–6 (House of Lords); the same presumption holds in the United States.

sterility would be sufficient to rebut the presumption; but medical evidence might be forthcoming to show that the sterility was not absolute or certain (e.g., where he merely has a low sperm-count). Some physicians make it a practice, when performing A.I.D., to mix the husband's semen with that of the donor, in order to give the couple at least the hope that the child is really the husband's. This practice may have a legal advantage, too, because it may make more difficult the rebuttal of the presumption of legitimacy. Another far-sighted practice of some physicians is to choose a donor whose blood group is the same as that of the husband; this prevents the child being bastardized by a blood test.

Supposing that the presumption of legitimacy is rebutted, the child is a bastard, and the husband has no rights in respect of him, unless the court is prepared to make new law by saying that there has been a quasi-adoption or semi-adoption. A New York court did this, in a case concerning the husband's right of visitation after separation.[1] The decision can be supported only as frank judicial legislation, since adoption in common-law countries is ordinarily the creature of statute. A more satisfactory basis for the particular decision would be to invoke the overriding interest of the child, which might be taken to justify the court in giving rights of access to one who is not its father. Such a principle would, however, be of no assistance on the general question of legitimacy, as if the issue related to inheritance rights.

If the child is regarded as illegitimate, there is a possi-

[1] Strnad v. Strnad, 190 Misc. 786, 78 N. Y. S. 2d 390 (Sup. Ct. 1948). Although holding that the A.I.D. child was not illegitimate for this purpose, the court left open the question of property rights. The decision was nullified by the mother moving to Oklahoma, where the court disagreed with the New York court and gave her exclusive custody on the ground that the husband was not the biological father: 28 *Indiana Law Journal* 620 n. 3. Another judicial opinion against Strnad v. Strnad is Doornbos v. Doornbos, Super. Ct., Cook Co., Ill., Dec. 13, 1954, noted 30 *N.Y.U.L. Rev.* 1016 (1955), 39 *Marquette Law Review* 146 (1955).

bility that the donor of the semen might be held liable to maintain the child under the bastardy laws: if so, since a single donor may have sired a hundred or more children, his theoretical liability is very large. This speculation gives considerable comfort and satisfaction to those who oppose A.I.D. In fact, however, legal proceedings for maintenance are most unlikely to be taken, the donor is protected by anonymity, and the bastardy laws of some jurisdictions deny maintenance when the mother was living with her husband when the child was born. On the second of these points, it is the invariable rule of physicians practising donor insemination to keep the identity of the donor an absolute secret even from the husband and wife, and conversely to keep from the donor all knowledge of the family into which his genes will enter. Among the reasons for this secrecy are the desire to protect the donor's reputation (think of the repercussions for his family if his adventures in paternity became common gossip!), and to eliminate the risk of the donor blackmailing the couple, as well as the risk of the wife transferring her affection to the donor. For all these reasons, as well as the protection of the donor from possible legal proceedings, some physicians make a practice of keeping no records of the transaction. Others, however, keep records,[2] and where they do so there is a slight risk that the secrecy of the transaction may be broken by the physician being subpœnaed to give evidence.

Whether the husband would be liable to maintain the child of donor insemination apparently depends on whether he is liable to maintain any other illegitimate child born to his wife. The law on this varies between different jurisdictions.[3]

Whether the child of donor insemination can inherit

[2] In New York City the Sanitary Code compels the keeping of a record (below p. 126).

[3] In England the husband was formerly liable to maintain illegitimate children born to his wife with whom he was cohabiting, but this liability has been removed by statute.

120

property on intestacy again seems to depend on whether it is regarded as illegitimate.[4] If it is, under the law of most jurisdictions it cannot inherit from the father, but can from the mother.[5]

Arizona has a progressive statute which aims at removing the status of bastardy by providing that "every child is the legitimate child of its natural parents."[6] An unintended result of this statute is that it apparently enables the child of donor insemination to inherit property from the donor of the semen.

The legal disadvantages of illegitimacy can mostly be avoided by making a will and/or adopting the child; but adoption proceedings have the drawback of at any rate some publicity—highly undesirable in a small town where such things are gossiped about and where some know-alls would be sure to assume that it is not even a case of artificial insemination, but of concealed adultery —and they tend to undo the emotional advantages given by artificial insemination as a near natural remedy for barren love. Yet another disadvantage is that since adoption requires consent of the child's natural parent, an inquiry would have to be made into the identity of the donor, which it is the whole object of medical practice to suppress. For all these reasons it would be infinitely preferable for legislation to be passed to legitimize children born of A.I.D. with the husband's consent. Bills for this purpose have been introduced into several of the states' legislatures, but so far without success.[7]

[4] For the grave difficulty of a theory of "semi-adoption" in property law see Schock in 46 *Dickinson Law Review* 271 (1942).

[5] Under the law of New York an illegitimate child cannot even inherit from its mother if she has legitimate children (N. Y. Decedent Estate Law, s. 83 [13]). This is a most unlikely situation in a case of A.I.D.

[6] Ariz. Code 1939, ch. 27.401.

[7] Indiana, New York, Virginia, Wisconsin. A bill introduced in Ohio proposed to declare A.I.D. illegal: this likewise failed to pass. For references see 8 *University of Florida Law Review* 314 (1955); and see ibid., p. 315 for the high state of feeling on the subject. In

A second group of problems relates to the concept of adultery. If A.I.D. had been dreamed up by the doctors for the express purpose of confounding and vexing the sister profession, it could hardly have been more effective for the purpose. Is A.I.D. adultery or not, and if so, who is the adulterer? All the traditional definitions of adultery presuppose some act of sexual intercourse or "criminal conversation"; but this is not conclusive, because the definitions were not advanced with artificial insemination in mind.[8] A stronger argument is that adultery can undoubtedly be committed not only without impregnation of the woman but even without the possibility of it, as where she is sterile. This makes it appear as though adultery consists in the sexual act rather than in the possibility or fact of illegitimate conception. A contrary argument, however, can be built upon the fact that sexual contact not amounting to intercourse in the natural sense but resulting in fecundation *ab extra* is ruled to be adultery,[9] even when the act apart from the fecundation would not be adultery. From this it may be deduced that

order to give a specimen of the legislation proposed, one of the New York bills (S. 801, 172d Sess.) provided: "A child born to a married woman by means of artificial insemination, with the consent of her husband, shall be deemed the legitimate, natural child of both the husband and wife for all purposes, and such husband and wife and such child shall sustain toward each other the legal relation of parent and child and shall have all the rights and be subject to all the duties of that relationship, including the rights of inheritance from each other." The bill also provided for the filing of the husband's written consent with the county clerk, to be open only to a court of competent jurisdiction.

As was mentioned above, Arizona has attacked the problem of illegitimacy by assimilating the position of the illegitimate to that of the legitimate child. Similarly Wisconsin (s. 237.06 [1947]) gives a child a right of inheritance from "the person who shall acknowledge himself to be the father of such child." This legislation is not, however, interpreted to give the child a right to share in the estate of a man who is not the natural father: (1950) *Wisconsin Law Review* 138.

[8] For a useful survey of judicial definitions see K. Rudlow in 28 *Australian Law Journal* 490 (1955).

[9] Per Lord Dunedin in Russell v. Russell, [1924] A.C., at 721.

adultery is a dual conception, meaning either sexual inter-course or fecundation. However, the authorities in these matters were laid down without A.I.D. in contempla-tion, and the fecundation *ab extra* in the case to which reference was made above (*Russell v. Russell*) was by bodily contact with a proximity of organs, which is some-thing very different from artificial insemination.[1]

The question of adultery arises chiefly in the law of divorce and maintenance. Where donor insemination is with the husband's consent, he cannot rely upon it as a ground for divorce or bar to a claim for maintenance, because his consent or connivance displaces this argu-ment. Where the insemination is not with his consent, it may not seem unreasonable to regard it as a violation of the marital agreement, and for the strictly limited pur-pose of divorce or maintenance to call it adultery. This view, at any rate, was taken by Mr. Justice Orde in an alimony case in the Supreme Court of Ontario [2]—the only judge in the British Commonwealth who has so far had a decision reported on donor insemination. He thought, *obiter,* that the essence of the offence of adultery was the voluntary surrender to another person of the reproduc-tive powers or faculties of the guilty person. This opinion seems to involve as its logical consequence that the donor of semen, if a married man, is guilty of adultery by giv-ing his semen, so that his own wife (if she does not con-sent) can obtain a divorce from him; it would follow, in addition, that he can be made co-respondent by the husband of the woman inseminated, and be made liable in damages for adultery—or perhaps even be made liable

[1] See the remarks of Lord Merriman in debates in the House of Lords, cited below, p. 124, n. 5.

[2] Orford v. Orford, 49 O.L.R. 15, 58 D.L.R. 251 (1921); cf. Doornbos v. Doornbos, p. 119, n. 1 above. A more satisfactory solution would be to enact that acceptance by a wife of A.I.D. without her husband's consent is itself a ground of divorce or judicial separation. A proposal to this effect was made in Britain by the Royal Commission on Mar-riage and Divorce, *Cmd 9678 of 1956,* paras. 90, 318.

in an action for criminal conversation in jurisdictions where that action still survives, and in the latter event the physician can be joined as co-defendant because he was a party to the act.[3] Another opinion, however, would hold that the part played by the donor is too remote, and that it is the physician who is the sole adulterer. This solution may look a little odd if the physician is a woman. Consequences of these kinds may be thought to be so absurd as to discredit the extended interpretation of adultery, and there is some authority against it.[4] Lord Merriman in a debate in the House of Lords, described the interpretation refreshingly as "absolute nonsense."[5] In practice, as said already, the donor is protected by the precautions taken by the physician to observe secrecy as to the donor's identity.

However the legal difficulties may be resolved, they are exclusively problems in the civil law pertaining to the family, and are therefore only indirectly relevant to the subject of the present book. It may be said with some confidence that artificial insemination is not itself an offence under the penal law. The only possible exception is in those states that purport to penalize adultery. This type of legislation is little enforced, either because public opinion has come generally to acquiesce in adultery, or because it is realized that the criminal law is not a suitable medium for the enforcement of sexual mores. Paradoxically, however, A.I.D. is precisely the

[3] To protect himself, the physician is well advised to have the husband's consent in writing; and if the man whom the woman introduces as her husband is not personally known to the physician, some make a practice of taking his (and her) fingerprints as well! See 107 *American Medical Association Journal* 1533 (1936); 116 ibid. 2747 (1941); 147 ibid. 250 (1951). For consents suggested in English practice see 12 *Medico-Legal and Criminological Review* 147–8 (1944).

[4] *Obiter dictum* of Judge Feinberg in Hoch v. Hoch, Cir. Ct., Cook Co., Ill. (1945), reported in *Time,* Feb. 26, 1945, p. 58.

[5] *Lords Debates,* vol. 161, col. 410 (March 16, 1949); vol. 169, col. 490 (November 23, 1950). See also H. A. Hubbard in 34 *Canadian Bar Review* 425 (1956).

unmeritorious type of case in which the aid of the criminal courts may be invoked, since sectarian feeling probably runs higher on this, regarded as a burning social and religious issue, than on adultery of the old-fashioned type. Assuming that a prosecution were brought, it seems inconceivable that a court would convict, provided at least that the donor insemination were performed with the husband's consent.[6] In New York, for instance, the Penal Law, section 101, makes adultery a misdemeanour, but section 100 defines adultery as "the sexual intercourse of two persons, either of whom is married to a third person." This definition would on any common-sense view be held to be inapplicable to A.I.D. Yet Mr. Justice Orde said, in the Ontario case: "If it was necessary to do so, I would hold that [A.I.D.] in itself was 'sexual intercourse.'"[7] If donor insemination is adultery in the law of New York, it is the only form of adultery for which the procedure has been put into legislative form. The Sanitary Code of New York City[8] contains regulations on the subject that are of sufficient interest for other jurisdictions to be worth reproducing in full.

REGULATIONS GOVERNING THE PROVIDING OF SEMINAL FLUID FOR ARTIFICIAL HUMAN INSEMINATION.

Regulation 1. A person from whom seminal fluid is to be collected for the purpose of artificial human insemination shall have a complete physical examination with particular attention to the genitalia at the time of the taking of such seminal fluid.

Regulation 2. Such person shall have a standard serological test for syphilis and a smear and culture for gonorrhea

---

[6] For an extended argument to this effect see 28 *Indiana Law Journal* 624–7 (1953).

[7] Orford v. Orford, p. 123, n. 2 above. The relevant statutes in some states, such as California (Penal Code s. 269a), limit the offence to living in "a state of cohabitation and adultery"; this clearly rules out A.I.D.

[8] S. 112 (1947, as amended in 1950).

not less than one week before such seminal fluid is obtained.

Regulation 3. No person suffering from any venereal diseases, tuberculosis or infection with brucella organisms, shall be used as a donor of seminal fluid for the purpose of artificial human insemination.

Regulation 4. No person having any disease or defect known to be transmissible by the genes shall be used as a donor of seminal fluid for the purpose of artificial human insemination.

Regulation 5. Before artificial human insemination is undertaken, both the proposed donor and the proposed recipient shall have their bloods tested with respect to the Rh factor at a laboratory approved for serology by the Board or Commissioner of Health. If the proposed recipient is negative for the Rh factor, no semen shall be used for artificial insemination other than from a donor of seminal fluid whose blood is also negative for this factor.

Regulation 6. Where artificial human insemination is performed, the physician performing the same shall keep a record which shall show:

(1) The name of the physician.

(2) The name and address of the donor.

(3) The name and address of the recipient.

(4) The results of the physical examination and the results of the serological examination, including the tests for the Rh factor.

(5) The date of the artificial insemination.

Such records shall be regarded as confidential and shall not be open to inspection by the public or by any other person than the Commissioner of Health, an authorized representative of the Department of Health and such other persons as may be authorized by law to inspect such records. The custodian of any such records, the said Commissioner or any other person authorized by law to inspect such records shall not divulge any part of any such records so as to disclose the identity of the persons to whom they relate except as provided by law.

The question whether A.I. performed without the woman's consent would be rape is too academic to be worth discussion. But a practical issue may conceivably arise as to so-called "statutory rape," where, although the woman consents in fact, she is below the statutory age at which an effective consent can be given to sexual intercourse. In some American states the age of consent is fixed so absurdly high (even as high as 18 in a quarter of the states) [9] that it is possible to imagine a vindictive prosecution being launched against the physician with some semblance of a legal argument in its favour.

Even if, as one hopes and believes, it should be finally determined that A.I. is not an act of sexual intercourse or of adultery, certain incidental questions of criminal law will remain. One is in relation to declarations of legitimacy—though this is not a problem peculiar to the case of artificial insemination. Suppose that a married woman commits adultery (real adultery, not the artificial kind), as a result of which a child is born; the husband forgives her, and registers the birth of the child with his own name as father. It may be that in so doing he technically commits the offence of making a false declaration. However, a prosecution for the offence would be inconceivable; the charge, if brought, would almost certainly fail for lack of evidence to rebut the strong presumption of legitimacy; and even if such evidence were forthcoming, it is by no means clear that a court would convict. Public policy certainly requires that the law should give its blessing to the reconciliation of the spouses and the *de facto* adoption of the child by the husband. It is not very difficult for the court to give effect to this policy by saying that no false declaration has been made, the word "father" in the registration being understood in the special sense of the husband of the mother at the time of the birth.

If this is so, the same interpretation must be adopted in the case of donor insemination, and it must be

[9] See the chart in Robert Veit Sherwin: *Sex and the Statutory Law, The Personal and Psychological Aspect* (New York, 1949), p. 89.

lawful for both the husband and for the attendant physician (in jurisdictions where the latter is required to register births) to enter the husband as father.[1] The usual view advanced by lawyers, however, is that such an entry would constitute an offence.

In order to make this legal position clearer, it would be desirable, as a minimum step, for statutes relating to the registration of births to be amended to allow the husband in all cases to be entered as such without reference to the question of paternity. This step has been taken in the governing Ontario statute, the Vital Statistics Act,[2] which provides that no indication of the paternity of the child is to be given in the registration of the birth of a married woman's child, though particulars of the husband may be given. Under this legislation, the problem of registration is solved. But there still remains the point that if, at any time during the child's life, either parent claims any property, allowance, or tax concession by representing the child as the child of the husband, an offence of false pretences or false declaration might be regarded as committed. Thus the only completely satisfactory solution is a statute legitimizing the child.

A not unimportant consideration is that lawyers tend to be hostile towards a medical practice that upsets established legal notions, and this hostility may result in doubtful legal issues being settled against it. One of the most interesting discussions of artificial insemination is in a symposium held jointly by the Chicago Bar Association and the Chicago Institute of Medicine,[3] which shows a marked contrast between the doctrinaire conservatism of the legal approach ("The mere fact that a woman wants a child, that she longs for a child, is no reason

[1] This argument is advanced in an able article in 113 *Justice of the Peace Journal,* at 442–3 (1949).

[2] R.S.O., 1950 c. 412.

[3] Published under the editorship of Samuel A. Levinson: *Symposium on Medicolegal Problems* (Philadelphia, 1948).

she should be gratified") and the empirical, imaginative humanitarianism of the medical one.[4]

The theological arguments

It is a remarkable fact that the Catholic and Anglican churches, which have made no pronouncement against the procreation of deaf mutes and other children doomed to serious congenital disability, gird themselves against donor insemination, which generally results in the birth of children above the average in their genetic endowment (since the donor is chosen with some care). Equally remarkable is the fact that although these churches have always been at pains to emphasize the view that the procreation and rearing of children is the principal if not the only legitimate end of marriage, as well as a duty of marriage, they reject a procedure that science has devised to serve that very purpose. The reason for their opposition seems to be a rather sad example of the theology of conceptions.

The Catholic decision was made as long ago as 1897, when, to the question whether artificial fecundation of women is permissible, the cardinals with the approval of Pope Leo XIII replied *"Non licere."* No reasons were then given; nor did Pope Pius XII add much enlightenment when, in an address to Catholic doctors on September 29, 1949, he condemned artificial insemination as "entirely illicit and immoral," with the sole exception where

[4] For other hostile legal discussions see Mr. Justice Vaisey and H. U. Willink in *Artificial Human Insemination, The Report of a Commission appointed by the Archbishop of Canterbury* (London, 1948), pp. 36ff., proposing that it should be made a criminal offence, and G. P. R. Tallin, Dean of the Manitoba Law School, in 34 *Canadian Bar Review* 1, 166 (1956). H. A. Hubbard's reply in 34 ibid., p. 425, while taking a different view of the law from Dean Tallin, concedes that A.I. is an "abhorrent practice."

it serves "as an auxiliary to the natural act of union of the spouses and of fecundation."

Only the marriage partners have mutual rights over their bodies for the procreation of a new life and these are exclusive, non-transferable and inalienable rights. So it must be, out of consideration for the child.

It is somewhat puzzling that the child should be referred to, when apart from the physician's help there would be no child. The reference to "the natural act of union" seems to show that the Catholic interpretation of the law of nature is again at work. The considerable Catholic literature on the topic that developed in the interim between these two pronouncements clarifies the official attitude. The fullest treatment is the Reverend William Kevin Glover's *Artificial Insemination among Human Beings,* published by the Catholic University of America Press in 1948. This lengthy study, though it purports to survey the moral aspects, manages to say not a word of the human and social advantages of artificial insemination. Since even a good end can never be sought by sinful means, and since the Divine Law is laid down for ever and can neither require nor receive alteration, all that has to be done is to examine and interpret the sacred writings and priestly pronouncements. In this way, A.I.D. is easily dismissed by saying that it amounts to adultery, which is sinful. A.I.H. is not adultery, but when it involves masturbation by the husband, as it usually does, it also is sinful. A.I.H. is, however, permissible when it follows a sexual union.[5]

Within the Church of England, the Most Reverend

[5] The Catholic physician who is considering whether to perform A.I.H. will first wish to satisfy himself that the husband has no adequate live sperm, but he is under severe religious disabilities in his effort to procure a specimen for examination. Roman theologians have given close attention to the various possible methods. Masturbation by the husband, or even ejaculation outside the wife's vagina, are definitely prohibited. Some theologians permit intercourse with a perforated condom; this allows some semen to be deposited in the wife's

Geoffrey Fisher, Archbishop of Canterbury, appointed a commission in 1945 to study the subject. Medical men and lawyers were included, under the chairmanship of the Bishop of London. This commission found no fault with A.I.H., but, with the sole dissent of Dr. W. R. Matthews, the Dean of St. Paul's, it followed the Roman opinion on A.I.D., condemned it in effect as adultery, or at least as conduct inconsistent with "the nature of marriage," and went so far as to suggest that (unlike "traditional" adultery) it should be made a criminal offence.[6] In a subsequent debate in the House of Lords, the Archbishop of Canterbury took the same line, saying that donor insemination was "wrong in principle and contrary to Christian standards."[7]

The Protestant churches, on the other hand, have not reacted strongly against artificial insemination, and many Protestants support it. The best discussion of the ethical question from a liberal Protestant point of view is in Joseph Fletcher's *Law and Medicine;* the Christian humanist approach in this book is at the opposite pole from that of dogmatic and authoritarian religion. Jewish opinion is similarly divided. A body of Jewish religious opinion is prepared to support the practice, one writer

vagina (and so renders the intercourse "natural"), while retaining some for examination. Others, however, reject the method, on the ground that all the semen must be left in the vagina. Some who take this view modify it by saying that after a "reasonable" time a specimen of the semen may be removed from the wife's vagina. Father Vermeersch suggested a brilliant solution of the whole difficulty: to remove semen direct from testicles by aspiration or from the vesicles by massage, thus carefully avoiding venereal pleasure. As will be shown later, Catholic opinion has now turned against this device. See generally Gerald Kelly, S.J.: *Medico-Moral Problems* (Dublin, 1955), pp. 111ff.

[6] *Artificial Human Insemination,* published by the S.P.C.K. (London, 1948). See also the report of a conference held under the auspices of the Public Morality Council, published by Heinemann (London, 1948).

[7] *Parliamentary Debates (House of Lords)*, vol. 161, cols. 400ff. (March 16, 1949). See the pungent comment of Joseph Fletcher: *Morals and Medicine* (Princeton, N. J., 1954), p. 216.

saying that "other than Jewish legal principles of the past must enter into the final judgment." [8]

The key to the debate evidently lies in the interpretation of the word "adultery" when used in a moral sense. It was because of the prohibition of adultery that the Primate thought A.I.D. "wrong in principle", and this, too, is the principal Catholic objection.

To a lawyer, theological discussions of the fundamentalist type make fascinating reading. They are legalistic in form, being rather reminiscent of interpretations of the Constitution of the United States, particularly before the advent of the "Brandeis brief." Deductions are drawn from the Bible, which is interpreted more or less (sometimes very much more, sometimes very much less) in the light of social conditions, knowledge of ordinary human nature, and the pressure of contemporary opinion. But the texts themselves, unless regarded in any particular case as interpolated, are authoritative and not open to dispute. They do not rest on human calculation but are the direct voice of God, the supreme lawgiver, and no human legislature can vote their amendment. In Christian theology we are thus subject to an unalterable law laid down some two thousand years ago—longer still if the Old Testament is invoked. Fortunately, there is always sufficient doubt and contradiction in the sacred texts to enable a common-sense result to be reached if the interpreter is willing to do so.

In regard to the word "adultery" this willingness is not evident. The word is used without explanation in the Seventh Commandment, where numberless problems are left unresolved. The concept of adultery presupposes an understanding of what is meant by marriage, and this in turn raises many questions. Who is to perform the marriage, and in what place? What kind of consent is necessary? What are the rules of capacity, and what the

[8] Rabbi Armond E. Cohen in *Therapeutic Abortion*, Harold Rosen, ed. (New York, 1954), p. 168.

prohibited degrees? Must the marriage be monogamous? May there be a marriage after a decree of divorce, and if so what are the rules of divorce? Only if the answers to all these and other questions are known can the meaning of adultery be known. They are all answered by the law, and many are answered by the church, though on some issues the church leaves the answer to the law; when the church gives its own answer, it is frequently different from that given by the law. In so far as the state is permitted by the church to alter the law of marriage and divorce, it is evidently permitted to alter the practical effect of the Seventh Commandment. The only alternative is to say that what is adultery in law need not be adultery within the meaning of the religious commandment, and *vice versa.* In whatever way this question may be settled for adultery, it is quite clear that the state can to some extent alter the scope of the Decalogue. For instance, the prohibition of theft in the Eighth Commandment makes sense only when the whole civil law relating to property is known; property is primarily a legal concept, and so theft is primarily a legal concept also. Religion or morality merely gives an added sanction to the legal position. The church does not have its own definition of property, and consequently it does not have its own definition of theft.[9]

[9] The point as to theft was well expressed by Morris R. Cohen in 49 *Yale Law Journal* 993–4 (1940): "Apart from existing law, it is hard to say what does and what does not morally belong to another. Especially is this true in modern society when no man can point to anything and say, 'This is exclusively the product of my own work in which I received no help from others.' For, in fact, the author of a book, or the farmer who raises crops, has been supported by others during his work, and the relative value of his services is largely determined by the conditions created by the legal system. The notion of theft is relatively clear if it denotes taking something in a way that the law prohibits. But on purely moral grounds, apart from the law, it is by no means clear. Is it immoral for a manufacturer to copy the brilliant ideas that his rival has developed? If the design of a dress should be made property by law on the analogy of copyright, then imitating it will become theft. Among many primitive people there is no sense of private property in food. But it is a grave theft for one

Returning to the question of adultery, evidently this word cannot be interpreted today in precisely the meaning it bore for the Old Testament patriarchs. On Old Testament principles one may marry several wives, even two sisters; and a married man may and should beget children for his dead brother.[1] When Sarah found herself childless, she advised her husband Abraham to go in unto her maid, so that she might obtain children by the maid.[2] Such acts, though evidently not adulterous within the original meaning of the Decalogue, would be regarded as adulterous by the laws and customs of Western society at the present day.

It may be legitimate for the moral philosopher to differ somewhat from the lawyer in his definition of what acts constitute adultery. For example, although sexual contact with a married woman by a third party resulting in fecundation *ab extra* is adultery, the same act without the resulting fecundation would not be adultery in law, and a married woman's masturbation of a man other than her husband is not adultery.[3] It is open to the moralist to say that the two last acts, whether or not they are to be called adultery, are as much a breach of the marriage bond and deserving of the same moral censure as adultery.

This leads to a consideration of the meaning of the word "adultery" as found in the New Testament. Jesus used it in two reported utterances. He said that a man who puts away his wife and marries another commits adultery, as does a woman who puts away her husband and marries again (Mark x, 11; Luke xvi, 18). He also said that "whosoever looketh on a woman to lust after

---

man to sing the personal song of another. Before the copyright laws, there was no conception of property in the literary composition itself. But when the legal rules in regard to property change, our moral ideas in respect to it change."

[1] Deut. xxv, 5–6.
[2] Gen. xvi, 2; cf. ibid. xxx, 1–13 (quoted by Fletcher: op. cit., p. 119).
[3] Sapsford v. Sapsford [1954] P. 394.

her hath committed adultery with her already in his heart" (Matt. v, 28). The first of these two contexts emphasizes the permanence of the marriage bond, which makes "adultery" even after divorce an act of faithlessness. The second takes the thought for the deed. I am not much concerned to evaluate these two remarks, though their uncritical acceptance would present great difficulties for moralists, psychologists, and lawyers. The first is not accepted by ordinary opinion in America and Britain: marriage after divorce is not regarded as adultery. The second is impossible as a rule of positive law or conventional morality, and would, if felt deeply as a matter of private conviction, give rise to irrational and unhealthy guilt feelings for transient thoughts that are a perfectly natural expression of sexuality. However this may be, it suffices for the present purpose to say that in both gospel contexts the word "adultery" refers to a kind of treason against the sexual bond that has been sanctified by marriage. It is not easy to see how either text settles the question of A.I.D., undertaken with the full consent and active desire of both spouses, which may in many cases do more than anything else to cement a marriage.

The point may be put in another way by considering sexual congress from two aspects: the pleasurable sexual act, and the fact of fertilization. These two aspects have always been severable, because the pleasurable sexual act may be planned in such a way or not to result in fertilization (e.g., through the practice of *coitus interruptus* or the use of the "safe period"). Conversely, it is now possible for the woman to be inseminated without her participation in the sexual act. In the past, "adultery" has always been thought to be committed by performance of the sexual act with someone other than the marriage partner; it makes no difference whether or not a child is born. This is obviously the meaning of the word "adultery" in the passage in Matthew. To discover in A.I.D. an act of adultery though there is no coitus or any ap-

135

proach to or thought of coitus in any reasonable sense
of the term is certainly to give the word a meaning that
it does not bear in the New Testament.

When one gets down to rock bottom, the real objection
to adultery is that it is a particularly gross kind of infidelity to the marital partner. One of the principal reasons—I do not say the only reason—in favour of conjugal
fidelity is that it is required for bringing up the young.
Thus, the European cuckoo, which does not make a nest,
is an exception to other birds in using any mate: its mating is just a brief encounter. Fidelity—at least seasonal
fidelity—is the characteristic of animals that have to combine to rear their offspring. A.I.D. in standard medical
practice is so far from being an act of infidelity that it is
intended by all parties to turn a barren marriage into a
fruitful one; and sometimes it repairs a marriage that,
because of the wife's sense of frustration, is on the brink
of disaster. (However, a physician will not perform
A.I.D. if he thinks the marriage unstable, unless the sole
irritant factor is the wife's barrenness.)

To sum up, although it is possible for the moral meaning of adultery to differ from the legal one, there is no
realistic way in which A.I.D. performed with the husband's consent can be said to be adultery in morals, even
if it is adultery in law.

The remaining theological issue is the Catholic contention that masturbation is not only a sin, but so sinful
that it cannot be permitted whatever good results may
follow from it. That masturbation is sinful, when it is a
means of obtaining venereal pleasure without the prospect of fertilization, follows, of course, from Augustinian
doctrine. But in this instance the donor does not perform
the act for this purpose; on the contrary, he performs it
for the biological purpose of begetting. Consequently,
the Catholic position needs some authority for saying that
masturbation is sinful *per se* and irrespective of its purpose. This authority it finds in two biblical texts: that

relating the sin of Onan, and St. Paul's remark (I Cor. vi, 9–10) that "effeminates" shall not inherit the kingdom of God. It was pointed out on a previous page that Onan, on the common-sense reading of the passage in Genesis, was guilty of *coitus interruptus* and not of masturbation,[4] and moreover that his act was committed in circumstances making him guilty of a type of fraud, and abandonment of his duty of the levirate. The Pauline text is equally inapposite, since the original Greek word translated "effeminates" in the King James Version meant homosexuals, and it is rendered by that word in the Revised Standard Version.[5]

It may not be out of place to add that the argument from biblical texts is a selective argument, used to reach a predetermined end. If attention is concentrated on individual texts, the Bible can be made dialectically to prove anything ("Even the Devil can cite Scripture to his purpose"). A biblical argument in favour of artificial insemination could easily be constructed by showing that it is the only form of virtuous propagation on the woman's side, being entirely free from sinful lust and approximating to the immaculate conception. Without using such a crude counter-thrust, the Dean of St. Paul's well expressed the objection to religious fundamentalism in his minority report to the Archbishop.

[4] It is true that the Catholic reading of the text is supported by the traditional Jewish interpretation. Mr. Joseph Wallfield tells me that from the early centuries of the Christian era down almost to the present day Onan's act has been traditionally interpreted as masturbation. He points to the Talmud, *Niddah*, fol. 13, which may be consulted in the German translation edited by Lazarus Goldschmidt: *Der babylonische Talmud,* vol. 9 (The Hague, 1935), pp. 739–42. But Mr. Wallfield adds that Heinrich Graetz, the greatest of Jewish historians, whose most valuable work treats of the Talmudic era, had to say on this vast compendium: "The Talmud . . . favours an erroneous exegesis of the Scriptures, with forced interpretations that are wanting in taste and often contrary to the sense of the text" (Graetz: *Geschichte der Juden,* 2nd ed., vol. 4 [Leipzig, 1866], p. 410). These words seem very apt to the text under discussion.

[5] Joseph Fletcher: *Morals and Medicine* (Princeton, N. J., 1954), p. 118.

I distrust the method of deducing moral laws from theological premises. We should never forget that one of the duties which has been deduced from theology by most of the churches is that of intolerance and the persecution of heretics. I do not find that Jesus deduced his ethical teaching from a theological system. He based it on his belief in God as Father. The Christian ethic springs from the one central conviction that God is love.

Apart from the scriptural texts, it is claimed that self-abuse is wrong because it is "unnatural." Whatever the meaning of this proposition may be, the fact is that "in all human communities investigated masturbation has been proved to be exceedingly common, if not universal; and that it is known also in a number of other mammalian species, e.g. some monkeys, dogs and rabbits." [6] Certainly this feature of the procedure for artificial insemination is unpleasant to contemplate, but so is much else in medical practice. To say that masturbation is unpleasant and regrettable is not at all the same as saying that it is wrong, and psychiatrists are emphatic that great harm is frequently done to young people by frightening them about their masturbation.[7] Even Catholic practitioners have come to see the wisdom of this view, and are therefore in the interesting position of having to tell patients who suffer from a compulsory habit of masturbation that they are guilty of mortal sin but are not to be

[6] Anthony Barnett: *The Human Species* (London, 1950), p. 52.

[7] Thus Dr. Kenneth Walker, discussing this aspect of A.I.D., said: "I, who have to deal with the sexual difficulties of the male, find that much of my work is the direct result of the tremendous stress which is laid on the deadly sin of masturbation. It has been the custom to try to cure boys of masturbation by telling them of the dreadful things that will happen to them in future years as a result of it. The number of neurotics and impotent husbands I see later, who are frightened that they have ruined themselves for life as a result of masturbation, is tremendous. I have even seen young men rendered suicidal as the result of this stupid and pernicious teaching and I am sure that some otherwise inexplicable suicides have been amongst its fruits." (In *Artificial Human Insemination* [London: Wm. Heinemann; 1947], p. 17.)

unduly worried by the fact![8] Another odd feature of the Catholic position is that whereas masturbation is forbidden absolutely to the male, it is allowed in certain cases to the female. According to Vicar-General D. Craisson, "if the husband should withdraw after ejaculation before the wife has experienced orgasm, she may then lawfully at once continue friction with her own hand in order to attain relief. In the same manner it is lawful for the woman to prepare herself by genital stimulation for sexual union in order that she may have orgasm more easily."[9] This concession is perhaps the result of the restricted methods of birth control open to those of the Catholic faith. Whatever may be thought of the expedient, the permission given to it is at least a recognition of the fact, insufficiently noticed in the old days, that the female has sexual necessities as much as the male; and it shows that even the rather morbid religious obsession with the guilt of masturbation is capable of giving way to human needs.

Finally, it may be pointed out that the instant question concerns not the general practice of masturbation but isolated and purposeful acts. As the Archbishop's Commission said in its report, "it cannot be the will of God that a husband and wife should remain childless because an act of this kind is required to promote conception." When the medical practice is not highly organized, more than one act may be required to accomplish fertilization. But since a single specimen of semen may be divided to perform twenty or more inseminations, and may be kept under refrigeration until used, it is possible for the donor's single act of masturbation to relieve the barrenness of two or more marriages.

[8] See Frederick L. Good and Otis F. Kelly: *Marriage, Morals and Medical Ethics* (New York, 1951), pp. 48–9, 136.
[9] *De Rebus Venereis ad Usum Confessariorum* (*On Sexual Matters for the Guidance of Father Confessors*) (Paris, 1870), p. 172, quoted by T. H. Van de Velde: *Ideal Marriage* (London, 1928), p. 193.

Another aspect of this question is the extent to which the same donor is used. In the United States, medical practitioners set no fixed limit to the number of donations. The British practice is to limit each donor to a hundred impregnations, though this limit is rarely if ever reached. In England, in the great majority of cases, no fee is paid to the donor, who gives his semen in the altruistic spirit of a donor of blood. In the United States it has been found so hard to enroll suitable and willing donors that the practice has arisen of using interns in hospitals, who are paid a small fee ($5 or $10) on each occasion. The position is, then, that these donors masturbate themselves in order to sell their bodily secretions. It is a natural reaction to regard this as not only repulsive but wrong. The parallel easily suggests itself between the donor—or rather vendor—of semen and the prostitute: both sell the use of their bodies in respect of their sexual or reproductive functions. However, the social problem of prostitution is obviously different from that of artificial insemination. The donation of semen presents no problem of communicating disease, disrupting family life, or creating a nuisance. The medical view is that the masturbation performed by the donor, if done without feelings of guilt, causes him no harm. Finally, there is nothing intrinsically wrong in selling a part of the body, e.g., hair. Although it is the English practice to give rather than to sell blood for transfusion, there would be no moral wrong in selling it; and in fact payments for blood are common in the United States.

It seems, then, that the somewhat repellent prospect of "human stud farms," though one of the things to be considered in passing upon the æsthetics or the social desirability of artificial insemination, is not a conclusive argument for repressing this practice by law. If the "human stud farm" produces a sufficient overplus of good, it can, at least on a utilitarian philosophy, be justified.

It seemed at one time that Catholicism would make no objection to A.I.H. when the semen was obtained otherwise than by masturbation, as by the rather painful operation of puncturing the testicle. According to one opinion, this practice was neither the "unnatural act" which condemned contraception in Catholic thought nor the "mutilation" which condemned sterilization.[1] However, the question was closed by a pronouncement of Pope Pius XII, on September 29, 1949, which condemned even A.I.H. unless this served "as an auxiliary to the natural act of union of the spouses." In a second address, on May 19, 1956, the pontiff explained that the church considered any method of obtaining semen from men outside the natural conjugal act as sinful. This question is, however, a somewhat academic one, because the method of collecting semen by puncture is not medically regarded as reliable.[2] The other possibility is for the seminal fluid to be collected, after normal intercourse, from the vaginal pool of the woman. In England this method is sometimes used for donor insemination, the donor's wife co-operating for this purpose, and the donor and his wife consenting to the physician's invasion of their privacy for the purpose of helping the barren couple. In the nature of the case it can rarely be used for A.I.H.

The social issues

Turning from religion and æsthetics, the question remains whether there are any real social evils in the practice of artificial insemination. When theological ar-

[1] See Joseph B. McAllister: *Ethics with Special Application to the Medical and Nursing Professions,* 2d ed. (Philadelphia, 1955), pp. 351ff.

[2] See Alan F. Guttmacher in 120 *American Medical Association Journal* 442 (1942).

guments condescend to examine the social implications of the practice, they generally resort to supposition and ignore the medical and social experience.[3] This is, of course, a common vice in theological, legal, and political discussions of social issues. E. S. Turner's *Roads to Ruin* deserves to be accounted a classic study of this mentality; it shows how the English reforms of the nineteenth century, which are now taken for granted, such as the abolition of the sweeping-boys and the legalization of marriage with the deceased wife's sister, were fought tooth and nail at the time by those who saw in the change every symptom of moral and social decay. The Deceased Wife's Sister Marriage Bill was resisted for years on the ground that if it were passed husbands would kill their wives in order to marry their wives' sisters. In the same gloomy vein, the Dean of the Manitoba Law School foresees that if artificial insemination becomes common it may cause wives to deceive their husbands. "A childless wife, after obtaining her husband's consent to resort to artificial insemination, would be able to carry on with impunity sexual intercourse with her lover, secure in the knowledge that she could attribute any pregnancy which might result to artificial insemination."[4]

A more usual objection is that A.I.D. may upset the psychological balance of a marriage, and that the husband may bear animosity against the child. These speculative evils are, fortunately, disproved by the universal testimony of doctors. The medical evidence accepted by the Archbishop's Commission was that "the couples who desire A.I.D. are of more than average intelligence, thoughtfulness, and responsibility," and that "it is usually the husband and not the wife who first comes to enquire about artificial insemination, and is eager that it should be tried; and he is as delighted as she when it is

[3] It may be said that this is true of Fr. Anthony F. LoGotto's treatment in 1 *The Catholic Lawyer* 267 (1955).

[4] G. P. R. Tallin in 34 *Canadian Bar Review,* at 4 (1956).

successfully carried out." Moreover "doctors who have observed the family life in which A.I.D. children are being brought up report that the husband and wife quickly appear to assume the roles of normal parents and the episode of insemination soon becomes unimportant." Having recorded these opinions without challenge, the commission saw no inconsistency in asserting, without a shred of evidence, as one of the practical objections to A.I.D., that "in the heat of a quarrel between husband and wife, particularly one provoked by the child's behaviour, it is only too probable that the husband will allude to the child's origin—perhaps in the latter's presence."[5]

Those who condemn A.I.D. have a slightly more effective argument in the magnificent words that Dr. Johnson applied to adultery: "Sir, it is the confusion of the progeny which constitutes the essence of the crime." But are the progeny really confused by A.I.D.? And even if they are, what harm is there in this if the husband consents? Almost the only apparent harm is when property has been settled on the husband and his issue: here the use of donor insemination may, it is said, enable a fraud to be perpetrated on the reversioner. But too much can be made of this objection. In the first place, the problem is not confined to A.I.D., since the fraud can also be practised in another way, namely, by the husband's acquiescence in the adultery of his wife. But, in the second place, it may be questioned whether there is any fraud in morals, whatever it may be called in law. Whether there is moral fraud depends upon what the person who settled the property would have intended if the question of artificial insemination had been brought to his notice. It may well be that most settlors would regard "test-tube babies" as sufficiently like natural ones to bring them within the gift to the husband's children. Emotionally, they are more closely identified with the husband than stepchil-

[5] The quotations are from the report, pp. 17, 18, 27, 53.

dren or even than adopted children. If the gift is to the wife's children, there is no difficulty, except the ancient and discreditable rule of construction that illegitimate children are not children.

If a statute is passed declaring that A.I.D. babies are legitimate and to be deemed to be the natural children of the husband and wife, almost all question of fraud, on which the Archbishop of Canterbury laid such stress, disappears. Any statement by the husband that the A.I.D. child is his child then becomes true in the statutory meaning of the words.

There might have to be statutory exceptions to such a principle, say in respect of entailed interests, and, in monarchical countries, in respect of royal and noble titles. Titles of honour have to be specially treated because here the public is emotionally interested in a continuity of "blood." It is possible to imagine A.I.D. being used as the equivalent of the warming-pan of the English history books, with sensational opportunities for court gossip. Here again A.I.D. does not create the problem, but merely plays a variation upon it.

An A.I.D. child brought up in ignorance of his true parentage (as doctors recommend) may make some innocent misstatement as to his biological ancestors, as in making a proposal for life insurance. But this may also happen to an adopted child brought up in ignorance of his adoption. So far as insurance companies are concerned, misstatements of this kind are a normal insurance risk.

It may be said that a child born as a result of A.I.D., not knowing the identity of his true father, and his legal parents not knowing it either, runs a very slight risk of marrying a near relative. But this risk need not be much greater than for foundlings and illegitimate or adopted children whose parents are not known, and it must be accounted altogether too remote to enter into the balance. The risk, such as it is, can be diminished by limiting the number of donations by a single donor, and by arrangements for taking donors who live at a distance from the woman inseminated; such arrangements would be greatly facilitated by the use of refrigeration. These are mere matters of detail, lying on the practical plane, and do not affect the question of principle.

Previous chapters discussed two rules on which at least majority opinion is in agreement; on the one hand, the duty not to kill children when they are born, and, on the other hand, the absence of duty to conceive or procreate. Between these two rules there lies an area in which even Protestant (and rationalist) opinion is divided against itself: the area signified by the word abortion. Is it a moral wrong, and to what extent is and should it be a legal wrong, to cause the death of a fetus before birth?

V

THE LAW OF ABORTION

The law of abortion raises social and religious problems of the first magnitude; and the purely legal problems are not inconsiderable. The present chapter will be chiefly concerned with the present law in Britain and America, while the chapter next following will consider religious attitudes, social difficulties, and the experience of countries that have largely legalized abortion.

Terminology

There is an unfortunate ambiguity in the term "abortion." In law, abortion (that is, induced abortion) means any untimely delivery voluntarily procured with intent to destroy the fetus. It may be committed at any time before the natural birth of the child. A synonym, used in the legislation of a number of jurisdictions, is "miscarriage." In medical and statistical usage, however, abortion generally means untimely delivery before the child is viable, that is to say, before it is capable of being reared.[1] A child is regarded as viable from the beginning

[1] See *Report of the Departmental Committee on Maternal Mortality, Cmd 5422 of 1937*, p. 194; F. J. Taussig: *Abortion* (St. Louis, 1936), p. 21. Untimely delivery after the child is viable is medically referred

of the twenty-eighth week of pregnancy, i.e., near the end of the seventh lunar month. At present children born before this rarely survive.[2] Those who advocate the extension of legalized abortion generally use the term in its medical sense. The changes that they propose would not, therefore, apply to operations performed after the fetus is viable.

Many doctors attempt to avoid what they consider to be the unsavoury connotations of the word "abortion" by speaking instead of a termination of pregnancy.

---

to as premature labour. "Miscarriage" is also used medically and popularly in a sense different from its legal one, namely, the premature expulsion of the contents of the uterus spontaneously, or as the result of an accident. Yet even medical usage is not fixed; for opposing definitions, see Sydney Smith: *Forensic Medicine* (London, 1949), p. 324; L. A. Parry: *Criminal Abortion* (London, 1932), p. 1. T. A. Gonzales, M. Vance, M. Helpern, and C. J. Umberger: *Legal Medicine, Pathology and Toxicology,* 2nd ed. (New York, 1954), p. 564, apply "abortion" to the first three months of uterine life; thereafter to the seventh month they use "miscarriage," and after the seventh month "premature birth." Stallworthy in *Obstetrics,* Sir Eardley Holland, ed. (London, 1955), p. 330, says that "the term miscarriage is now accepted as a synonym of abortion, and the old distinction between abortion (for a pregnancy ending before the sixteenth week) and miscarriage (for one ending between the sixteenth and twenty-eighth week) no longer exists."

Criminal abortion (miscarriage) implies that the fetus is killed; the normal obstetrical procedure of inducing labour is not criminal. Parry: op. cit., is in error as to this. But see below p. 191 as to removal of a dead fetus. The legislation of some jurisdictions punishes a mere attempt at abortion, whether the woman is pregnant or not.

According to Gonzales and others: op. cit., p. 571, the word "fetus" is customarily reserved for the period after the fifth week of pregnancy. For the first two weeks it is an "ovum," and from the third to the fifth week an "embryo." But not all medical writers follow these distinctions. The fertilized ovum is referred to as a zygote, which through cleavage becomes a blastocyst: see W. J. Hamilton, J. D. Boyd, and H. W. Mossman: *Human Embryology* (Cambridge, England, 1945), pp. 4, 28.

[2] It has been found that of infants born at about 28 weeks, weighing 2–3 lbs., 33 per cent survive; of those weighing 2 lbs. (presumably born before the 28th week) only 5 per cent survive. See Keith Simpson, ed.: *Modern Trends in Forensic Medicine* (London, 1953), p. 7.

History of the law of abortion

The practice of artificial abortion is as old as history. The earliest abortifacient recipe is more than 4,600 years old,[3] and primitive peoples all over the world have been found to practise abortion as well as infanticide in order to prevent an increase in their numbers.[4] Both Plato and Aristotle approved abortion for this purpose, the latter suggesting that a mother should be compellable to commit abortion after she had borne an allotted number of children.[5] In Greece and Rome abortion was practised not only for economic reasons but even from shame at the illegitimacy of the child, or fear that childbirth would detract from the mother's appearance. There was some move to repress abortion in the later Roman Empire, regarding it rather as a wrong to the husband in depriving him of children than as an offence to the unborn child,[6] but it appears to have been ineffectual. The Christian church, on the other hand, set its face against abortion as sternly as against infanticide, and for the same reason: the sanctity of the life of the child.[7]

[3] Taussig: op. cit., p. 31.

[4] Westermarck: *The Origin and Development of the Moral Ideas* (London, 1906), I, 413ff.; Lecky: *History of European Morals,* 3rd ed. (London, 1911), II, 20ff.; *Enc. Soc. Sci.,* s.v. "Abortion"; W. G. Sumner: *Folkways* (Boston, 1911), Chap. 7; Taussig: op. cit., p. 41; George Devereux in *Therapeutic Abortion,* Harold Rosen, ed. (New York, 1954), pp. 97ff.; same, *A Study of Abortion in Primitive Societies* (New York, 1955).

[5] *Politics* vii. 16; cf. Plato *Republic* v.

[6] *Digest of Justinian* 47. 11.4. The woman who procured her own miscarriage was guilty of an *extraordinarium crimen,* but not under the Lex Julia against homicides. It is not stated whether the consent of the husband would have been a defence.

[7] The earliest mention of the subject in English law seems to be in the *Leges Henrici,* LXX, 16 (Liebermann, I, 589), from which it appears that abortion was then punishable only by religious penalties.

All Christian countries, affected by these teachings, introduced laws forbidding the practice.

At present both English law and the law of the great majority of the United States regard any interference with pregnancy, however early it may take place, as criminal, unless for therapeutic reasons. The fetus is a human life to be protected by the criminal law from the moment when the ovum is fertilized. It is not generally realized that this rule is not older than the beginning of the last century. Before 1803 the legal prohibition of induced abortion was confined to the period after the fetus had quickened, that is, moved in the womb. This goes back to an ancient speculation as to the time when life commenced. It was formerly believed by many that the fetus did not begin to live until some time after conception had taken place, but the exact time was not agreed, and such theories as were put forward were naturally devoid of any experimental or rational basis. Aristotle put it at "about" 40 days after conception for the male fetus, and "about" 90 days for the female.[8] Hippocrates put the two periods at 30 and 42 days respectively.[9] The Stoics thought that the fetus did not become animate till it breathed at birth,[1] but the later Roman view took 40 and 80 days after conception for the male and female fetus respectively; later still the time was settled in the civil law as 40 days after conception for both sexes, and this time, too, was accepted by Galen.[2] Various other writers, however, had their own speculations to put forward.[3] Before the fetus became animate it was regarded as merely *pars viscerum matris,* so that the destruction of it could not be homicide, though it might be made

[8] *Hist. Anim.* vii. 3.
[9] *Lib. de Nat. Puer.* No. 10.
[1] Plutarch's *Morals* iii. 230.
[2] *Opera, de Usu Partium* xv. 5.
[3] See generally Theodrick R. Beck and J. B. Beck: *Elements of Medical Jurisprudence,* 11th ed. (Philadelphia, 1860), pp. 461–2, from whose account the last three footnotes are taken.

some lesser offence. Whether its destruction after the supposed time of animation was homicide in law was an issue that was long in doubt.

In theology the question of the time of animation was bound up with theories of the origin of the soul. According to Traducianism, defended by Tertullian, Apollinaris, and a few other heretics, the human spiritual soul is transmitted to the offspring by the parents. This theory, and the closely similar theory of Generationism, naturally led to the conclusion that the soul was coeval with impregnation. Both theories were, however, combated by Creationism, which held that the soul was in every instance the creation of God. Creationism could invoke the support of Genesis ii, 7: God made the body of Adam from the dust of the ground, and only after the body was made did he breathe life into it. To meet this, Traducianists made an exception for Adam from their theory. Creationists were naturally led to assert that the soul did not enter the embryo until some time after conception, and in choosing this time they were usually influenced by the views of the classical writers upon the time of animation. Thus St. Augustine, following the Septuagint reading of Exodus xxi, 22, drew a distinction between *embryo inanimatus* and *animatus*. Before the embryo has been endowed with a soul it is *embryo informatus,* and its artificial abortion is to be punished with a fine only, being merely an act preventing a life from coming into being; but the *embryo formatus* (i.e., organized in human shape) is an animate being, and to destroy it is murder, a crime punishable with death. In another of his writings, however, Augustine expressed the opinion that though there was a point of time in embryonic development at which life came in, no human power could tell when this time was. Augustine was even prepared to contemplate, in one place, that the soul might originate in the act of parental generation, postulating for this purpose a *semen incorporeum* which gave rise to the soul. Indeed, to be consistent with his own theory of inherited original sin Augustine had to suppose that the soul was in some way inherited in its tainted form from the parents, but this assumption was contrary to his own religious bias in favour of the notion of individual Creation. Augustine confessed that he was unable to make up his mind finally on the issue.[4]

The distinction between the *embryo formatus* and *informatus,* though rejected in some of the earlier canons of the church, was accepted by Gratian in his *Decretum* (about the year 1140). Gratian announced definitely that abortion is not murder if the soul has not been infused into the fetus. He did not commit himself as to the time of this animation. The glossators upon Gratian's text assumed that vivified or *animatus* was the same as "formed"; and between the fourteenth and sixteenth centuries it slowly came to be accepted by the canonists, as it had been in the Roman period, that the time of formation and animation was the fortieth day for the male fetus and the eightieth day for the female.[5]

The hesitations of the canonists as to the time of animation gave Englishmen the opportunity to settle the question in their own special way. St. Thomas Aquinas defined the soul as the first principle of life in those things that live, and he added that life is shown principally by two actions, knowledge and movement.[6] It was easy to imagine that the *animus,* life or soul, entered the body of the unborn infant when it turned or moved in the womb. Hence the rule of the common law, dating from the time of Bracton (a contemporary

[4] For the above writings of Augustine see William Reany: *The Creation of the Human Soul* (New York, 1932), Chap. 2 and pp. 83–6; Roger J. Huser: *The Crime of Abortion in Canon Law* (The Catholic University of America, Canon Law Studies No. 162: Washington, D.C., 1942), p. 15.

[5] Ibid., pp. 41–2, 45, 55, 64–5.

[6] *Summa Theologica,* Part I, Question 75, Art. I; see also ibid., Question 76, Art. III ad 3, Question 118, Art. II ad 2.

of St. Thomas) that life is taken to start not at a fixed time after conception but at the moment of "quickening," which usually takes place about mid-term. "Life," said Blackstone, "begins in contemplation of law as soon as the infant is able to stir in the mother's womb."[7] (An amusing illustration of the interest formerly taken in quickening is the entry in Pepys's diary for January 1, 1662/3: "Lady Castlemaine quickened at my Lord Gerard's at dinner.") Influenced by this medical and theological doctrine, Bracton[8] said that the killing of the fetus after quickening was murder; Coke, however, denied this, and asserted such a killing to be a misdemeanour ("great misprision") only.[9] Abortion before quickening was no crime. So the law remained in England (though hardly, if at all, enforced) until 1803, when it was put on a statutory footing and changed in an important particular: abortion before quickening became a crime for the first time, but not punishable so severely as abortion after quickening; both were felonies.[1] The change in the law was of great significance because nearly all women who procure their own abortion do so in the early months of pregnancy before quickening.

The present law: England

For England, the crime now rests on the Offences against the Person Act, 1861, s. 58, which establishes a uniform maximum punishment of imprisonment for life whether the abortion is attempted before or after

[7] *Commentaries,* I, 129.

[8] Folio 120b.

[9] Coke's *Institutes* III 50; D. R. S. Davies: "The Law of Abortion and Necessity," 2 *Modern Law Review,* at 133–4 (1938); *Report of Interdepartmental Committee on Abortion,* 1939, p. 27.

[1] Davies: op. cit., at 134.

quickening. The law of abortion being theological in origin, and resting on the view that the fetus has an immortal soul equally with an adult, one would expect the punishment to be the same as for murder. Although it is not, the maximum punishment is more severe than would be expected on utilitarian grounds. The Act covers two cases: (1) where a pregnant woman uses any means with intent to procure her own miscarriage, and (2) where any one else unlawfully uses means with such intent whether the woman is pregnant or not. Instances of means given in the statute are "poison or other noxious thing" and "any instrument." [2] It will be seen that the crime consists not in the procuring of miscarriage but in the attempt to do so. It is immaterial that the attempt is unsuccessful or even that (where someone other than the woman herself is charged) the woman is not with child. The maximum penalty is remarkably severe for a mere attempt. In contrast, the maximum for attempted rape, which most people would think a much worse crime, is only seven years' imprisonment. If the woman dies as the result of the illegal abortion, the offence is manslaughter,[3] for which again a life sentence is possible. In practice, nothing near the maximum is imposed.

In its treatment of the consenting mother English law is theoretically one of the most ferocious in the world, allowing her to be sentenced to imprisonment for life. In practice, however, she is not prosecuted at all. The police confine their attentions to those men and women who act as professional abortionists—the "back-street surgeons." It might be sufficient to justify this attitude by saying that prosecutions, even if instituted, would be futile to deter. The law can do nothing with women who

[2] The statute is apparently not confined to these two instances, and it has been extended to an abortion attempted by manipulation with the hand. See Rex v. Spicer, (1955) *Criminal Law Review* 772.

[3] Murder according to some of the older authorities, which are partially retained in Wharton: *Criminal Law*, 12th ed., I, § 441. It seems clear that at the present day the more lenient view would be taken.

are governed by the one fixed determination that their baby shall never be born, and who are prepared to risk health and life itself in order to prevent it. But this, of course, is not a consideration that weighs with the police, who are influenced to show indulgence to the mother chiefly by the fact that her evidence is required against the professional abortionist, who through his unskilled ministrations is patently the real source of mischief. Even though the mother has operated upon herself, or taken drugs without the intervention of another, she will frequently cause herself such injury as to need qualified help, and it would be most undesirable that she should be deterred from seeking this help through the threat of punishment. Yet another reason for not prosecuting her is the difficulty of persuading a jury to convict the mother for what many regard as an imaginary crime, and the unlikelihood that even if convicted she will receive anything but an immediate discharge. But perhaps the most decisive reason for the indulgence is an unavowed change of attitude towards the crime of abortion. The chief evil of an abortion is no longer thought to be the loss of the unborn child, but the injury done to the mother by the unskilled abortionist. That this is so—subject to one contradiction to be mentioned in a moment—is evidenced by the fact that the reluctance to convict the mother has infected even judges. On one occasion a magistrate refused to issue process for abortion against the mother herself.[4] No application was made to the Divisional Court for a mandamus, so that it cannot be said with confidence whether the refusal was lawful. But some indication that the magistrate would have been upheld is afforded by a case of 1932,[5] where it was ruled that a woman who gave evidence could not claim to refuse

[4] 9 *Journal of Criminal Law* 1.
[5] Rex v. Peake, 97 J. P. 353; *The Times* (London), November 18, 1932.

to answer a question whether she had suffered an abortion, on the ground that this answer might incriminate her, because there was no substantial possibility of a prosecution being instituted against her. This seems to give judicial approval to the demise of the abortion statute as regards the mother herself. The logical next step would be to take the medical profession out of the Act; but apart from an exception for therapeutic abortions this is a controversial issue. Therapeutic abortion is to be discussed presently, and the general policy of the law of abortion will be considered in the next chapter.

The indulgence shown to the mother is extended in lesser degree to the father. In a case of 1949,[6] the trial judge sentenced a husband who had tried to abort his wife and killed her to five years' penal servitude, but owing to the particular circumstances the Court of Criminal Appeal reduced the sentence so that, having regard to the date of the conviction, the defendant was discharged immediately. The Lord Chief Justice said:

It is because the unskilful attentions of ignorant people in cases of this kind often result in death that attempts to produce abortion are regarded by the law as very serious offences. In the present case the sentence is that which is usually passed on a professional abortioner. In the case before us the appellant, who certainly deserves the description of being a devoted husband, was living with his wife and two children in circumstances which were truly deplorable. They were all living in one small room, and the prospect of another child being added to their number was such as might have moved any one to the greatest pity. . . . The circumstances were that this man and his wife were trying to prevent another little life from being brought into the conditions in which they were living. The offence is a serious one, but there are circumstances which enable the court to take a merciful view.

It may be commented that the first remark in this en-

[6] Rex v. Tate, *The Times* (London), June 22, 1949.

lightened judgment is not altogether true. Abortion is, in law, just as serious an offence for the skilled obstetrician as it is for the "back-street surgeon" with her knitting-needle. If the real aim of the law were to prevent deaths from unskilled abortion, there would be an exemption for the medical profession; but in fact doctors are treated not only by the abstract law but in the sentencing policy of judges just as severely as lay abortionists.

The position in the United States

Abortion is a statutory crime throughout the United States.[7] Some statutes apply only where the woman is in fact pregnant; others are violated if the woman is merely supposed to be pregnant. Punishment varies, but in all states the maximum for attempted abortion is lower than in England. Some statutes impose an increased punishment where the offence is completed by the destruction of the fetus or death of the mother; they frequently treat the crime as manslaughter. Some states, such as New York,[8] follow the English rule that a pregnant woman who commits or attempts an abortion upon herself is guilty; others exempt her. Similarly, in some states the consenting mother is held to be an accomplice;[9] elsewhere, not.[1] The question is not practically

---

[7] For a comprehensive review of the statutes and cases see Louis J. Regan in *Legal Medicine* Gradwohl, ed. (St. Louis, 1954), Chap. 30; also Note, 23 *Southern California Law Review* 523 (1950).

[8] N. Y. Penal Law ss. 81, 1052 ("quick with child"); cf. s. 1050.

[9] People v. Peyser, 44 N.E. (2d) 58 (Ill. 1942); cf. Steed v. State, 170 So. 489 (Ala. 1936).

[1] State v. Carey, 56 Atl. 632 (Conn. 1904); State v. Shaft, 81 S. E. 932 (N. C. 1914); Commonwealth v. Turner, 112 N. E. 864 (Mass. 1916); State v. Willson, 230 Pac. 810 (Ore. 1924); State v. Tennyson,

important as regards the punishment of the mother, because, as in England, it is not the custom to prosecute her,[2] but it has an indirect effect in respect of the rule that the evidence of an accomplice must be corroborated. In those jurisdictions where the mother is not held to be an accomplice, her evidence against the abortionist does not require to be corroborated, in the absence of a statute to the contrary.[3] This is, of course, a substantial advantage to the prosecution.

Quickening still has legal significance as regards punishment in Arkansas, Florida, Kansas, Michigan, Minnesota, Missouri, New Hampshire, New York, North Dakota, Pennsylvania, South Dakota, Washington,[4] and Wisconsin; also, by judicial construction, in Georgia.[5] The argument in favour of this was stated by a Wisconsin court as follows:

> In a strictly scientific and physiological sense there is life in an embryo from the time of conception, and in such sense there is also life in the male and female elements that unite to form the embryo. But law for obvious reasons cannot in

---

[2] N. W. (2d) 833 (Minn. 1942); People v. Wilson, 153 Pac. (2d) 720 (Cal. 1944); Cahill v. State, 178 Pac. (2d) 657 (Okla. 1947); People v. Alvarez, 166 Pac. (2d) 896 (Cal. 1946). The Rhode Island and Vermont statutes expressly exempt the mother from punishment.

[2] Otto Pollak: *The Criminality of Women* (Philadelphia, 1950), 45–6.

[3] See cases cited on p. 156 nn. 8, 1. The Kentucky statute provides that for the purpose of testimony the mother is not considered an accomplice; North Dakota, South Carolina, and Utah adopt the opposite policy of expressly requiring her evidence to be corroborated. Some states, such as New York, require her to testify, but give her immunity. Where corroboration is required, it is not settled whether evidence that the woman visited the defendant and had a miscarriage afterwards is corroboration. See People v. Josselyn, 39 Cal. 393 (1870); State v. Holden, 20 O.N.P. (N.S.) 200 (1917).

[4] See State v. Hart, 175 P. (2d) 944 (Wash. 1946).

[5] Guiffrida v. State, 7 S. E. (2d) 34 (1940), interpreting Code, Crimes and Punishment, s. 26–1101; but cf. s. 26–1102. The interpretation depends upon the use of the word "child" which is held to mean a quick child.

its classifications follow the latest or ultimate declarations of science. It must for purposes of practical efficiency proceed upon more everyday and popular conceptions, especially as to definitions of crimes that are *malum in se*. These must be of such a nature that the ordinary normal adult knows it is morally wrong to commit them. That it should be less of an offense to destroy an embryo in a stage where human life in its common acceptance has not yet begun than to destroy a quick child is a conclusion that commends itself to most men.[6]

In Mississippi the legislation is so worded that destruction of a fetus before quickening is no crime. Where the legislation does not refer to quickening, it is generally held to punish abortion whether before or after quickening;[7] but in South and North Carolina the statute is held impliedly to preserve the common-law distinction, so that here, too, criminal abortion cannot be committed if the child is not quick.[8] In some jurisdictions third parties can be punished whether the child is quick or not, but the woman herself only if it is quick.[9]

The requirement of quickening appears to make the legislation somewhat impractical, where the mother is dead or otherwise unavailable to become a witness, for it would seem to require the prosecution to give evidence that in many cases can be supplied only by the mother. There is no fixed time in the gestation at which medical evidence can assert that quickening invariably takes place.[1] Moreover, the requirement of quickening raises

[6] Foster v. State, 182 Wis. 298, 196 N. W. 233 (1923).
[7] Mills v. Commonwealth 13 Pa. 626 (1850); Commonwealth v. Wood, 77 Mass. (11 Gray) 85 (1858); State v. Ausplund, 167 Pac. 1019 (Ore. 1917); *Re* Vince, 67 A. (2d) 141 (N. J. 1949).
[8] State v. Steadman, 51 S. E. (2d) 91 (S. C. 1948); State v. Green, 53 S. E. (2d) 285 (N. C. 1949). This interpretation is reached although the statement is in the alternative ("either pregnant or quick with child").
[9] *Re* Vince, n. 7, above.
[1] W. J. Hamilton, J. D. Boyd, and H. W. Mossman: *Human Em-*

a problem in proving the mental element requisite for the crime (*mens rea*), for a woman who is pregnant for the first time may not feel movement until after the sixth month, or, if she feels it before, realize what it is; on the other hand she may mistakenly believe that she has quickened. On principle it would seem that in those jurisdictions where the crime requires quickening to have occurred, the mother must have felt it; and there is authority for this view.[2] But often it would be impossible to prove what the law requires. A leading American work on medical jurisprudence assumes that proof by post-mortem examination that the fetus has reached the fifth month of development is evidence of quickening;[3] but this neglects the necessity for proving the mother's feeling. A post-mortem cannot show whether the fetus has in fact moved, still less whether the mother was aware of it.

In the United States the risks incurred by a practitioner in performing an abortion are not only those resulting from the possibility of criminal prosecution or professional discipline. In addition, a majority of states permit a woman to bring a civil action for damages against a practitioner for performing a non-therapeutic abortion upon her even though she consented to the operation. A substantial minority disallow recovery,[4] and this view is preferred in the American Law Institute's *Restatement*

---

bryology (Cambridge, England, 1945), p. 100, states that fetal movements are usually first detected by the mother during the fifth month; ibid., p. 273 says that such movements can usually be detected, with the stethoscope, at about the fourteenth week, but are not felt by the mother until the sixteenth or seventeenth weeks.

[2] Evans v. People, 49 N. Y. 86 (1872); State v. Steadman, 51 S. E. (2d) 91 (S. C. 1948).

[3] T. A. Gonzales, M. Vance, M. Helpern, and C. J. Umberger: *Legal Medicine, Pathology and Toxicology,* 2nd ed. (New York, 1954), p. 566.

[4] See 35 *Iowa Law Review* 267–8.

of the Law of Torts (§ § 60–1) and would probably be adopted also in England.

The exception for therapeutic abortion

Most of the American legislation (including that in New York) provides expressly that abortion is lawful if necessary to preserve the life of the woman. In the governing English statute, the Act of 1861, no exception is expressed for therapeutic abortions. This is not surprising, for the operation was regarded as dangerous only twenty years ago, while in 1861 it would have been ridiculous to call it therapy. When, however, the child-destruction statute was passed in England in 1929, it was provided that no person should be found guilty unless it was proved that the act was not done in good faith for the purpose only of preserving the life of the mother. The proviso was necessary because it had long been the accepted medical practice to destroy the child *in utero* where this was essential to prevent the mother's life from being gravely endangered.

It is an example of the haphazard methods of English law reform that although this proviso was seen to be necessary in 1929, no exception to the same effect was inserted by amendment in the abortion statute of 1861, though the question of policy is the same under both. Indeed, child destruction, which is committed in respect of a viable fetus, is much more serious than an abortion in the early months of pregnancy, so that the recognition of therapeutic feticide must logically be followed by the recognition of therapeutic abortion. The inference that this is possible even under the abortion statute as it stands is assisted by the fact that the draftsman of the latter statute took the precaution to insert in it the blessed word "unlawfully" ("whoever shall unlawfully . . ."), which has long been undersood in the medical world to imply that some abortions are lawful. This view was upheld by Mr. Justice Macnaghten in *Rex v. Bourne*,[5] in a direction to the jury which has been much admired on both sides of the Atlantic. The effect of his ruling is to read into the abortion statute the same exception as that in the child destruction statute, and to interpret "preserving the life of the mother" in an extended sense to include preserving the longevity of the mother.

The facts of the Bourne case were dramatic. A girl of fourteen had been shockingly raped by a number of soldiers, with the result that she became pregnant. Her medical advisers decided that for the sake of her physical and mental health it was necessary to break off the pregnancy, and they appealed to Mr. Alec Bourne, a gynæcologist and obstetric surgeon in the front rank of his profession, to perform the operation. Although therapeutic abortions had long been performed by some courageous surgeons, there was nothing in the written law to sanction them. Even if they were permissible, there was no definition of the limits of permissibility, so that it could not be said with any approach to certainty that the psychiatric indication, for example, would be accepted by a judge and jury. Mr. Bourne, however, not only consented to act but announced that he would make it a test case in order to secure the clarification of the law. "I have done this [operation] before," he declared, "and have not the slightest hesitation in doing it again. I have said that the next time I have such an opportunity I will write to the Attorney-General and invite him to take action." It was thus through his own de-

---

[5] [1939] 1 K.B. 687. The case is also reported in [1938] 3 All E.R. 615, but the variations between the two reports, in omissions and additions, are so great that Macnaghten J. must have almost rewritten his judgment for the Law Reports version. For the background of the case see Lilian Wyles: *A Woman at Scotland Yard* (London, 1952), pp. 221ff.

liberate choice that **Mr.** Bourne found himself in the dock at the Old Bailey, charged with a felony that in point of view of possible punishment must be reckoned one of the most serious known to the law.

The judge's direction to the jury, which resulted in Mr. Bourne's acquittal, is a striking vindication of the legal view that the defence of necessity applies not only to common law but even to statutory crimes. It is true that the direction proceeded in some slight degree on the analogy of the child destruction statute, which contains an express exemption for the preservation of the life of the mother; but the exception in the one statute was not in itself a ground for reading a similar exception into another. The only legal principle on which the exception could be based was the defence of necessity. It is true, also, that Mr. Justice Macnaghten proceeded in part on the ground that the abortion statute contained the word "unlawfully," which he regarded as implying that some abortions are lawful. The word does not, however, specify which abortions are lawful, and again the only principle indicating the extent of legality is the defence of necessity. The defence of necessity involves a choice of values and a choice of evils, and the choice made by the judge appears clearly from his statement that "the unborn child in the womb must not be destroyed unless the destruction of that child is for the purpose of preserving the yet more precious life of the mother." [6] Apparently the interest of the mother in living a single extra day is preferred to the life of the child. This may sound like pushing the argument to an extreme, but it is submitted that legal certainty requires the rule to be an absolute one. In practice these matters cannot be estimated to periods of days.

[6] From the report in [1938] 3 All E.R., at 620. Almost the whole of this page of the All England Report is omitted from the Law Reports version.

The attitude of the Bourne case is adopted also in those American jurisdictions where the governing statute makes no express saving for therapeutic abortions. This point will be taken up presently.

Six questions arise as to the scope of the exception for therapeutic abortions.

(1) Is it limited to cases where the operation is performed for the purpose of preventing the mother from having her days cut short?

In England, so far as the judgment in *Rex v. Bourne* goes, there is no hint that the exception extends beyond saving the life or preserving the longevity of the mother. Not only did Mr. Justice Macnaghten's direction confine itself to this case, but his reasoning proceeded in part on the analogy of the child destruction statute, where the exception is limited to the preservation of the mother's life. It is true that at one place the learned judge directed the jury to find whether the accused believed that the continuance of the pregnancy would make the patient a physical or mental wreck;[7] but this must be read in the light of his earlier intimation that the case was one in which health was depressed so much that life was shortened,[8] and his concluding direction, which was confined to the preservation of the girl's life.

Looking at the question on principle, there seems to be no good reason why the defence should not be extended to cases where pregnancy is terminated for the purpose of preventing serious physical injury to the mother, even though that injury is not of such a character as to affect the duration of life (for example, impairment of sight or hearing). The reason is that the mother's life must be considered in relation to its quality as well as to its duration. Serious physical injury to the mother, who is a human being with the full human capacity for pain, is an

[7] [1939] 1 K.B., at 694.
[8] At pp. 692-3.

evil greater both morally and socially than the destruction of the fetus, at any rate if the fetus is in an early stage of development. It is true that the offence of abortion does not discriminate between an operation performed in the earlier and later stages of pregnancy; but an operation performed in the later stages falls within the law of child destruction, which contains no defence in respect of the health (as opposed to the life or longevity) of the mother.[9] It may seem reasonable that there should be greater freedom of interfering with pregnancy in the earlier stages than very late. Alternatively, the opinion may well be held that the health of the mother should be preferred to the life of the fetus at all stages.

The view that all therapeutic abortions are lawful is generally entertained in the English medical profession[1] (though not always acted upon by doctors in practice), and is slightly supported by the later case of *Rex v. Bergmann and Ferguson* (1948),[2] which seems to indicate that where serious injury to health is feared, the court will not look too narrowly into the question of danger to life.

The legislation of most of the United States refers to "preserving" or "saving" the mother's life; perhaps there is no difference of meaning between the two verbs, but the first is arguably wider. It seems likely that the American courts, like the English, will allow the surgeon to operate in order to prevent the curtailment of the mother's life; he need not expect her death during the

---

[9] Presumably the express exception in the child-destruction statute would prevent the courts reading in other exceptions under the doctrine of necessity. It may be thought that this is a point that the legislature should reconsider.

[1] E.g., (1952) 1 *British Medical Journal* 915; Parry: op. cit., pp. 11–12.

[2] Central Criminal Court, May 1948. The quotations later in this chapter are from the official transcript of Morris J.'s direction to the jury. There is a short account of the case in (1948) 1 *British Medical Journal* 1008.

period of gestation or in delivery.[3] There is as yet no judicial guidance on the question whether the quality of life is regarded under statutes referring merely to the preservation of the life of the mother. It would certainly be a grave thing to hold that operations to preserve the mother's health (as distinct from life) are illegal, when these operations are already performed by the medical profession with beneficial results.[4] A decision that they are illegal would run counter to the ethical convictions of the medical profession and the community as a whole. The legislation of some states has wording sufficiently wide to make a liberal interpretation easy. In Maryland the operation is lawful to "secure the safety of the mother" (a formula that must have been intended to cover something beyond saving life); in Alabama and the District of Columbia it may be performed to preserve the life or health of the mother, and in Colorado and New Mexico it may be performed to prevent serious and permanent bodily injury to her. In a few states, no reference is made to the question of saving the mother, whether in life or in health,[5] but a Massachusetts court nevertheless felt itself able to imply into such legislation the defence of necessity, not only in respect of saving the mother's life[6] but in respect of preventing serious

[3] Since this is the position even in states that have no exception for the preservation of the life of the mother (Commonwealth v. Wheeler, below), it seems to be so *a fortiori* where there is such an exception in the statute.

[4] Even in states confining legal abortion to the purpose of saving the life of the mother, it is the practice of some of the best physicians to allow social and moral factors to influence decisions—which means that in effect health rather than life is being considered. This is so, for example, in Iowa: see Moore and Randall in 63 *American Journal of Obstetrics and Gynecology* 28 (1952).

[5] Florida; Louisiana; Massachusetts (using the word "unlawfully"); New Jersey ("maliciously or without justification"); Pennsylvania ("wilfully . . . unlawfully").

[6] This point had already been decided in State v. Rudman, 136 Atl. 817 (Me. 1927).

impairment of her health, mental or physical; and actual necessity was not required, but only the physician's *bona fide* belief in necessity, provided that his judgment corresponded with the general opinion of competent practitioners.[7] In a later case in New Jersey, however, the trial judge refused to extend the exemption to considerations of health as distinct from life; the appellate court left this question open; but held that the woman's "well-being" was not the test of legality.[8]

(2) Is the exception for therapy limited to cases where the threat to the mother's life or health is a somatic (bodily) illness? Clearly the law will take account of mental as well as physical ill-health. This appears in the Bourne judgment, with its reference to the mother becoming a "physical or mental wreck." The Bourne case concerned a girl who had been the subject of rape, and such sexual assaults upon young girls (whether by way of rape or of incest) are recognized in present medical practice as being capable of giving rise to mental illness, which may justify the emptying of the uterus; though it may frequently be a matter of extreme difficulty to decide upon the best medical course.[9]

The importance of the psychiatric indication has advanced greatly in recent years as that of the somatic indication has receded. Owing to medical advances and

[7] Commonwealth v. Wheeler, 53 N.E. (2d) 4 (Mass. 1944). The extraordinary situation in Massachusetts is that although a physician can thus abort a woman on health grounds, the law against contraception forbids him to go on to give her advice on how to avoid another pregnancy: Commonwealth v. Gardner, 15 N.E. (2d) 222 (1938).

[8] State v. Brandenburg, 58 A. (2d) 709 (1948).

[9] The mere youth of the mother (even where her age is between 13 and 16) is said to be no indication for therapeutic abortion: (1932) 2 *The Lancet* 131; (1940) 2 *The Lancet* 61. A psychiatrist wrote: "Where pregnancy is the result of rape, the fact of rape does not in itself constitute a reason for termination. The mental strain consequent upon the birth of a child so conceived must, however, be a potent factor in determining the post-natal condition of the mother's psychic, and therefore also her physical, health." (Dr. Eustace Chesser in [1949] 1 *British Medical Journal* 727.)

discoveries, there has been a steady reduction in the indications for therapeutic abortion on account of somatic
disease. Indeed, the number of cases where the operation
is needed to save the mother from impending death has
dwindled one might almost say to insignificance. One of
the major reasons for this reduction is a change of attitude towards pulmonary tuberculosis, for which an abortion is now performed much less often than formerly.
Women are also carried through pregnancy with hypertension when some years ago it would have been terminated. Severe and advanced degrees of cardio-vascular-
renal disease in pregnancy; some other serious cases of
cardiac disease; an occasional case of disease of the
primary urinary tract with renal decomposition—these
constitute almost the sum total of cases on which there is
still general medical agreement that the operation is
needed for pressing medical reasons of a somatic nature.[1]
It is only if the physician is allowed to provide against a
probable shortening of the expected span of life, and for
this purpose to take into account some psychiatric, family, and social factors, that the operation comes to have a
more general application.

In assessing medical trends in abortion it is hard to
disentangle the triumphs of new discovery from changes
in attitude. At Los Angeles County Hospital, for example,
the average incidence of therapeutic abortion fell from 1
in every 106 deliveries in 1931 to 1 in every 2,864 in
in 1946–50; in 1950 only 1 in 8,000 pregnancies was
terminated.[2] These figures are sometimes cited as indicating the virtual disappearance of the need for therapeutic abortion, but other commentators find that they

[1] See Moore and Randall in 63 *American Journal of Obstetrics and Gynecology* 38 (1952); Alan F. Guttmacher and David C. Wilson in *Therapeutic Abortion,* Harold Rosen, ed. (New York, 1954), pp. 12, 189.
[2] Keith P. Russell in (1953) 151 *Journal of the American Medical Association* 108, extracted in (1953–4) *Year Book of Obstetrics and Gynecology* 32.

merely show a change of policy in the particular hospital. Thus Dr. Harry G. LaForge, after quoting the Los Angeles record, observed: "Therefore, I venture to say they are being done in other hospitals because in 8,000 cases there are bound to be a number of cases of Grade 3 or 4 heart disease, severe hypertension, etc." [3] That the striking reduction in abortions in Los Angeles is not entirely to be explained on medical grounds seems to be shown by the fact that in other hospitals no such steep decline has taken place. It is reported, for example, that in the Chicago Lying-in Hospital the incidence of the operation has remained unchanged, in the aggregate, between 1931 and 1954. There was a drop in the number of operations performed on the pulmonary indication, but an increase in the number of cardiac indications. The psychiatric indication remained constant at a cautious 15 per cent, but a new indication, called maternal-fetal, became recognized towards the end of the period. [4] At some other hospitals the psychiatric indication has risen to balance a drop in the somatic indications.

There can be little doubt that fear of the law is a determining factor in the policy adopted by hospitals and surgeons, both in the United States and in Great Britain. A few regard themselves as entitled to accept the report of a psychiatrist without question, performing or authorizing the operation to be performed whenever he advises it. In Britain this appears to be true of only one hospital. A larger number control or usurp the discretion of the psychiatrist. Thus many obstetricians refuse to act upon psychiatric advice unless they themselves—though not psychiatrists—think there is "something in it." Some, probably most, hospitals require three concurring opinions, with the assent of the head of the department of

---

[3] 56 *New York State Journal of Medicine* 1610 (1956).
[4] See Myrna F. Loth and H. Close Hesseltine: "Therapeutic Abortion at the Chicago Lying-in Hospital," 72 *American Journal of Obstetrics and Gynecology* 304 (1956).

gynæcology and obstetrics.[5] Many hospitals in the United States, and one or two in England, have set up boards of review to consider applications for therapeutic abortion. Psychiatrists are naturally in a minority on these boards, and the general effect is to restrict the operation. Others, again, ignore the psychiatric ground altogether.

As already noticed, the position is made more difficult in those jurisdictions where the governing legislation refers only to saving or preserving the life of the mother. In New York, where the statute uses the word "preserving," the medical interpretation of the law varies, one physician expressing the opinion that "the only legally valid psychiatric reason for terminating pregnancy in this state is danger of suicide,"[6] and another contradicting this by quoting the dictionary definition of "preserve"—"to save, to keep safe or secure from injury, loss or destruction. To defend or guard from harm, evil or hurt, to protect."[7]

One of the chief legal problems in connection with the psychiatric indication is the mother's threat of suicide. Is a psychiatrist justified in advising an abortion where he believes that if it is refused there is a strong possibility that the mother will commit suicide? On the one hand, it may be argued that threats of suicide are generally not seriously intended, and that if the mother's threat of suicide is taken as justifying the operation, the mother is enabled to have an abortion whenever she desires. Perhaps it was for these reasons that a Wisconsin court in a rather old case held that the threat of suicide could not turn an abortion into a therapeutic one.[8] On the other

[5] See, e.g., A. F. Guttmacher in 21 *Journal of the Mount Sinai Hospital* 111 (1954).

[6] Robert B. McGraw, "Legal Aspects of Termination of Pregnancy on Psychiatric Grounds," 56 *New York State Journal of Medicine* 1605 at 1607 (1956).

[7] Harry G. LaForge, ibid., at 1609.

[8] Hatchard v. State, 48 N.W. 380 (Wis. 1891), regarding death from suicide as not "from natural causes."

hand, it may be said that enlightened medical practice does at present take account of such a threat. A mere threat of suicide, or even an attempt at suicide, is not regarded in itself as a medical indication; for the threat may be merely an attempt to blackmail the surgeon into performing the operation, and the attempt may be merely staged, or performed in circumstances that are not likely to be repeated. On the other hand, there may be a history of previous psychiatric illness, or symptoms of an obsessional state, which give force to the threat. It must be for the psychiatrist to decide, in the light of his knowledge and experience, whether the threat of suicide is likely to be carried into effect, and if so whether a termination of the pregnancy is the best treatment.[9] If he advises a

[9] The following medical opinions are of interest. Dr. Eustace Chesser expressed the view that "where a patient is in so disturbed a mental condition as to warrant continual watching for the prevention of suicide, that in itself would seem to be strong evidence of such severe mental conflict as may lead to complete breakdown. . . . In genuinely doubtful cases I consider it wiser to give the mother the benefit of the doubt:" (1949) 1 *British Medical Journal* 728. Books on forensic medicine, not being written by psychiatrists, sometimes take a stiffer position. Thus F. E. Camps and W. B. Purchase: *Practical Forensic Medicine* (London, 1956), pp. 31–2, say: "The doctor may find that the basic fact is that the woman threatens suicide if the pregnancy goes on. If she is married and living with her husband, the prevention of her suicide is a matter for the spouse and is not necessarily a reason for aborting her." But they add that if the woman has been deserted by the father of the child she may be in such a state of depression that a psychiatrist can express a firm opinion that suicide would be likely, and that pregnancy should be terminated.

Dr. Robert B. McGraw: "Legal Aspects of Termination of Pregnancy on Psychiatric Grounds," 56 *New York State Journal of Medicine* 1605 at 1607 (1956), quoted statistics supplied by Dr. Milton Helpern, Chief Medical Examiner of New York City. "In 1953, 231 women reported suicides; 119 were between fourteen and fifty years of age; 60 were autopsied; one was pregnant." But Dr. McGraw, although he took a restrictive attitude towards abortion on psychiatric grounds, expressed the opinion that "threats are not to be taken lightly, although they may be made for effect. Threats made to others, obvious mental anguish, constant weeping, sleeplessness or terrifying dreams, loss of appetite and weight, history of previous attacks or suicidal attempts, and history of suicide of siblings and relatives are all significant. It

termination on the psychiatric indication, the surgeon may properly regard himself as entitled to act on the psychiatrist's report. The question is, after all, a medical one, and it would be a serious thing for the courts to interfere with the medical practice.

A variation of the suicide question occurs where the woman evidences a determination to abort herself in a way that is likely to endanger her life. The question might have arisen in an Iowa case, where a girl of fifteen, being pregnant, was in a highly nervous condition, threatened to kill herself, used instruments on herself, and jumped several times from a height of eight or ten feet in a haymow. The physician who decided to empty the uterus testified that he did so because he found the fetus dead. On this evidence being given, it was held that the physician could not be convicted.[1] The case is not, therefore, a neat authority on the question raised above. It may, however, be submitted, if the point ever calls for decision, that there is no essential difference between fears for the mother's life resulting from her fixed intention to commit suicide and similar fears resulting from her fixed intention to abort herself dangerously.

Some additional comments may be directed to both Question 1 and Question 2.

So far there has been no indication in the American or English cases that abortion would be legally justified on the ethical ground that the mother was raped or the intercourse obtained by threat or fraud, or on the eugenic ground that the father or mother is feeble-minded or affected with a transmissible disease, or that the intercourse was incestuous; or on the economic ground that the parents cannot well support another child, or that the mother is unmarried and to have the child would result in her losing her employment or would interrupt

---

is in appraising the danger of suicide that it is proper to consider social and economic factors in the total picture."

[1] State v. Dunklebarger, 221 N.W. 592 (1928).

an expensive course of training. It seems unlikely that the judges will ever feel themselves able to stretch either the words of statutes or the doctrine of necessity to cover any of these considerations. Still less is abortion likely to be permitted where it is claimed only because of the social disgrace of giving birth to an illegitimate child. However—and this cannot be too strongly emphasized —some of these considerations may enter indirectly (at least in those jurisdictions where the mother's health as well as her life can be considered) by giving rise to the practitioner's belief that it would be injurious to the mother to allow her to give birth to the child. In particular, severe worry about the consequences of having the child is one of the factors that may affect the mother's mental health.

The legality of an operation becomes much more problematical when the surgeon's fear does not relate to the gestation or childbearing itself, or their later effect upon the mother's physical or mental health (the purely medical indication), but relates only to the strain of rearing the child (the socio-medical indication). If the law allows the doctor to take account of the strain that would be imposed on the mother's health by bringing up the child after birth, it will have taken a long step towards allowing abortion on social grounds. The mother, for example, may already have a large family, and she may have to do all the work in the house herself, as well, perhaps, as outside work. Her strength is already taxed to the limit. She may be able to give birth to the child without predictable illness; but it may reasonably be feared that the rearing of yet another child will so drain her strength as to cause a breakdown. In a sense the indication is a medical one; but it differs from the purely medical indication in that abortion is not in theory the only way of dealing with the situation. The child might be permitted to be born, and, if the mother can be persuaded to give her consent, placed in a foster-home. There may be practical difficulties in this course which might make abortion (if this is the course that the mother desires) the only effective solution. Whether a court would regard it as legal must remain a matter of speculation. It is, at all events, the present practice of some of the most reputable members of the profession to terminate a pregnancy on some socio-medical grounds. Where, for example, the mother is suffering from pulmonary tuberculosis, one medical opinion has it that childbearing of itself cannot be shown to have an adverse influence upon the disease, and there is good prospect of a healthy child being born. Nevertheless, where the social circumstances are unfavourable, it may be foreseen that the added work, worry, and possible financial strain of caring for the infant are likely to lead to a retrogression; and here a surgeon may consider himself justified in operating.[2] The same remark applies where the patient suffers from cardiac trouble,[3] or where the upbringing of another child is likely to lead to mental illness.[4]

In some illnesses an obstetrician is enabled to take into account illegal considerations—e.g., eugenics—under cover of the legal ones. An illustration is supplied by some cases of diabetes, where the therapeutic indication for abortion may be somewhat thin, since the maternal mortality of diabetics is low and the worsening of the diabetic state caused by gestation and birth is usually only temporary. There is, however, a very strong eugenic reason for terminating the pregnancy if both parents

[2] See on this example Raymond C. Cohen in *Obstetrics,* Sir Eardley Holland, ed. (London, 1955), p. 468.

[3] A. F. Guttmacher in *Therapeutic Abortion,* Harold Rosen, ed. (New York, 1954), p. 21.

[4] Cf. the words of G. W. B. James: *Obstetrics,* Sir Eardley Holland, ed. (London, 1955), p. 1101: "It is commonly said that eugenic, economic and social factors do not justify therapeutic termination of pregnancy. Psychiatrists must be cautious in supporting such views if at the same time they teach that such factors are of importance in the ætiology of psychiatric illness."

have a pronounced family history of diabetes, since a child will probably develop the disease at some stage in its life. (This is less likely if only one parent is affected.) A surgeon who complies with the woman's demand for an abortion, acting in reality for the eugenic reason, may still find himself adequately protected by arguments looking to the therapeutic indication, for example, the inability of the patient to remain within easy reach of expert supervision throughout pregnancy.[5]

Under cover of therapy, eugenic considerations are coming to be avowed in some reports of American obstetricians. They are termed the "fetal indication," but it is explained that this expression is used for brevity and convenience—"actually it is only partially fetal because in most of these cases the pregnancy is terminated because of emotional stress in the mother, as well as the prevention of serious or irremediable hereditary or congenital defects in the fetus."[6] The emotional stress is the legal reason for terminating, while the eugenic consideration may be uppermost in the mind of the physician. How does the emotional stress come about? The answer generally given is that the expectation of giving birth to a defective or nonviable child causes the expectant mother to worry. She may realize the danger through knowledge of her own defect which brings about the risk, as in the case of Rh incompatibility. Or

[5] The various indications are given by J. H. Peel in *Obstetrics* (cited last note), pp. 482–3.

[6] Myrna F. Loth and H. Close Hesseltine: "Therapeutic Abortion at the Chicago Lying-in Hospital," (1956) 72 *American Journal of Obstetrics and Gynecology* 304 at 307. The authors say that fetal indications were accepted in 7 per cent of the therapeutic abortions performed at their hospital in 1939–54.

M. S. Guttmacher in *Therapeutic Abortion,* Harold Rosen, ed (New York, 1954), p. 183, quotes Studdiford as saying that most physicians justify their eugenic abortions by stating that they are preventing the mother from developing a psychosis. He adds: "This is certainly an acceptable scientific rationalization for a socially necessary procedure."

she may herself have repeatedly suffered the loss of infants at birth, due perhaps to erythroblastosis. Or again
she may know that her germ plasm is faulty because the
mating has previously yielded amaurotic idiots, succes-
sive microcephalics, children with cleft palates, hæmo-
philiacs, or children with muscular dystrophy. As soon
as the expectant mother becomes despondent on one of
these accounts, an abortion may be performed which is
professedly therapeutic but in substance eugenic. A supporting therapeutic reason is that it will be bad for the
mother's health for her to have to bring up an ailing
infant;[7] but, as already pointed out, it is not certain
whether this socio-medical indication, relating rather to
the rearing of the child than to giving birth to it, can be
recognized under the present law.

One of the anomalies of this excuse for eugenic abortion is that it makes the legality of the operation depend upon the mother's intelligence and temperament.
For example, one of the standard eugenic indications
for termination is where there has been therapeutic
radiation to the mother's pelvic organs during undiag-
nosed early pregnancy.[8] But the expectant mother will

[7] This ground is taken by C. T. Polson: *The Essentials of Forensic
Medicine* (London, 1955), p. 389: "Even if the mother is unaware of
the possibility [that her child will be born defective], but it seems
that her personality is of a kind which the delivery of a [defective]
would create a real risk of mental breakdown, it would follow that
therapeutic abortion may be performed in good faith in order to
preserve her health."

[8] A. F. Guttmacher in *Therapeutic Abortion,* Harold Rosen, ed.
(New York, 1954), p. 20. Another eugenic indication that, at least
until recently, was well established in Anglo-American surgical practice
was where the mother contracted German measles (rubella) within
the first three months of pregnancy; Australian doctors reported that
this created a strong probability of the baby being born with one
or more of serious abnormalities (cardiac lesions, microcephaly, congenital cataracts, deafness, etc.); and English and American surgeons
therefore made a practice of terminating the pregnancy. See A. F.
Guttmacher: loc. cit.; (1952) 1 *British Medical Journal* 915. But Loth
and Hesseltine, loc. cit., say: "Attitudes have become less certain on
the likelihood of fetal injury from maternal rubella in the first

not be worried by the fact that she had radiation treatment during pregnancy unless she happens to have come to know of the eugenic risk, as by reading an article in a popular magazine. The legal course is apparently for the doctor to tell the mother of the risk in order to bring on the worry, and then to abort on account of the worry. This plan doubtless works well enough unless the mother happens to be feeble-minded, in which case her child must be allowed to be born.

(3) The third question is this: When necessity is a defence, must it be shown that the act was objectively necessary (that is, necessary in the view of the jury), or is the surgeon's belief in necessity a defence? The answer is clear in the law of a few of the United States (such as Virginia and West Virginia), where the local legislation does not require necessity in fact, but gives a defence whenever the act was done in good faith with the intention of saving the life of the mother. Others achieve much the same result by providing that the operation should either be necessary to preserve the mother's life or be advised by physicians to be necessary for that purpose; here the mere advice of the physicians creates the defence.[9] Whether, where the statute merely excepts an operation necessary to preserve the mother's life, it will be interpreted to allow a defence based on good faith, is the subject of a difference of judicial opin-

---

trimester. The trend in recent years has been less toward termination of the pregnancy. It appears that these infections in the United States have not been as damaging to the fetus as was reported from Australia."

In England Lord Justice Denning, in an address to a medical school, expressed the opinion that the medical practice of abortion in regard to German measles was lawful ([1956] 2 *British Medical Journal* 821). He did not give reasons for his opinion.

[9] But where the advice of the requisite number of physicians has not been given, it has been said, *obiter,* that such a statute does not confer immunity upon a person who operates under a personal belief that the operation is necessary: in such circumstances "he acts at his peril of the fact": State v. Hatchard, 48 N.W. 380 (Wis. 1891).

ion,[1] but the better view seems to be in favour of the more lenient construction. As has been seen (p. 165), a Massachusetts court allowed the defence of *bona fide* belief in necessity even though the ruling statute did not mention excuses at all. This is consonant with principle, for the surgeon's belief that the operation is necessary to prevent injury to the mother excludes a guilty mind, *mens rea,* on his part, and on principle this should be so whether the belief was reasonable or not. It is true that there is a requirement of reasonableness according to the Massachusetts case just mentioned, because the physician's judgment is required to correspond with the general opinion of competent practitioners. The facts before the court, however, were peculiar. A physician was prosecuted for procuring his wife's abortion, and defended himself by alleging that the abortion was necessary to preserve his wife's mental health. It was held that evidence that the defendant had not complied with the accepted medical practice of consulting a fellow practitioner before operating, or as to the place of the operation, was properly admitted as bearing upon his criminal intent. The peculiar circumstances obviously cast grave doubt on the *bona fides* of the defence.

In England it seems that the only requirement is of good faith. This view of the law is supported by the direction in *Rex v. Bourne,* where the learned judge laid it down that a defence to the charge of abortion arises where the act was "done *in good faith* for the purpose only of preserving the life of the mother."[2] It is true that later in his direction he slipped in the words "on reasonable grounds,"[3] but still later he reverted to

[1] Yes in Iowa: State v. Dunklebarger, 221 N.W. 592 (1928). Not in Maine (State v. Rudman, 136 Atl. 817 [1927]), Maryland (Adams v. State, 88 A. [2d] 556 [1952]), Wisconsin (Hatchard v. State, 48 N.W. 380 [1891]), or apparently Washington (State v. Hart, 175 P. [2d] 944 [1947]).

[2] [1939] 1 K.B., at 691.

[3] At p. 694.

the simple statement of "honest belief." [4] The point was made clearer in *Rex v. Bergmann and Ferguson,* [5] where Mr. Justice Morris addressed the jury in the following terms:

You are not concerned with the question as to whether Dr. Ferguson arrived at the right conclusion; you have not to decide whether Dr. Ferguson did or did not make a mistake. Between medical people there may often be differences of opinion; sometimes it is difficult to assert which of two opinions is to be preferred; but you are not here to weigh up whether Dr. Ferguson was correct or incorrect in the view she had formed. You have to be satisfied by the prosecution that she expressed a dishonest opinion, and that when she advised, if you think she did advise, the termination of pregnancy by her letters in these two cases, you will have to consider whether you are persuaded by the evidence called by the prosecution that that lady gave a dishonest opinion, did not act in good faith, and was therefore advising something that was unlawful.

If this is so, some remarks of Mr. Justice Macnaghten in *Rex v. Bourne* seem to need qualification. The learned judge said that the defence of necessity "could not be available to the professional abortionist," and "members of the medical profession alone could properly perform such an operation." [6] This restriction is intelligible if reasonable belief is required, but not if the question is merely one of belief. A quack may in fact believe that he is saving the woman's life. However, a jury would be slow to credit him. The question is really one of evidence as to belief, not of drawing a rigid legal line between qualified and unqualified practitioners.

From the social point of view it is highly desirable

---

[4] At p. 694, l. 6; cf. [1938] 3 All E.R., at 620 E-F. It should be noted that the adjective "honest" as applied to belief is superfluous. Either there is or there is not belief; there is no such thing as a dishonest belief. So also with *"bona fide* belief."

[5] Above, p. 164 n. 2.

[6] [1938] 3 All E.R., at 617 D-E, 621 D; [1939] 1 K.B., at 695.

to prevent unqualified persons from performing the operation, even on therapeutic grounds. In some of the United States the operation, to be lawful, is expressly required to be performed by or under the advice of a qualified medical practitioner; and some require it to be performed in a licensed maternity hospital, unless an emergency prevents.

Although the opinion of the practitioner is legally conclusive, this does not mean that the practitioner does not have to justify his opinion in court. In practice he has to, for otherwise the jury may not believe him when he swears as to his belief. This matter will be considered further when we come to the question of burden of proof.

(4) The fourth question is whether the necessity must always be known to the actor, or whether one can (so to speak) act by accident from necessity. A surgeon performs the operation of abortion. He does it in order to earn his fee, and makes no inquiry whether it is necessary to preserve the life of the mother. In fact, however, he performs the operation competently, and it is proved that the operation did probably save the mother's life, owing to cardiac weakness of which the surgeon was unaware. Can he defend himself on this ground? It is submitted that he can, if he is charged under legislation which penalizes a completed non-therapeutic abortion. Although he has the *mens rea* of the offence, he has not committed the forbidden act, the *actus reus*.[7] However, there is no reason why such a surgeon should not be convicted of attempting a criminal abortion. The law of attempt is the recognized means of punishing one who has a criminal state of mind though he fails to achieve

[7] A case apparently against this view of the law is Commonwealth v. Wheeler, 53 N.E. (2d) 4, at 6 (Mass. 1944). But in favour of it see Hatchard v. State, 48 N.W. 380 (Wis. 1891), where it was contemplated that a defendant could plead the statutory defence of the advice of two physicians even though the advice was not given to or known by him but only to and by his co-defendant.

his criminal purpose. In England, indeed, the abortion legislation is worded only in terms of attempt, it being immaterial for the purpose of the offence whether the abortion itself is effected or not. It is submitted that a practitioner could be convicted under this legislation of performing what is in fact a therapeutic abortion where he believes it to be non-therapeutic.

(5) There is nothing in the American or English authorities to require the surgeon who performs a therapeutic abortion to operate without fee. It does not matter in the least whether he acts solely in the duty of his profession, or whether his motive is tinctured by a desire to earn his own living.[8] Nevertheless, so great is the fear of the law felt by eminent surgeons, psychiatrists, and others, that some make a practice of charging no fee for participating in therapeutic abortions, as an insurance against misrepresentation afterwards.

It need hardly be added that there is nothing in law to prevent a surgeon specializing in therapeutic abortions; in fact such specialization has great advantages from the medical point of view. Legally, however, it carries some risk. Especially regrettable is the judicial habit of allowing a surgeon to be cross-examined upon other abortions that he has performed, without proof or even suggestion by the prosecution that these other operations were unnecessary for medical reasons.[9] Evidence of this kind has no probative value and can only prejudice a jury.

(6) The problem of burden of proof has given rise to a good deal of difference of opinion. Although this is merely a matter of the law of evidence, it is of some importance to medical practitioners to know who has the burden of proof in respect of the therapeutic quality of an operation. The law of England[1] and most of the

[8] In England this follows from the case of Rex v. Bergmann and Ferguson, p. 164, n. 2, above, where Dr. Bergmann charged a fee.

[9] E.g., State v. Powers, 283 Pac. 439 (Wash. 1929).

[1] As stated in Rex v. Bourne.

United States requires the prosecution to prove that the operation was not necessary (or not believed to be necessary) for the permitted purpose,[2] but a minority of the states (including New York) place the burden on the defence.[3] The reason given for the minority view is that the facts are peculiarly within the knowledge of the defendant; but this reason fails to discriminate properly between the persuasive and the evidential burden. It is true that the burden should be on the defence to particularize the issue by introducing some evidence of necessity. The prosecution should not be liable to be met

[2] State v. Wells, 100 Pac. 681 (Utah 1909); State v. Brown, 85 Atl. 797 (Del. 1912); State v. Ausplund, 167 Pac. 1019 (Ore. 1917); State v. Montifoire, 116 Atl. 77 (Vt. 1922); State v. Goodson, 252 S.W. 389 (Mo. 1923); State v. Darrow, 217 N.W. 519 (N.D. 1928); People v. Davis, 200 N.E. 334 (Ill. 1936); Guiffrida v. State, 7 S.E. (2d) 34 (Ga. 1940); Fitch v. Commonwealth, 165 S.W. (2d) 558 (Ky. 1942); State v. Fitzgerald, 174 S.W. (2d) 211 (Mo. 1943); State v. St. Angelo, 52 A. (2d) 513 (R.I. 1947). See Note, 23 *Southern California Law Review* 523 (1950).

It has been held in Iowa that the prosecution must prove not only that the operation was not necessary to save the life of the mother, but also that the doctor did not in good faith believe that it was so necessary: State v. Dunklebarger, p. 177, n. 1, above; cf. State v. Anderson, 33 N.W. (2d) 1 (Iowa 1948).

In Ohio, where the statute is in the alternative, stating an exception where the miscarriage is necessary to preserve the mother's life, or is advised by two physicians to be necessary for that purpose, it is held that the state must offer evidence that the abortion was not necessary to preserve life, while the burden is on the defendant to show that it was advised by two physicians, because this fact is readily available to him: Bridge v. State, 20 O.C.C. (N.S.) 231 (1912). Cf. Hatchard v. State, 48 N.W. 380 (Wis. 1891), holding that the defendant need prove the fact of advice only on the preponderance of evidence.

[3] State v. Lee, 69 Conn. 186 (1897); People v. McGonegal, 62 Hun 622, 17 N.Y.S. 147 (1891), aff'd 32 N.E. 616; Johnson v. People, 80 Pac. 133 (Colo. 1905); People v. Hammer, 194 App. Div. 712, 186 N.Y.S. 132 (1921); Williams v. United States, 138 F. (2d) 81 (D. C. 1943); State v. Hart, 175 P. (2d) 944 (Wash. 1946); Adams v. State, 88 A. (2d) 556 (Md. 1952). There is no relevant difference of wording in the statutes in force in the states adopting the majority and minority views. The Michigan statute is unique in expressly removing the burden from the prosecution.

by a submission of "no case" merely because it fails to negative the defence before it has been raised, and the surgeon's failure to adduce evidence in support of his belief may well be taken as corroboration of the prosecution's case that he did not have it. This, however, is not the same as saying that the persuasive burden is on the defendant; when all the evidence is in, the jury should be instructed that the persuasive burden on the issue of necessity remains with the prosecution, for this is the general rule of criminal policy.

In the majority jurisdictions where the burden is placed on the prosecution, it seems that the evidential as well as the persuasive burden is placed upon it. The rule is, however, mitigated by another. This is that proof that the woman was previously in good health is sufficient to shift the evidential burden in respect of necessity to the defence.[4] According to some decisions, failure by the prosecution to give evidence that the woman was previously in good health may be regarded as failure to discharge the burden of proof.[5] This view may make it impossible for the prosecution to succeed where the woman was in indifferent health, even though the circumstances may to the eye of common sense suggest strongly that the operation was performed merely for gain, and even though the defendant does not set up a case of necessity. A clearer distinction between the evidential and persuasive burden would solve the difficulty.

Some other rules of evidence may be mentioned. In

---

[4] Hatchard v. State, 48 N.W. 380 (Wis. 1891); State v. Goodson, p. 181, n. 2, above; State v. Ausplund, 167 Pac. 1019 (Ore. 1917); State v. Shortridge, 211 N.W. 336 (N.D. 1926); State v. Rowley, 248 N.W. 340 (Iowa 1933); Guiffrida v. State, p. 181, n. 2, above; Fitch v. Commonwealth, p. 181, n. 2, above; State v. Fitzgerald, p. 181, n. 2, above; People v. Malone, 185 P. (2d) 870 (Cal. 1947); People v. Ramsey, 189 P. (2d) 802 (Cal. 1948). In State v. Decker, 104 S.W. (2d) 307 (Mo. 1937), it was even held sufficient to show that the woman was in her usual and ordinary condition of health before the operation.

[5] State v. Wells, 100 Pac. 681 (Utah 1909); State v. Smith, 76 S.W. (2d) 1077 (Mo. 1934).

those jurisdictions where the burden of proof is on the prosecution, it has been held that lack of consultation with another medical practitioner,[6] or still more the fact that the defendant is not a medical practitioner,[7] or attempts to conceal the cause of death,[8] or even fails to tell the mother that the operation is to save her life,[9] is corroborative evidence of the non-necessity of the operation. So also the fact that the defendant has performed other abortions is sometimes held to weaken the presumption that the particular abortion was necessary.[1] As already indicated, from a medical point of view this last rule is absurd, for if applied with any severity it would inhibit specialization. In fact the rule is directed against the lay abortionist or medical "black sheep." It would not be needed if the evidential burden were frankly placed upon the defence. Placing the evidential burden on the defence would be no embarrassment to the *bona fide* practitioner, because all he has to do to satisfy the burden of raising the issue is to give evidence of the reason why he thought the operation necessary. Once he has done this, the jury will be directed that the persuasive burden of proof rests (in case they be in any doubt) upon the prosecution.

Rules of medical etiquette and prudence

It has been shown that under the law of some of the United States there is a legal advantage for a surgeon

[6] Commonwealth v. Wheeler, p. 179, n. 7, above; cf. Guiffrida v. State, p. 181, n. 2, above.

[7] Copus v. State, 224 Pac. 364 (Okla. 1924).

[8] State v. Shortridge, p. 182, n. 4, above.

[9] State v. Holden, 120 O.N.P. (N.S.) 200 (1917).

[1] People v. Hagenow, 86 N.E. 370 (Ill. 1908); cf. State v. Lewis, 57 S.E. (2d) 513 (W. Va. 1949). But see State v. Willson, 230 Pac. 810 (Ore. 1925), refusing to admit such evidence even on the issue of intent.

who terminates a pregnancy on therapeutic grounds to have the concurring opinion of one or two other practitioners. Even when there is no express requirement of this, it is common practice. The course generally recommended to the practitioner in manuals of forensic medicine is to protect himself by consultation, if possible with an obstetrician or gynæcologist, otherwise with a senior practitioner of standing.[2] Another opinion is that he should consult a specialist in the disease from which the patient is suffering.[3] Most frequently in England the advice of two other medical practitioners is sought. There is no other therapeutic operation in which the unanimous opinion of three doctors in favour of the operation is considered to be necessary before it can be performed, still less one in which all three doctors act under the threat of punishment and loss of livelihood if their conduct is afterwards misinterpreted by a jury.

The requirement of a second opinion is not the guarantee of *bona fides* that is sometimes supposed. Abortion is such a profitable business that it can well support two or three practitioners who are in it together. It should be pointed out that there is nothing in English or American law to *require* a second opinion. When Mr. Bourne operated he did not obtain a second specialist opinion; he was himself a consultant and so considered himself as the second opinion in the case. But a surgeon who operates solely on his own responsibility runs the risk of having the jury's attention called to this fact as some evidence of criminal intent.[4]

Sydney Smith's *Forensic Medicine* advises the doctor in addition to obtain the express permission of the husband or guardian,[5] and in no circumstances to act with-

[2] Sir Sydney Smith and F. S. Fiddes: *Forensic Medicine,* 10th ed. (London, 1955), p. 323; John Glaister: *Medical Jurisprudence and Toxicology,* 9th ed. (Edinburgh, 1950), p. 382.

[3] (1952) 1 *British Medical Journal* 915.

[4] Commonwealth v. Wheeler, 53 N.E. (2d) 4 (Mass. 1944).

[5] Sir Sydney Smith and F. S. Fiddes: *Forensic Medicine,* 10th ed.

out this permission. This advice is probably wrong. If a surgeon failed to perform a necessary operation because of the husband's refusal to consent, where the woman consented to the operation, the surgeon would quite possibly be liable for negligence, and if the woman died he might be guilty of manslaughter. A medical practitioner should, of course, inform the husband and listen to his comments; but the decision upon the necessity of the operation must be the practitioner's, not the husband's. Where the operation cannot be shown to be necessary for therepeutic reasons there is some advantage in obtaining the husband's consent, because this will prevent him from bringing the action in tort against the surgeon that may otherwise be open to him.

Another unsound piece of advice given by the same writer in the ninth edition of his work is as follows: If a woman comes to a medical man after suffering an illegal operation, and he thinks that it was performed by a professional abortionist, he should refuse to have anything to do with the case unless the patient gives her permission to inform the police. The advice seems to be not only cruel to the patient but unwise for the

(London, 1955), p. 323. Cf. Taylor: *Medical Jurisprudence* (London, 1934), II, 141; Russell S. Fisher in 42 *Journal of Criminal Law and Criminology* 243 (1951); (1952) 1 *British Medical Journal* 915; G. W. B. James in Sir Eardley Holland, ed.: *Obstetrics* (London, 1955), p. 1100. The advice appears also in the two latest English works on forensic medicine. C. T. Polson: *The Essentials of Forensic Medicine* (London, 1955), p. 388, declares that the consent of the husband is necessary for a therapeutic abortion. Francis E. Camps and W. B. Purchase: *Practical Forensic Medicine* (London, 1956), p. 31, go still further, and require the consent of the husband to be given in writing, implying that an oral consent has no legal effect. This is certainly not the law, even though it may be a practical precaution to have written evidence. Glaister: op. cit., merely recommends the consent of the husband to be obtained "if possible." There is more to be said for obtaining the consent of the parents of an unmarried woman who is a minor; such consent is necessary in principle to any operation upon the minor, though it may be that minority for this purpose ends before the usual age of 21.

doctor. If the advice is followed and the patient, having refused her consent to betray the abortionist and herself, dies or is injured as a result of lack of medical aftercare, she or her executor will probably have an action against the doctor, and he may as before be criminally responsible for manslaughter. He may also be held accountable for professional misconduct. The council of the British Medical Association and the Royal College of Physicians have resolved that a medical practitioner is not bound to disclose to the authorities information that he has obtained from the patient in his professional duties, and the Royal College of Physicians expressly contradicted the advice given in Smith's work.[6] The current (tenth) edition continues the advice but qualifies it by confining it to cases where the woman's condition is not dangerous. This qualification, while it does not remove the objection to the advice, seems to deprive it of most of its practical effect. No reference is made to the authoritative resolutions just mentioned. It ought to be remembered that if a woman who has been tampered with by inexpert hands feels that she cannot go to her doctor without having what she has done reported to the police, she will tend to postpone her resort to medical treatment until grave danger is present.[7]

[6] See the resolutions printed in Parry: op. cit., p. 178; Taylor: op. cit., pp. 136–8; Glaister: op. cit., p. 387. Smith's advice is also given in Francis E. Camps and W. B. Purchase: op. cit., pp. 31–2; but Polson: op. cit., pp. 397, 513, quotes the resolution of the Royal College of Physicians. Technically, a practitioner who fails to report a criminal abortion could be charged with misprision of felony; but this offence is almost obsolete and there is no example of its use against a medical practitioner. The medical practice varies; a compromise view is that the practitioner should not disclose confidential information without the patient's consent, but may, without disclosing the patient's name, inform the police that such-and-such an abortionist is working in a given neighbourhood ([1952] 1 *British Medical Journal* 916). By not disclosing the patient's name, the doctor saves her from being mixed up in legal proceedings, which would deter women from seeking medical advice.

[7] Taussig; op. cit., p. 448; 19 *Medico-Legal Journal* 90 (1951).

In some of the United States the matter is covered by legislation. Some states require physicians to report to the coroner, or to the sheriff or chief of police, deaths due to abortion or to other criminal act (in some states this is extended to criminal injury short of death). The legislation is commonly interpreted to refer to the death of or injury to the mother, not to every case where the infant dies as a result of abortion. In New York City an ordinance of the Department of Health requires physicians and hospitals to report all abortions to the department. Such legislation purports to compel what would in other jurisdictions be regarded as a serious breach of professional etiquette. It is believed, however, that many hospital physicians fail to make the returns of criminal abortions that are theoretically required. A medical writer, dealing with the difficulty where the mother refuses to disclose her condition and its cause, suggests that the physician should do the best he can for her up to the time that it seems probable that she will die as a result of the criminal abortion. At that stage, he should afford the district attorney a chance to obtain a statement from the patient.[8]

Medical practice

The trend of legislation and judicial decision in favour of therapeutic abortion has ameliorated the law, but has not yet taken full practical effect. Some medical practitioners are said to be still chary to act, except in

[8] Article in 55 *Wisconsin Medical Journal,* No. 1 (1956). The same writer also suggests, as a counsel of prudence, that when a woman comes for assistance suffering from the effects of an abortion, the physician should insist that an independent physician be called in before treatment is given. In an emergency, when no other physician is available, the physician should insist that the woman sign a state-

the clearest cases, partly because they fear that public opinion may not be in favour and partly because they are not certain how far the law protects them. This difficulty is particularly felt in England, where the exception for therapeutic abortions does not rest on a statutory footing.[9] Some doctors are afraid that the decision in the Bourne case will be reversed in some future case in which they themselves are prosecuted.[1] It may safely be said that this fear is unfounded. It is true that according to the technical rules of the doctrine of precedent some other judge might refuse to follow the direction in *Rex v. Bourne,* and his decision might be upheld by the Court of Criminal Appeal. Every lawyer knows that this is not a practical possibility. The decision in *Rex v. Bourne* has received far too much approbation for such a situation to be conceivable. Even in the unlikely event of the Court of Criminal Appeal doubting *Rex v. Bourne* as an interpretation of the law, that court would not

---

ment before witnesses reciting the facts of the abortion and including the name of the abortionist. The necessary treatment should then be given only after an understanding that the physician may use the statement in the event he requires it for his protection. The writer does not consider the situation that would arise if the patient refused to comply.

[9] See Dr. Eustace Chesser: "The Law of Abortion," 72 *Medical World* 495 (1950).

[1] Medical men rely on books on medical jurisprudence which are rarely written by lawyers and are often inaccurate or misleading on the law. Thus Sydney Smith and F. S. Fiddes: *Forensic Medicine,* 10th ed. (London, 1955), p. 323, say of the ruling in the Bourne case that it "cannot be regarded as binding for the future. . . . The attitude of juries is not a safe field for prophecy." The authors do not consider the volume of legal comment in support of the ruling, nor do they mention that it has been followed by another judge. Contrast the advice given in F. E. Camps and W. B. Purchase: *Practical Forensic Medicine* (London, 1956), p. 31: "Law will certainly not interfere if the pregnancy is terminated for a substantial medical reason that can be supported by the opinions of more than one practitioner who has examined the patient and if it is agreed that the health (and a fortiori, the life) of the patient is endangered if the pregnancy is allowed to go on." Polson: op. cit., p. 385, is to much the same effect.

retrospectively reverse a decision in the realm of criminal law upon which medical men have acted.

Although a legal adviser may be firmly of this opinion, it remains the case that some members of the medical profession are still doubtful. The mere fact that a prosecution is unlikely to be successful is not sufficient reassurance. No one wants the publicity of a jury trial, and even an unsuccessful prosecution may be professionally ruinous.

One consequence of these doubts, on both sides of the Atlantic, is that while the ordinary practitioner is frequently reluctant to involve himself in an abortion, some practitioners make a profitable specialty of it, giving abortion to all comers under pretence of therapy, protecting themselves by working in teams, and charging fees commensurate with the risk that they consider themselves to run. Hence the law of therapeutic abortion tends to be one for the rich and another for the poor.[2]

In London and one or two other large English towns the position is ameliorated by the action of hospitals under the National Health Service granting therapeutic abortions in all cases that appear to be proper. For example, a large London hospital operating under this service has published, in one of its annual reports, figures to show that 46 therapeutic abortions were performed in the year 1953, as compared with 9 in 1938. An interesting feature of the statistics is that the proportion of abortions performed in this particular hospital on the psychiatric indication shows a steady rise through the years, from 21 per cent in 1938 to 52 per cent in 1953. Even so, the

[2] See Dorothy Thurtle: *Abortion: Right or Wrong?* (London, 1940), pp. 18ff. Dr. Harry Roberts denied that in his experience poor people had difficulty in obtaining therapeutic abortion (F. W. Stella Browne and others: *Abortion* [London, 1935], p. 141), but Mrs. Thurtle quotes instances to the contrary. See to the same effect, for the United States, Sophia J. Kleegman in *Therapeutic Abortion*, Harold Rosen, ed. (New York, 1954), p. 256; Moya Woodside: *Sterilization in North Carolina* (Chapel Hill, N.C., 1950), p. 58.

total of no more than about one termination a week at a large and exceptionally progressive hospital shows that therapeutic abortion is not being abused; rather the inference is that it is not performed on a scale commensurate with the need. Much of the blame for deficiencies in the service must rest with general practitioners, who, either through fear or through ignorance, tend to say categorically to the patient seeking therapeutic abortion that she cannot have it, thus deterring her from pressing her case further in the lawful way. But many hospitals appear to be just as restrictive in their attitude to abortion. Roman Catholic doctors never terminate a pregnancy, and use their influence in hospitals to prevent operations being performed.

One result of the decision in *Rex v. Bourne* is, as Mr. Justice Macnaghten himself pointed out, that if a doctor unreasonably refuses to perform the operation when it is necessary to save the life of the mother, and if in consequence the mother dies, the doctor can be convicted of manslaughter. The position appears to be the same in American law. This is capable of being a serious rule for the Roman Catholic practitioner. The view may well be held that any attempt to enforce the law against a Catholic would be not only unwise but unjust. The operation of abortion must be recognized to be one on which there are strong and sincere differences of opinion, and it would not be right to compel any practitioner to destroy a fetus against his beliefs. On the other hand it would certainly be wise and fair for the Catholic practitioner, if he feels a conscientious objection to acting, to put the situation fully to his patient, and if necessary to surrender the case to a colleague. A compromise of this kind might well be embodied in the law, and might make it easier to pass in England a statute giving the sanction of the legislature to the ruling in *Rex v. Bourne*. One of the reasons for the strong Catholic opposition to such a measure is, no doubt, the fear

that it will help to establish in medical practice an operation in which their religion forbids them to participate.

The removal of a dead fetus

American courts interpret the usual wording of
the abortion statutes, quite remarkably, to prohibit the
removal of a dead fetus from the mother.[3] The social
reason for this interpretation is that it enables the lay
abortionist, who has perhaps brought about the mother's
death or caused her serious injury, to be convicted, because it deprives him of the defence, perhaps difficult
to negative, that the fetus was already dead when he
operated. The qualified practitioner is not affected, because he can of course bring himself within the exception for preserving the mother's life.[4] These useful social
results of the interpretation are perhaps sufficient to
justify it, although it certainly represents a perversion of
the historical intention underlying the abortion legislation, which was passed for the protection of the unborn
child and not as a form of control of unregistered medical
practitioners.

[3] Commonwealth v. Nason, 148 N.E. 110 (Mass. 1925); Wilbanks
v. State, 152 S.E. 619 (Ga. 1930); State v. Cox, 84 P. (2d) 357
(Wash. 1938); Territory v. Young, 37 Hawaii 150 (1945); Anderson
v. Commonwealth, 58 S.E. (2d) 72 (Va. 1950). To the contrary effect
see Commonwealth v. Wood, 77 Mass. (11 Gray) 85 (1858); also
Hans v. State 25 N.W. (2d) 35 (Neb. 1946), where the statute
referred to the death of the fetus. The statute in force in Wisconsin
expressly forbids the removal of a dead fetus, while that in Maryland
expressly allows it. The interpretation covering the dead fetus is
adopted also in Australia: Rex v. Trim (1943) V.L.R. 109.

[4] State v. Dunklebarger, 221 N.W. 592 (1928).

VI

THE PROBLEM OF ABORTION:
MORALITY AND THE
SOCIAL FACTS

The religious attitude to therapeutic abortion

Nearly all Protestants have come to accept therapeutic abortion.[1] Beyond this, Protestant opinion is divided, though it is quite possible that majority opinion would support the legalization of abortion upon an extended list of grounds. Jewish opinion is in much the same position.[2]

The Church of Rome, on the other hand, remains adamantly opposed even to therapeutic abortion.[3] On this view, induction is not morally permissible even to save the life of the mother. The prohibition is extended to an operation like craniotomy, designed to reduce the bulk of the mature fetus, which intentionally sacrifices the fetus in order to save the life of the mother.[4] The prohibition of therapeutic abortion was reaffirmed in an encyclical of October 29, 1951, and occasioned many adverse comments in the non-Catholic press. In view of this

[1] See Curran in *Therapeutic Abortion*, Harold Rosen, ed. (New York, 1954), pp. 153ff.

[2] See Cohen, Gerstein, and Glasner in *Therapeutic Abortion*, pp. 166ff.

[3] For the historical attitude see Roger J. Huser: *The Crime of Abortion in Canon Law*, The Catholic University of America, Canon Law Studies No. 62 (Washington, D.C., 1942). A recent defence of the Catholic position is Frederick L. Good and Otis F. Kelly: *Marriage, Morals and Medical Ethics* (New York, 1951).

[4] Huser: op. cit., p. 124, citing decisions of the Holy Office in 1884 and 1889.

unwelcome publicity the Pope issued a further statement on November 28, 1951, which explained that the prohibition was confined to a "direct killing." If, for example, he said, the saving of the future mother's life, independently of her pregnant state, should urgently require a surgical act or other therapeutic treatment which would have as an accessory consequence, in no way desired or intended, but inevitable, the death of the fetus, "such an act could no longer be called a direct attempt on an innocent life." This distinction was not a new concession but a well-recognized application of the Catholic rule of "double effect" or "indirect killing." The permission to operate applies to a surgical removal (hysterectomy) of a pregnant uterus for malignant ovarian tumor, or an operation to control hæmorrhage during pregnancy before viability. In these instances what is done to the mother can be justified (so it is said) without reference to the pregnancy. The permission does not apply to the common case where the danger to the mother arises purely and simply because of her pregnancy: here the Catholic obstetric surgeon must allow the mother to die, if that is otherwise unavoidable, and must pin his hopes on being able to rescue the child, either before or after the death of the mother, perhaps by Cæsarian section.

The historical reason for the Catholic objection to abortion is the same as for the Christian Church's historical opposition to infanticide: the horror of bringing about the death of an unbaptized child. Dying in original sin, without the sacrament of baptism, the child is condemned to eternal punishment. This doctrine appears to have been the invention of Origen, who was perhaps the most important doctor of pre-Augustinian Christendom. Origen was one of the stern ascetics of the early Church, who carried his principles to the extent of acting literally upon the commendation of those who "made themselves eunuchs for the kingdom of heaven's sake." He became acquainted at Cæsarea with the custom of infant baptism, which in the third century was not universally practised, or even universally known, amongst Christians. When and how this practice originated cannot be said with certainty, but Dr. N. P. Williams conjectures that it was the result of popular sentiment rather than of reasoned logic, and may well have been suggested by certain Jewish and pagan practices.[5] However this may be, it attracted Origen's attention, and an explanation had to be found for it. Given the rightfulness of the practice, which it did not occur to him to dispute, there had to be some theological justification for the administration of a sacrament to newly born and unconscious infants. This sacrament was the same purificatory ceremony as was thought needful for converted adults, and it was thus clear to Origen that some sort of sinfulness must be supposed to inhere in human nature as such, from the very moment of birth. The sinfulness could only be explained in terms of the story in Genesis, and Origen accordingly arrived at the theory that Adam's pollution had somehow become transmitted by the processes of generation and birth. Adopted by Augustine (and by him associated with the theory that Adam's sin was sexual lust), this became orthodox Christian doctrine. Its effect was to give a dire importance to infant baptism. St. Fulgentius, in the sixth century, expressed the position clearly. "Be assured," he wrote, "and doubt not, that even little children who have begun to live in their mother's womb and have there died, or who, having just been born, have passed away from the world without the sacrament of holy baptism, must be punished by the eternal torture of undying fire."[6]

[5] N. P. Williams: *The Ideas of the Fall and of Original Sin* (London, 1927), pp. 221–2. I am indebted to this authoritative work for the account given above of Origen's views.

[6] *De Fide* § 70, cited by Lecky: *History of the Rise and Influence of the Spirit of Rationalism in Europe* (London, 1904), I, 362; he quotes testimonies of the later Fathers to the same effect.

Origen's hand has lain heavily upon posterity. The fear of an appalling fate for their offspring is still nourished among mothers by the Catholic insistence upon the importance of baptism, and, in pursuance of this policy, somewhat elaborate rules are laid down for emergency baptism by Catholic doctors and nurses. The subject is fully treated by Professor Joseph McAllister, of the Catholic University of America, in his book *Emergency Baptism,* published with the usual Catholic imprimaturs;[7] and it is also glanced at in the *Code of Ethical and Religious Directives for Catholic Hospitals* prepared under the auspices of the Catholic Hospital Association of the United States and Canada.[8] Professor McAllister states that "when in the ordinary course of divine Providence baptism is a necessary condition for eternal salvation, death without baptism must be regarded by every Christian as tragic and has to be avoided if at all possible." In emergency baptism the use of holy water blessed by the Church is preferable but not necessary; for medical reasons it must be sterile, and by a decree of the Sacred Office in 1901 it is lawful to use a proportion of bichloride of mercury in the water for the sake of antisepsis. On the other hand, the magical nature of the ceremony is emphasized by the fact that the baptismal formula must be word-perfect, or it is void. Another absolute rule is that the water must touch the infant's skin. Unborn children are baptized by syringing on the forehead if that has come forth and death seems imminent; if some member other than the head presents, this may be baptized, though it is not certain whether such a baptism is effective. If a pregnant mother dies, the fetus is ex-

[7] Bruce Publishing Co., Milwaukee, 1945. See also Good and Kelly: op. cit., pp. 99, 116, and Chapter 10; Gerald Kelly: *Medico-Moral Problems* (Dublin, 1955), pp. 77ff.

[8] Reprinted in an appendix to Joseph B. McAllister: *Ethics wtih Special Application to the Medical and Nursing Professions,* 2nd ed. (Philadelphia, 1955); also in Gerald Kelly, S.J.: *Medico-Moral Problems* (Dublin, 1955).

tracted, and, if it may be alive, baptized. If the child is not viable, there is a difference of opinion whether baptism may be performed in the womb.[9] An abortive fetus may be baptized at any stage of development to be on the safe side, though it is not certain whether this is spiritually effective in the first couple of months of development, because of the doubt when a rational soul begins to animate the fetus. Presumably, if the soul has not yet entered, there is no one standing in danger of eternal torment.

It has seemed worth while to set out these rules of religious practice, because they show how the ancient belief has persisted to support the present-day ban upon abortion. It must now be added that the Catholic rules of emergency baptism may perhaps be regarded at the present day as concessions to the faith of the more unsophisticated members of the sect, for the Roman priesthood seems to have surrendered the distinctively religious or eschatological approach to the problem of abortion, and to base itself instead upon the less vulnerable doctrine of natural rights. According to this, every man has a right to his own life, which may not be taken from him by the act of another. An embryonic child is as much a human being, and therefore has as much right to life, as an adult; consequently all abortive operations are murder. Being sinful (and, moreover, "intrinsically" sinful), they cannot be justified by a good end. It need hardly be said that this position is maintained with the utmost fervour and sincerity.

It will be remembered (p. 150) that, according to many of the early canonists, the soul was not infused into the infant's body until some time after conception. How, then, has it come to be maintained that abortion

---

[9] No according to McAllister; yes according to Gerald Kelly. Taussig: op. cit., p. 399, states that some surgeons operating upon a pregnant woman of the Catholic persuasion will try to still her fears by first introducing sterile holy water into the uterus.

is sinful at all times during gestation? The subject is studied by the Reverend William Reany in his work *The Creation of the Human Soul.*[1] The author shows that many enactments of the Catholic Church on abortion presupposed that the soul does not make its entry until some time after pregnancy; but in 1869 the distinction disappeared, in the sense that the punishment of excommunication was pronounced for those who caused an abortion without regard to the question whether the fetus was endowed with a human soul. The theory behind the new doctrine is that even if the abortion occurs before the advent of the soul, it is still, in the words of Cardinal Lepicier, an "anticipated homicide." This doctrine extricates the theologians from their difficulty in timing the entry of the soul, and leaves the question of this entry unresolved. Most modern Catholic writers who attempt to justify the prohibition of abortion do not investigate the problem, but assume, expressly or impliedly, that the soul enters at conception, or at any rate that there can at that moment be a killing of a human being. Thus Professor McAllister says simply that "abortion is wrong because the embryo is a person from the first moment of fertilization,"[2] and the *Code of Ethical and Religious Directives for Catholic Hospitals* is likewise content to say that all therapeutic abortion is illegal where the killing is direct.[3]

The assumption that the fetus has the same right to

[1] New York, 1932. See also Joseph Fletcher: *Morals and Medicine* (Princeton, N.J., 1954), pp. 89-90.

[2] *Ethics with Special Application to the Medical and Nursing Professions,* 2nd ed. (Philadelphia, 1955), p. 223.

[3] Ibid., p. 395.
One of the few modern theologians (not a Catholic) with the courage or innocence to revive the ancient question of the soul is E. L. Mascall in his Bampton Lectures, *Christian Theology and Natural Science* (London, 1956), p. 276. Dr. Mascall professes himself a Creationist; but as to the moment of animation of the human fetus by the soul he can only remark that "it is obviously impossible to speak with confidence."

life as the born child is dogma, but is not open to conclusive objection on that account. Every moral position
is dogmatic and ultimately unprovable—if you will, a
matter of faith. However, the logic of the Catholic position seems to some extent to be assailable even within
its own presuppositions. If the fetus has a right to life,
so has the mother. Situations occur in which a surgeon
has to choose between destroying the fetus in order to
save the mother's life, and allowing the mother to die in
the hope of saving the fetus. Such a situation presents a
moral choice which is inescapable. The Catholic preference of doing nothing to assist the mother amounts in
fact to a preference of the fetus over its mother, if not to
a sentence of death for both. Such a preference was
logical at a time when emphasis was placed upon the
paramount importance of baptism; but if that argument
is given up it appears difficult to defend.

The proposition that a sinful act cannot be justified
by a good end is in itself tautologous, since to describe
the act as sinful when its intention is good begs the
question. According to the general opinion, some acts
that would otherwise be wrong are rendered rightful
by a good purpose, or by the necessity of choosing the
lesser of two evils. Those who maintain the absolute
irrelevance of ends to means nearly always preserve
some verbal form of escape for difficult situations. For
example, Catholic orthodoxy permits a killing in self-
defence, and in this instance an act that would certainly
be regarded as sinful apart from its purpose is recognized
as justified—and by what other than by its purpose or
effect? Again, the Catholic religion permits killing in
the course of a just war, and this killing may even involve infants who are in no wise responsible for the war.
Evidently these concessions cannot be reconciled with
the Catholic doctrine of ends and means except by highly
tendentious reasoning.[4]

[4] Orthodox religious thinking on the subject of war has not gone

Every ethical system proposes certain positive values to which it attaches importance; but the compilation of such a list has to face the difficulty occasioned by situations in which one value conflicts with another. Merely to describe the values as natural rights does not solve this problem. The conflict may be either quantitative (one value conflicting with an equal or greater quantity of the same value) or qualitative (one value conflicting with another value). An example of a quantitative conflict is the following. Suppose that a dike threatens to give way, and the actor is faced with the choice of either making a breach in the dike, which he knows will result in one or two people being drowned, or doing nothing, in which case he knows that the dike will burst at another point involving a whole town in sudden destruction.[5] In such a situation, where there is an unhappy

much beyond the discussion of Augustine, who, in his *City of God* (Bk. I, para. 21), justified killing in just war and capital punishment, apparently on the ground that these were special divine exceptions from the general rule against homicide. The argument involves the assumption that all the powers that be are in some way ordained by God. It was, in fact, a concession made by the church to procure partnership with the state.

Joseph V. Sullivan: *Catholic Teaching on the Morality of Euthanasia* (Washington D.C.: Catholic University of America; 1949), pp. 36–7 reports the opinion of Father Cronin that the only lawful killing in war is "indirect": you wish merely to incapacitate the enemy, and it is through no desire of yours that you happen to kill him. But, he adds, other modern Catholic writers say that in a just war the killing of the enemy may be "direct," i.e., intended. The only way of reconciling this with the Catholic doctrine of ends and means is by invoking supernatural permission, as Augustine did.

It is relevant to point out one particular implication of the Catholic permission to kill by way of defence. Usually the person so killed will be not only an aggressor but a wrongdoer, but this is not necessary. For instance, it is both legally and morally right to kill a lunatic who attacks one, where one can by no other means save one's own life, even though the lunatic is not responsible for his actions. And a man may defend another, as by killing a lunatic who is attacking his wife. Why, then, should one not be allowed to kill the unborn child who, however innocently, is through his presence bringing a woman into peril of death?

[5] The illustration is given in a discussion of the legal doctrine of

choice between the destruction of one life and the de-struction of many, utilitarian philosophy would certainly justify the actor in preferring the lesser evil. A philosophy that, like the Catholic, purports absolutely to forbid the doing of evil in order to procure a greater good, may seem at first sight to counsel a policy of inaction in such circumstances. There is, however, a Catholic doctrine that may be used, if the canonists so desire, to reach the utilitarian result. This is the doctrine of double ef-fect. It is sometimes found that an act has two conse-quences, one good and one evil. If the actor intends the good consequences, his act may be rightful in Catholic eyes although he realizes that it will also have the bad consequence, provided that he does not "will" the bad consequence, but only "permits" it to take place, and provided that the good consequence is of a positive value equal to or greater than the consequence here called evil.

The doctrine of double effect thus admits a choice of the lesser evil; but it is allowed to be used only when both effects are the immediate result of the act. The doctrine is not applied if the good effect is the result of the bad one, because that would violate the dogma that evil cannot be done that good may come.[6]

Apply this to the case of the dike. Making a breach in the dike has two effects. (1) It relieves the pressure on the dike and so saves the town. (2) It causes the death of one or two persons. Since consequence (1) is good, and the evil consequence (2) is not intended (though foreseen as certain, and, in Catholic phraseology, "per-mitted"), the act is justifiable under the doctrine of double effect. The unintended killing is said to be an

necessity by Wechsler and Michael in 37 *Columbia Law Review* 738 (1937).

[6] Statements of the Catholic position will be found in Frederick L. Good and Otis F. Kelly: *Marriage, Morals and Medical Ethics* (New York, 1951), Chap. 2; Gerald Kelly, S.J.: *Medico-Moral Problems* (Dublin, 1955), pp. 16ff., 173ff.

"indirect killing" because it is supposed not to be "directly willed." It will be observed that the good consequence (1) follows "directly" from the act and not via the evil consequence (2). If the good consequence were the result of the evil consequence, the doctrine of double effect could not be used and the act would become sinful.

Similar considerations apply where the conflict of values is qualitative, i.e., one of kind. Common-sense ethics would construct a hierarchy of values, allowing a lower value to be sacrificed to a higher. Even where values are, from an abstract point of view, of the same kind, circumstances may, in case of necessity, cause one to be preferred to another. In Catholic philosophy, if a value is once recognized as a religious absolute it cannot be sacrificed to any other value by conscious choice. But this, again, is subject to the verbal escape-mechanism of the doctrine of double effect.

It will be remembered that the doctrine of indirect killing (which is only a particularized name for the doctrine of double effect) was used by the Pope to allow a therapeutic abortion where the operation could in some way be justified independently of the concept of abortion—e.g., where the uterus is dangerously diseased.[7] A second application of the doctrine is in respect of ectopic or extra-uterine pregnancies, where a fetus grows in the ovary or abdominal cavity or (the commonest case) the Fallopian tubes, instead of in the womb. No absolute prohibition is now maintained of an operation to terminate such a pregnancy, because if the operation is not performed the death of both mother and child would be practically certain. It is of some interest to

[7] This is recognized in the *Code of Ethical and Religious Directives for Catholic Hospitals,* reprinted in McAllister: op. cit., p. 396. Joseph V. Sullivan: op. cit., p. 39, defines an indirect killing as "an action or omission having some other immediate effect in addition to the death of a person."

notice that there has been a shift in the Catholic position on this. In 1902 the Congregation of the Holy Office ruled, with relentless religious logic, that the surgical removal of a nonviable ectopic fetus was not lawful. "Such a removal is a direct killing of the fetus and is therefore forbidden." [8] It made no difference that refusal to operate spelt the doom of the mother in addition to that of the fetus. This ruling, which must have gravely frustrated Catholic surgeons, compelled by their faith to allow young wives and mothers go to useless death, was too crassly stupid even for the most rigid religious conformism. Hence, without any explicit retractation by the Holy Office, and with theologians divided in their opinions, Catholic doctors have come at last to take the view that operation upon a tubal pregnancy is permissible, because the killing is not direct but indirect.[9] The point is ingeniously explained by Professor McAllister: a tubal pregnancy, he says, causes hæmorrhage; "this can and should be stopped, not by attacking the fetus but blocking the cause of the hæmorrhage, by clamping the arteries. The fetus will die but as the indirect result of interrupting the blood supply to stop the hæmorrhage. Then the tube and the dead fetus should be removed." [1] Little is to be gained by too minute an examination of this logic, but it may be pointed out that the hæmorrhage is caused by the pregnancy, and according to the pontifical prouncement of 1951, quoted on

[8] Quoted by Fletcher: *Morals and Medicine* (Princeton, N.J., 1954), p. 150; cf. ibid., pp. 19–20. See also the fuller discussion by Gerald Kelly, S.J.: *Medico-Moral Problems* (Dublin, 1955), pp. 24–33.

[9] See the Code of Directives cited above, p. 201, n. 7. See also the discussion by Huser: op. cit., pp. 134ff.: he suggests that the operation is permissible because "almost every ectopic pregnancy will, sooner or later, engender a pathological condition which then, independently of the pregnancy itself, constitutes a serious danger to the mother's life." Could not the same be said of every pregnancy seriously threatening the mother's life for which Protestant surgeons are accustomed to operate? For the division of opinion that still exists among Catholic theologians on ectopic pregnancies see Gerald Kelly: **op. cit.**

[1] McAllister: op. cit., p. 228.

page 193, above, an operation on a pregnant woman which kills the fetus is justifiable only where the pathological condition is independent of the pregnant state.

It will be seen from Professor McAllister's statement that the desire to avoid the appearance of "direct killing" controls the way in which the operation is performed. This is further emphasized by another pair of Catholic writers, who say: "Let us make it plain that one cannot, even for the desire to baptize the fetus, open the tube and remove the fetus and then remove the tube. The tube must must be removed with the ectopic pregnancy still in the body of the tube, and then the tube may be opened and baptism given." [2] If the fetus is dead the baptism will be too late to be spiritually effective, but one must not directly kill the fetus even for the sake of its eternal salvation.

Whatever may be thought of the dialectic by which the life of the mother is now permitted to be saved, the change of thought is an encouraging one because it shows that the Catholic mind is not, as is sometimes supposed, completely closed to the practical effect of its distinctive beliefs in this department of conduct. At the same time, the distinction made as to the intention of the surgeon seems to be difficult to defend. To the eye of common sense, a result that is foreseen as certain, as a consequence of what is done, is in exactly the same position as a result that is intended. Imagine two surgeons: both remove a tubal fetus, but the one desires to save the mother and laments the destruction of the fetus, while the other decides to destroy the fetus in order to save the mother. Apparently the second surgeon sins, while the first is without sin. Yet in substance both of them do and both may intend precisely the same thing: there need be no more than a verbal difference between them. It is this kind of reasoning that has earned casuistry its bad name.

[2] Good and Kelly: op. cit., p. 97.

Justifiable casuistry in ethics faces the whole situation with open eyes, and makes the moral judgment depend on all the circumstances. It prods us out of the comfortable armchair of simple general solutions, holding at all time for everybody. Catholic casuistry, on the other hand, attempts to keep a preconceived rule verbally intact and stable by drawing distinctions that often seem to have no moral relevance.

It may be said that if, in the situation under discussion, Catholicism reaches the same result as commonsense ethics, the verbal means by which it does so are unimportant. However, the doctrine of double effect is used so restrictively that it fails to accord with common sense in a large number of cases. Suppose that a surgeon terminates a pregnancy in order to save the life of the mother who is suffering from heart disease; or suppose that he performs craniotomy upon the unborn child in order to save the mother when normal birth is seen to be impossible. In Catholic theory, he is not allowed to say that he did not desire the death of the fetus and desired only to save the mother's life. His act, in the Catholic view, is sinful, and accordingly Catholic surgeons are not allowed to perform these operations. It is not immediately obvious to a person outside the Catholic fold why the doctrines of indirect killing and double effect, if valid at all, should not be applied here. After all, it is not the death of the fetus, as such, that benefits the mother, but its removal. The removal of the fetus has two effects: it causes the fetus to die, and it benefits the mother. Causing the fetus to die is not, in itself, desired or intended (if the word "intention" is not used to include foresight of certainty). Therefore the case should fall within the doctrine of double effect. Thus Catholic reasoning on the subject of therapeutic abortion is inconsistent with its own principles.

At present, however, the ectopic pregnancy is merely one of a small number of exceptions to the general Cath-

olic ban on therapeutic abortion. Its distinguishing feature is that the surgeon who operates for an ectopic pregnancy does not prefer the life of the mother to that of
the fetus, for the fetus must die anyway. It is, however, a
case where the death of the fetus is permitted to be accelerated by human action, the life of the fetus having
no substantiality in probable duration. From this point of
view, the precedent will be worth remembering when
we come to the Catholic attitude towards voluntary euthanasia.

The objection of the Roman hierarchy to therapeutic
abortion takes on an added importance because of the
close control exercised over the actual practice of Catholic physicians and nurses. Catholic medical students are
enjoined to attend courses on medical ethics given by
Catholic theologians, and practitioners are associated in
Catholic medical guilds which regard it as part of their
function to instruct their members in the divine law. No
parallel to these activities exists in the Protestant medical world, where practitioners are left to follow the dic-
tates of their own conscience moulded by the actualities
of their medical experience. Hence arises a lamentable
gulf between the practice and attitudes of Catholic and
non-Catholic physicians, and the fate of the patient will
frequently depend entirely on the religion of her adviser
and the denomination of her hospital. This situation is
evidently one calling for toleration and charity in both
religious camps, and some wise words of Dr. Eustace
Chesser deserve careful attention.

On numerous occasions, Roman Catholic doctors when
dealing with such cases have been known to request that the
patient should seek the opinion of a non-Catholic colleague.
That is a just attitude, worthy of all respect. Unfortunately
there are still many who do not practise so objective an approach, and who make the patient suffer for their own personal belief.

There is another side to this question, too, and one even

more frequently neglected. While a doctor should not attempt to force upon a woman the practice of his own religious beliefs, neither should he try to force upon her the practice of his own scientific beliefs where these conflict with her spiritual convictions.

It may well be that a doctor, having arrived at the conclusion that on grounds of physical or mental health a pregnancy should not be permitted to continue, will find the expectant mother's spiritual beliefs in conflict with the course of action he advises.

In such a case he has no right to do more than make his honest and sincere recommendation. If the mother chooses to set it aside he should not take umbrage. It is not sufficiently appreciated by many doctors in general practice that the right of final decision *here* belongs to the mother. If she chooses to risk life and health either from passionate desire to bear a child or from religious conviction, he has no right to do more than warn.

There is, after all, a strong psychological factor to be reckoned with if such a mother is persuaded into doing violence to strong wishes or beliefs, and concurrence with his viewpoint may set up in her such conflict and conviction of guilt that irremediable harm may be done.

In the case of Roman Catholics, of course, this applies very strongly, and where a woman cannot finally decide on her correct course it would surely be well to suggest that she should consult her spiritual adviser. If it were her wish, it might be very satisfactory for doctor and priest to meet to discuss the case. Such co-operation, entered into with mutual respect and understanding, might be fruitful of much good.[3]

The social facts of abortion

Neither religious dogma nor legal command has ever entered fully into the popular mores. When a

[3] Chesser: *The Unwanted Child* (London, n. d.), p. 135. Contrast

woman is faced with the prospect of having a child that will tend to impoverish her existing family, or that will disgrace her in the eyes of others, she does not generally regard an early termination of pregnancy as wrongful, though she may shrink from it for other reasons. Dr. Taussig wrote: "Every physician will testify that it is without any feeling of guilt that most women speak of induced abortions in the consultation room."[4] It is partly because of this that although abortion laws exist in all Western countries, there has been a remarkable lack of enforcement. Another reason is the inherent unenforceability of a statute that attempts to prohibit a private practice where all parties concerned desire to avoid the restriction.[5] The result is that the trade of abortionist is conducted with a large measure of impunity. As an English woman police officer said, "it is gratitude to the person who has relieved them of an unwanted burden that keeps the victims of abortion silent. For this type of help, gratitude wells up in the heart to subdue every other sense. Even when dying they hug their secret gratefully, refusing to divulge the name of the person who has brought them to this impasse."[6]

The extent of the problem in the United States was shown by an authoritative study by a leading demographer[7] in which 22,657 women (whites and Negroes) were questioned. They were all married and living in

---

the Catholic opinion that a Catholic physician cannot rightfully refer a patient to a non-Catholic colleague who will do something forbidden to a Catholic: Good and Kelly: op. cit., p. 26. Catholic hospitals also refuse to allow non-Catholics to perform operations offending their creed: Gerald Kelly, S.J.: *Medico-Moral Problems* (Dublin, 1955), p. 8.

[4] Taussig: op. cit., p. 403.
[5] 35 *Columbia Law Review*, at 91, 94 (1935); D. V. Glass: "The Effectiveness of Abortion Legislation in Six Countries," 2 *Modern Law Review* 97, 227 (1938); Taussig: op. cit., pp. 438ff.
[6] Lilian Wyles: *A Woman at Scotland Yard* (London, 1952), p. 227.
[7] Raymond Pearl: *The Natural History of Population* (London, 1939), pp. 222, 237.

wedlock. Taking the number of admissions made by these women as to criminal abortions that they had undergone, it was calculated that 1.4 of each 100 pregnancies among white women were ended by criminal abortion, and .5 of each 100 pregnancies among Negroes. Among the whites, the rate varied little between the different socio-economic groups, being 1.3 for the very poor, 1.5 for the poor, 1.3 for those in moderate circumstances, and 1.0 for the well-to-do and rich. Nor were the differences between religious groups as high as might have been expected. The largest percentage of criminal abortions were confessed by Jews (2.56 per cent of pregnancies); next to them were those with no religion (1.56), followed by Protestants (1.39) and Catholics (1.13).[8] These figures are obviously minimal: an unknown number of abortions were probably not confessed. It must also be remembered, for whatever effect it may have upon the figures, that the data were obtained only from families living together in wedlock.

Another careful study was made in 1941–2 by interviewing 1,080 couples: it was found that the number of illegal abortions stated by the women were, according to the data assumed, between 1 per cent of all pregnancies (a figure which was thought undoubtedly to underestimate the frequency) and 1.9 per cent of all pregnan-

[8] Similarly it was found in Iowa that 12 per cent of patients accepting therapeutic abortion were of the Roman Catholic faith: Moore and Randall in 63 *American Journal of Obstetrics and Gynecology* 29 (1952). In interpreting the figures for Catholics, the distinction must be borne in mind between "good Catholics" who attend church regularly and "nominal Catholics" who attend irregularly: the former have a much higher average of children than the normal, while it is the latter who are more likely to practise and favour birth control and abortion. See Ernest W. Burgess in *The Abortion Problem: Proceedings of the Conference Held under the Auspices of the National Committee on Maternal Health, Inc., 1942* (Baltimore, 1944), pp. 118–20. It may also be remarked that Catholics who do not practise an efficient method of contraception are the more likely to find themselves in the desperate situation in which abortion seems the only way out.

cies (a figure which was thought probably to exaggerate the frequency).[9]

It has been calculated that there were 2,750,000 pregnancies in the United States in 1940.[1] If the proportion of criminal abortions was 1.5 per cent, this would give a total of more than 41,000 such abortions. Other writers, however, using different methods of calculation, arrive at a much higher total. Many accept Taussig's estimate (for the year 1935) as a conservative one. He assumed 700,000 abortions per year of which a minimum of 30 per cent were criminal: this gives the stupendous total of 210,000 criminal interruptions of pregnancy in the year. Since there is nothing to indicate that the abortion rate has declined since 1935, the gross number has probably increased owing to the considerable growth of population; in that case, and if Taussig's estimate for 1935 is accepted, illegal abortions must now be running close on a thousand a day. This figure has been put forward as a serious estimate by Dr. Russell S. Fisher.[2] It is not, however, necessary to accept it in order to believe that the abortion problem in the United States is a very serious one.

The number of convictions for abortion is not known, but it is certainly only a minute fraction of the number of offences. Thus in Michigan over a forty-year period there were only forty convictions.[3] Dr. Fisher, who in 1951 guessed the annual number of criminal abortions in the United States at 300,000, put the number of convictions at 2,500.[4] A conviction rate as high as this (1:120) would be much better than that in England, as will be

[9] See P. K. Whelpton in *The Abortion Problem* (cited in last note), p. 18.

[1] Halbert L. Dunn in the same work, p. 10.

[2] In *Therapeutic Abortion*, Harold Rosen, ed. (New York, 1954), pp. 3, 6. John H. Amen, in *The Abortion Problem* (cit. p. 208, n. 8, above), p. 139, estimated a total of more than 100,000 criminal abortions performed in New York City alone, during the three-year period 1936–9.

[3] 35 *Columbia Law Review* 91 (1935).

[4] 42 *Journal of Criminal Law and Criminology* 244 (1951).

shown in a moment; but it may be that the rate is unreliable and that both figures are put too high.

In England in 1955 there were 52 prosecutions for abortion, with 49 convictions; and this is a representative figure. In contrast, the number of illegal abortions, though not precisely known, is agreed by all to be very large in that country, running into tens of thousands each year. For the benefit of English readers, who will be prone to disbelief, I must try to substantiate this figure. Professor Glass thought it "not at all improbable that there are each year about 100,000 illegal operations in England and Wales."[5] The Interdepartmental Committee on Abortion, after referring to certain statistical studies by medical officers, accepted the suggestion that there were between 110,000 and 150,000 abortions every year, and that two fifths of these were criminal.[6] Dr. Keith Simpson,[7] like Professor Glass, thinks this likely to be an underestimate. Dr. Eustace Chesser[8] says that his own most conservative estimate is that the figure cannot be less than a quarter of a million every year. Unfortunately these writers do not state the way in which they arrived at their conclusion. But that the problem exists in England on a large scale is indicated by Dr. Marie Stopes's report that she had over 10,000 people who wrote to her asking her to perform abortion.[9] It is pointed out that the practice is not confined to illegitimate pregnancies, but is widespread among the married, and in all classes of society.[1] One consultant gynæcologist has estimated

[5] *Population Policies and Movements* (Oxford, 1940), p. 429.

[6] H.M.S.O., 1939, pp. 9, 11. It may well be that a higher proportion should be regarded as criminal. A. Davis found that of 2,665 cases of abortion admitted to hospital, only 10 per cent were spontaneous; the rest must have been criminal. See (1950) 2 *British Medical Journal* 123.

[7] *Forensic Medicine* (London, 1947).

[8] "The Law of Abortion," 72 *Medical World* 495 (1950).

[9] Quoted L. A. Parry: *Criminal Abortion* (London, 1932), p. 18.

[1] Sir Sydney Smith and F. S. Fiddes, *Forensic Medicine,* 10th ed.

that 90 per cent of illegal abortions are suffered by wives who have had as much as they can cope with, and are prepared to risk their lives and health in back-street surgery.[2] The police generally hear only of cases where death or very severe illness results.

It seems sufficiently accurate, then, to say that there is not in England more than one prosecution to every thousand criminal abortions.[3] A figure of this order, even if ten times too high, demonstrates beyond all argument that the law is ineffective. In the overwhelming majority of cases the illegal operations are performed not by proper medical practitioners (for these are successfully intimidated by the law), but by unqualified persons under septic conditions. The business is often well organized and capable of showing high profits.[4] It is conducted quite brazenly, with door-to-door canvassers for custom

(London, 1955), p. 324. Dr. Lewis-Faning obtained statistics on behalf of the Royal Commission on Population by arranging for the questioning of over 7,000 women; 1 per cent admitted to having procured abortion, but Dr. Lewis-Faning remarks that it would be rather remarkable if such confessions of crime were anywhere near the actual figure. See *Papers of the Royal Commission on Population* (London, 1949), I, 165ff.

[2] That the proportion of illegal terminations generally rises with the number of pregnancies a woman has undergone is shown by the following table from Whelpton's study, cited above, p. 209, n. 9.

| | WOMEN PREGNANT | | | | | |
	ONCE	TWICE	THRICE	FOUR	FIVE OR SIX	SEVEN OR MORE TIMES
Number of illegal abortions, per cent	—	0.4	1.2	0.4	4.2	2.9

The common idea that abortion is particularly associated with sexual immorality is erroneous. A. Davis studied 2,665 abortions, and found that 88 per cent of the women were married: (1950) 2 *British Medical Journal* 123.

[3] This estimate of Rentoul (Parry: op. cit., p. 88) is confirmed by the Interdepartmental Committee's figure in the text above.

[4] For a description of an American abortionist's practice see J. E. Bates: "The Abortion Mill," 45 *Journal of Criminal Law and Criminology* 157 (1954).

in slum areas; [5] some American medical practitioners are said to refer cases to the better type of abortionist for a share of the fee. In addition, there are many women who will wield a syringe, a hat-pin, or a stick of slippery elm, for a small reward. Thus the effect of the law is not to eliminate abortion but to drive it into the most undesirable channels. The lay accoucheur, if unlucky enough to be convicted, can expect to spend six months to a year in prison, unless the prosecution is brought for a patient whom he (or she) has killed, in which case the sentence will be for several years.

Even if a doctor performs an operation, he frequently (if he is acting illegally) does so in secrecy, which prevents proper attention being given to the patient subsequently.

The other mode of unlawful abortion is for the woman to attempt it herself by resort to harmful drugs. Works on forensic medicine explain in detail the steps taken by women in their frantic efforts to end pregnancy, and no one can read them without being moved by horror and pity. The evil effects of these attempts may include insanity, blindness, paralysis, and death. [6] Taussig remarks that "a considerable portion of our knowledge of poisonous drugs is derived from the human experiments made upon themselves by women desirous of an abortion." [7]

The number of deaths following from clandestine abortions is not precisely known. In England the Interdepartmental Committee of 1939 quoted figures of between 411 and 605 deaths per annum attributable to or associated with abortions, criminal and non-criminal, but the committee admitted that this probably understated the

[5] See the Report of the Interdepartmental Committee. "The ramifications of this business are wide; it appears to have its agents everywhere": Wyles: loc. cit.

[6] Smith: op. cit., pp. 331ff.; Parry: op. cit., pp. 25ff., 148.

[7] Taussig: op. cit., p. 352.

position.[8] In the United States it was calculated that in 1935 there were 8,000 deaths annually from abortion; assuming 700,000 operations performed annually, this would make one death for each 87 abortions, or about 1.2 per cent.[9] If a smaller number of operations is assumed, the proportion of deaths becomes larger. It is probable that with the new antibiotics the illegal abortionists have bettered their results and reduced their death rate; one authority puts it now at .5 per cent.[1] This figure may be compared with the position in Russia between 1920 and 1936, when abortion was legal and was performed in special hospitals by doctors who developed skill in the operation of curettage. It is said that the death rate was only one in 10,000 cases.[2] The difference in the mortality rate would appear to be due primarily to the abortion laws, which prevent the operation being performed under proper conditions and by proper persons. Both in England and in America therapeutic abortion performed by expert hands in hospitals is not an abnormal risk.[3] Apart from causing death, unskilled abor-

---

[8] Dr. Teare, a London pathologist, discussed 51 deaths from criminal abortion in a paper published in 19 *Medico-Legal Journal* 81 (London, 1951). He gives a vivid idea of the risks associated with the operation when it is performed illegally.

[9] Taussig: op. cit., pp. 27–8. But Simpson: op. cit., p. 163, declared that the mortality from illegal abortion in England was only .3–.4 per cent.

[1] Fisher in *Therapeutic Abortion* Harold Rosen, ed. (New York, 1954), pp. 8–9. But illegal abortion sometimes causes instantaneous death by air embolism, and the common use of a syringe creates particular danger of this.

[2] *Interdepartmental Committee on Abortion,* 1939, p. 21.

[3] In 301 therapeutic abortions performed at one hospital over a fifteen year period, there was no immediate postoperative mortality, and of the patients who were followed over a period of time, only three were known to have died, one of malignant hypertension five months after operation, and two of chronic glomerulonephritis four months and three years, respectively, after therapeutic abortion. Sixty-four per cent of the operations were thought to have had good results; only 4.3 per cent were considered unsatisfactory or poor. 18.3 per cent were

tion is gravely injurious to health, and medical practitioners are frequently called in to attend to the complications following unskilled operations.

It is hard to visualize the total misery and wreckage of life that must result from this hidden social canker. The following survey of a single year's press cuttings in England (1952) may, however, assist the imagination.

Nearly one half of the deaths from abortion were caused by the bungling efforts of unqualified "helpers," and in two of the cases the helper was the woman's husband. One husband, a man of "hitherto unblemished character" was discharged, the judge declaring he had "suffered enough punishment." The other husband, described as being "devoted to his wife" was sentenced to a year's imprisonment. Other sentences varied from ten days to four years. Many of the accused stated that women had implored their help, and one woman who pleaded guilty to having performed several operations (with no deaths) said that her standard fee was five shillings.

About one fifth of the inquests, despite, in some cases, months of police inquiries, did not disclose evidence to show who was responsible for the victim's death. In two cases the body was found dumped in a ditch.

About one seventh of the fatalities were found to be the result of self-induced abortion; and amongst the causes of death were blood poisoning, embolism, myocardial failure, tetanus, and gangrene infection. In a case where a patient survived attempted abortion, the doctor described a rent that had been found on the floor of her pelvis, and stated that the woman was still pregnant.

Three mothers of five children, each expecting a sixth, committed suicide by gas poisoning; another mother of four children was charged with attempted self-abortion; one expectant mother threw herself in front of a train; and a woman charged with using an instrument gassed herself rather than face the remanded hearing.

---

undetermined. See Myrna F. Loth and H. Close Hesseltine, "Therapeutic Abortion at the Chicago Lying-in Hospital," 72 *American Journal of Obstetrics and Gynecology* 304 at 310 (1956).

In one case of attempted blackmail, the accused was sentenced to four years' imprisonment for threatening to inform the police that a doctor had performed an abortion.

Four doctors were actually charged with abortion; three were sentenced and later removed from the Medical Register. A local clergyman testified in court his praise for the professional devotion of one of the convicted doctors, and 3,000 local people signed a petition asking for leniency; but he was sentenced to two years' imprisonment. After the second doctor had been sentenced to three years' imprisonment, 10,000 signatures were presented to the General Medical Council in a fruitless attempt to influence the members in his favour.[4]

The remedy sometimes suggested for this state of affairs is a more severe enforcement of the abortion laws. What has already been said should make it clear that such a solution can be ruled out. A more drastic scale of punishment would not make evidence any easier to obtain, and would quite possibly lead to a refusal on the part of juries to convict.

These facts raise the question whether the church and the state made a mistake in attempting to extend the protection of human personality to the moment when the microscopic ovum is fertilized. It was a brave attempt, and might have succeeded. Perhaps the odds against success initially seemed no greater than for infanticide: yet infanticide has been all but suppressed while abortion is still rampant. The reason for the difference is not far to seek. The infant child is felt as a human being, so that protective feelings are easy to arouse: but the embryo is not. The question to be considered is whether it would not be wise to recognize that the legal prohibition has broken down, and to fix some lesser limit of protection that is more in accordance with human needs, public opinion, and the possibilities of enforcement.

[4] Summary supplied by courtesy of Mrs. Alice Jenkins, Hon. Secretary of the Abortion Law Reform Association in London.

Proposals for reform

The evil results of the abortion law as it now stands are still regarded with indifference by the leaders of opinion. The church, firm in its interpretation of the Sixth Commandment (the only biblical text capable of being construed as forbidding abortion), is interested in the statistics of abortion and post-morbidity merely to the extent that these indicate the existence of a certain volume of feminine sin. The church does not have to consider revising the moral law, because only God can do this; and hardly any theologian at the present day considers the possibility that the Sixth Commandment was not intended to protect embryos. The attitude of the legislator may, however, be different, not only because he may take a different view of the moral law from the ecclesiastics, but because human law does not necessarily have to enforce the whole of morality. In the words of the Roman jurist Paul, *"Non omne quod licet honestum est."* If legislation works badly, it may be repealed without altering the ideal that it was intended to embody.

Thus there has arisen at least the beginning of a movement for reform, particularly among medical men who have more opportunity to perceive the social results of the law than have lawyers. Among English lawyers, Mr. Justice McCardie and Mr. Claud Mullins [5] were the first to raise their voices. The former said, in a trial at Leeds Assizes:

The law of abortion, as it exists, ought to be substantially modified. It is out of keeping with the conditions that prevail in the world today. Here is a woman of most excellent char-

[5] *Marriage, Children and God* (London, 1933), pp. 150–3, which, however, suggests no positive conclusion.

216

acter, brave in the midst of sorrow and much burdened. She has had seven children born in poverty, reared in poverty, almost doomed to poverty all of their lives. She has had no money; her husband was lazy and earned nothing. The burden fell on her. She was tired out with this burden of bearing children to a husband who would not support them. They were living on charity. I think it should be recognised that we live in the world of 1931 and not in the medieval world.[6]

Change in the law was guardedly suggested by a committee of the British Medical Association in 1935.[7] Before that, the argument against the existing position had been stated by Dr. Charles Mercier in 1918 as follows:

The procuring of abortion with the consent of the woman wrongs no one. It prevents the fœtus from attaining complete development, but the life of the fœtus is scarcely begun, and it is yet far from being conscious, and has not even an independent existence. It would strain the meaning of words intolerably to look upon the action as a wrong done to the fœtus, nor can it be considered a wrong to the mother, who freely and eagerly consents to it. It does, indeed, endanger the life of the mother, but I know of no instance in which an act, otherwise innocent, is regarded as a crime because it endangers the life of the actor, or in which an operation, freely consented to by the subject for the benefit to be obtained by it, is considered on the same ground a crime. No. The only ground upon which the procuring of abortion can be held to be a crime is that it infringes the racial principle. It deprives the community of a potential citizen. . . . As the potential citizen is farther from the stage of actuality than the infant, it should seem that the crime is of less gravity than infanticide; but it is in fact reprobated more severely and punished with greater severity,[8] and the reasons seem to be

[6] Quoted by Taussig: op. cit., p. 395.
[7] *Medical Aspects of Abortion*, B.M.A. House.
[8] That is to say, in practice. In 1918, when Mercier wrote, infanticide was in English law a kind of murder, as it still is if the jury are not satisfied of mental unbalance, or if the prosecution chooses to charge murder instead of infanticide. Convictions for murder by way of neonaticide have always, however, been hard to obtain; and the capital sentence is regularly commuted.

two: first, it attracts to itself none of the sympathy that is felt for the mother who kills her illegitimate child, and who is usually assumed to be an innocent, confiding creature who has been led away by the arts of the seducer; and second, that around the practice of abortion clings some of the odium that attaches to the arts of the pander. Both reasons seem destitute of foundation. The mother of an illegitimate child is as often as not the seducer rather than the seduced, and the women who apply to have abortion procured are in many cases married and chaste. I can discover no sound reason in ethics for the great severity with which the procuring of abortion is punished by law.[9]

Mercier's concession of the point that induction endangered the life of the mother was unnecessary, for American and English as well as Scandinavian and Soviet experience has proved that if the operation is performed under proper conditions in the early months it does not do so. This is not to say the operation is without some risk of post-morbidity; but the risk is a small fraction of that where the operation is performed illegally and inexpertly. Experience shows that the induction of abortion, if properly performed, does not present any extraordinary hazard for the life of the mother, but that there is a possibility of sequelæ later, such as neurosis, particularly when the women has had no previous normal parturition. Against this must be balanced the risk of mental or emotional disturbance if an unwanted child is carried to term. Besides that, a humanitarian will wish to point to the appalling cruelty still committed against unwanted children.[1] Lack of parental love for the unwanted child is not merely a tragedy in the child's early youth; it is one of the major predisposing factors to

---

[9] Mercier: *Crime and Criminals* (London, 1918), pp. 196–7. The passage is virtually repeated from the author's earlier book *Crime and Insanity* (Home University Library, n.d.), pp. 216–17.

[1] See *Parlimentary Debates (House of Commons),* December 12, 1949, cols. 2431ff.; November 20, 1951, cols. 180ff.

juvenile delinquency, and so can lead to a ruined career.[2]

The whole question was considered by an English Interdepartmental Committee in 1939. With one dissentient, they viewed the position with calm and rejected all proposals for change in the law, except the proposal to clarify the law relating to therapeutic abortions. Even this has not been acted upon. The Committee pointed to the fact that the Soviet Union discontinued in 1936 its practice of permitting abortion (except for medical and eugenic reasons), professedly on the ground that the operation had been found to have undesirable effects on the patient. The committee rather took the Russian explanation at its face value; but another opinion would attribute the Russian change of policy to a desire to build up population for military reasons, in response to the population policies of Germany and Japan.[3] There is no doubt

[2] It is an odd fact that reformers who seek the causes and cure of delinquency hardly ever look to the law of abortion. A clergyman wrote to *The Times* (London), June 18, 1952: "After five years recently spent in prison work I am quite convinced that the greatest single class of criminal is the unwanted child. I do not think it is any exaggeration to say that 90 per cent of all prisoners today are in one form or another unwanted children, and the greatest single factor in producing these children today is . . . the facilities for easy divorce." It is not immediately obvious how the divorce of an estranged couple causes an unwanted child to be born, or how the refusal of such a divorce would cause an existing unwanted child to be wanted. Would not the letter have shown better logic, if less orthodoxy, if it had declared the greatest factors in producing unwanted children to be the lack of proper contraceptive advice and facilities for abortion?

[3] Wolff: "Some Aspects of Marriage and Divorce Laws in Soviet Russia," 3 *Modern Law Review* at 293 (1949); cf. Harold J. Berman: *Justice in Russia* (Cambridge, Mass., 1950), p. 246. Ibid., p. 286 states that popular opinion was strongly against the change, and this is borne out by the documents printed by R. Schlesinger: *The Family in the U.S.S.R.* (London, 1949), pp. 254ff. Concurrently with the ban on abortion, the literature on contraception suddenly disappeared from the Russian bookshops (Hermann Mannheim: *Criminal Justice and Social Reconstruction* [London, 1946], p. 40). The eugenic grounds for abortion still permitted after 1936 included "presence in the prospective mother, father or one of their children of one of the following hereditary diseases: hemophilia, idiocy, genuine epilepsy, severe schizophrenia or manic-depressive psychosis, blindness, hered-

that Russian obstetricians regarded abortion as an evil, but some at least took the view that the legalized form of it was a lesser evil.[4] It is of some significance in this respect that abortion has once again become legal in the Soviet Union since the end of 1955, and this time no restriction is placed upon it, provided that the operation is performed by qualified persons in hospitals or other health institutions. The reason given for the new law at the time of its introduction was the danger to the health of women through illegal abortion.[5]

It seems from the papers printed by Dr. Schlesinger [6] that a contributory factor to the difficulties experienced in the first Russian experiment was the shortage of facilities for preventing conception. Abortion appears to have been treated by the populace as a normal form of birth control, instead of being (as it should be) a last-ditch measure where the birth of a child is particularly undesirable. The result was that abortion had to be carried out on a scale that was patently injurious. This shows that, whether abortion is legalized or not, it is essential to reduce the scale of the problem by energetic education in contraception.

In 1952 and 1954 bills were introduced into the British Parliament to give limited legality to the operation of abortion, but owing to the limitations of Parliamentary time neither proceeded beyond the initial stages. These bills would merely have declared the legality of therapeutic abortion, but a later form of wording put forward

---

itary deaf-mutism, hereditary progressive diseases of the nervous system." (F. Lorimer: *The Population of the Soviet Union* [Geneva, 1946], p. 128.)

[4] Taussig: op. cit., p. 418; for views against abortion as such, see Schlesinger: op. cit., pp. 172ff. The Russian authorities adopted the "lesser evil" attitude from the beginning in 1920 when the law was enacted; ibid., p. 44. See also on the general medical question the editorial footnote in *Therapeutic Abortion,* Harold Rosen, ed. (New York, 1954), p. 178.

[5] *The Times* (London), December 1, 1955.

[6] Op. cit., pp. 254ff.; cf. ibid., p. 18.

by the Abortion Law Reform Association and sponsored by the Magistrates' Association proposed in addition to legalize certain eugenic abortions.[7]

In the United States opinion has not yet crystallized even to this small extent, but a good deal has been written on the evil of the situation. Perhaps the most important contribution, in its potential effect on public opinion, was a recent article in a widely read women's paper which showed the chaos of the present position.[8]

The three fears

The laws against abortion owed their origin to metaphysical notions concerning life and the soul, combined with the interpretation of the Sixth Commandment, but it is no longer on that ground only that they

[7] The text of the second bill was as follows:

There shall be added the following proviso to Section fifty-eight of the Offences against the Person Act, 1861 (which makes it a felony to administer drugs or use instruments to procure abortion)—

Provided that—

(a) no registered medical practitioner shall be found guilty of an offence under this section unless it is proved that the act charged was not done in good faith for the purpose of preserving the life of the mother;

(b) no registered medical practitioner who acts with the concurring opinion of a second registered medical practitioner shall be found guilty of an offence under this section unless it is proved that the act charged was not done in good faith—

    (i) for the purpose of preventing serious injury to the mother's physical or mental health, or

    (ii) in the belief that there was grave risk of the child being born grossly deformed or with a physical or mental abnormality which would be of a degree to require constant hospital treatment or hospital care throughout life.

[8] Morton Sontheimer: "Abortion in America Today," *Woman's Home Companion*, October 1955, reprinted by the Planned Parenthood Federation.

are judged. Many level-headed persons whose opinions can generally be respected, and who are prepared to consider the abortion laws in a strictly secular way, may yet be heard to express one or other of three fears concerning repeal. These are that the legalization of abortion would be unjustified on medical grounds, that it might lead to a population problem, and that it might result in a breakdown of sexual restraint. I believe that these three fears are either fanciful or logically irrelevant to the issue or both.

There is no doubt that abortion, even when performed by skilled hands, is capable in some cases of leaving bad effects. However, Western medical opinion in Protestant countries, while regarding the operation as undesirable in itself, is prepared to regard it in some circumstances as the lesser evil. Mr. Bourne, for example, regarded it as the lesser evil in the case in which he was prosecuted. The author of the leading medical treatise on the subject, Dr. F. J. Taussig, did not favour unrestricted abortion, but he did advocate its legalization in a number of cases not now provided for by the law. The full study of the Swedish experience by Professor Ekblad, which will be referred to later, is also reassuring.

This, however, is not the most important answer to the fear. To seek to justify the present abortion law by reference to medical considerations is really to confuse ethical and medical issues. The original reason for all laws against abortion was the religious one that it was thought to be wrong. If abortion is no longer thought to be wrong, it is not permissible to turn around and attempt to justify the abortion laws on medical grounds, even if the operation is regarded as medically undesirable, because it is not for the legislature to pronounce upon this. Had such an attitude been adopted in the days before Pasteur, the law might logically have forbidden all surgical operations, which killed as often as they cured;

but fortunately medicine was left to do its best and to improve its methods. The invocation of medicine to justify the abortion laws is to use the name of science to forbid scientific progress.

This is, then, not a question of medicine but one of the proper limits of the criminal law. There is no other branch of medicine in which the legislature attempts to prescribe what is good for the patient. Even an operation like lobotomy (prefrontal leucotomy), which has marked effects upon character, is not regulated by law. In general we are accorded liberty in respect of our own bodies, even the liberty to abuse them. No one seriously suggests that we should be compelled to keep regular hours, to take exercise, and to eat moderately, even though such courses would undoubtedly improve the health of many of us. It is under this banner of personal liberty that a feminist movement has arisen throughout Europe, maintaining that a woman has exclusive right in respect of the functioning of her own body, including the freedom to decide whether she shall continue a pregnancy.[9] All abortion laws have been made by males, and when feminine opinion is tested it is found to be in support of modification.[1] The movement for reform has been successful in some countries, as will appear later.

An important medical result of legalizing abortion would be that it would enable the patient to take proper

[9] Havelock Ellis: *Studies in the Psychology of Sex* (Philadelphia, 1924), VI, 607ff. In Britain the Abortion Law Reform Association (founded in 1936) advocates reform "within such limitations as may be considered advisable," and conferences of women's organizations have passed resolutions in favour of amendment of the law.

[1] Opinion polls in Denmark and Germany are quoted by Taussig: op. cit., p. 391. On January 15, 1956, the *Sunday Mirror* (London) reported the results of a questionnaire answered by 2,000 women. A substantial proportion favoured abortion for health reasons only. By a narrow majority (51 per cent) the women returned an unqualified "Yes" to the question: "Do you think abortion, carried out by qualified doctors, should be permitted by law and carried out at the request of the mother-to-be?"

professional advice. It is, of course, always open to a doctor to dissuade his patient from the operation by pointing out any harmful effects that he thinks it may have. From this point of view it is far better that the woman should consult her own physician, from whom she will get honest advice, than be driven to a charlatan who will give her no advice at all.

The population argument for the present law hardly merits serious attention, for if valid it should lead us to penalize not only abortion but celibacy, contraception, and emigration. The argument can hardly apply to unmarried women. Even if an adequate population is necessary, it must be shown that this cannot be achieved without recourse to the criminal law. Many other legal and administrative measures could be taken to stimulate fertility, in countries where that is thought desirable, in particular by decreasing the financial disadvantages of bringing up children. The truth is that this argument, like the medical one, is only a rationalization for the retention in law of what is in essence a religious offence.

An argument that is sometimes advanced, but more often perhaps is only half conscious, is that to permit abortion would be to license incontinence. It seems an odd idea that a woman is to be punished for the sin of sexual intercourse by being forced to bring an unwanted life into the world—odder still when the mother is feeble-minded or psychopathic, so that the child, if only because of the upbringing it will get, is likely to be no asset to the community. If the argument is a valid one, it would seem to require a prohibition of contraception, and even a ban on the cure of veneral disease—because fear of this disease is a potent check on promiscuity. Moreover, the argument does not justify the whole law of abortion, for that is not confined to illegitimate pregnancies. In fact, it has been estimated in the United States that nine tenths of criminal abortions occur among married women with three or more children,[2] and it was mentioned before that a similar calculation is made for England.

If these three fears are dismissed as the irrelevancies that they are, we seem to come back to the question of philosophy. Is the sanctity of the embryo or fetus a moral absolute, or are we to be allowed to look to utilitarian considerations? In utilitarian philosophy, the welfare of every member of society must be considered, even when he is breaking the law. Punishment is an evil that can be justified, but only when the evil of punishment (including its indirect consequences) is less than the evil to be apprehended from the want of penal restraint. Americans painfully learnt that the indirect evils of Prohibition far exceeded the evil at which the law was directed, and the question is whether the same proposition is not true of the law of abortion.

A re-examination of the theological attitude towards the unborn child

On the moral plane, no utilitarian argument has any effect upon the opinion that the unborn child is as much entitled to protection as the adult. This is the central moral issue upon which agreement is so difficult to secure. To a large extent it defies rational inquiry and solution, since it pertains to metaphysics or emotion and not to empirical facts. The view that human personality mystically begins with the fertilization of the microscopic ovum cannot be refuted any more than it can be proved. There are, however, some observations that seem to be worth making.

[2] Sophia J. Kleegman in *Therapeutic Abortion,* Harold Rosen, ed. (New York, 1954), p. 255.

We may begin with a piece of formal logic. The current theological objection to abortion is the conclusion of a syllogism which may be stated, not strictly in Aristotelian form, as follows:

> Killing human beings is wrong.
> The unborn child is a human being.
> Therefore killing the unborn child is wrong.

Here the first or major premise, the general value-judgment, is not in question. The second (minor) premise is a partial definition of the middle term "human being." It defines the application of this word in an extensive way at one of its temporal extremes. This extension involves drawing the line at impregnation. It is not the only line that can be drawn, and we saw in the previous chapter that at different periods in the past other times were taken. The question is: why does the moral theologian now draw the line at impregnation rather than some time else—say, the time of quickening, or of viability? If the line is to be drawn by reference to social considerations and human happiness, then pretty obviously the time of impregnation is the wrong one to take. What other argument is there for taking this time? The theologian may perhaps claim some direct access to the mind of God. If so, it can only be said that moral dogmatism of this kind cannot be dealt with on an intellectual level.

It may help to correct exaggerated sentiments as to the beginning of human personality if one points out that abortion often occurs spontaneously during the early months, and the woman may not even realize that it has taken place.[3] This is sometimes because of lethal genes,

[3] It is estimated that 60 per cent of all abortions in the U.S.A. and England are natural, or at any rate non-criminal events: (1952) 1 *British Medical Journal* 915. Seven to eleven per cent of pregnancies are found to end in spontaneous abortion: but this estimate probably omits many abortions occurring during the early months which are mistakenly regarded as menstrual irregularities: *Papers of the Royal Commission on Population* (London, 1950), IV, 4.

so that spontaneous abortion has in part a eugenic effect. The "deaths" of these embryos pass without public notice or obsequies; they do not go into the statistics of infant mortality, and our sentiments are not engaged to any marked degree. The mother may naturally feel grief, but it is over the loss of the prospect of a child—not over the loss of a child. Evidently we do not regard a miscarriage, when it occurs naturally, as the death of a human being —even as an accidental death.

When, in 1803, the English Parliament extended the law of abortion to cover the embryo before quickening, it made not merely a legal pronouncement but an ethical or metaphysical one, namely that human life has a value from the moment of impregnation. A statement of moral values cannot be proved or disproved by reference to facts, but it is perhaps worth pointing out that in the year 1803 very little was known of man's biological beginnings. De Graaf, a young surgeon of Delft, had discovered what we now call the Graafian follicles in the female in 1672, and had conjectured the existence of the ovum; three years later his fellow townsman, van Leeuwenhoek, a retired draper with a passion for microscopes, discovered the existence of spermatozoa, which he called "animalcules." These two discoveries were not combined to give the conclusion that male and female contributed equally to the formation of the offspring; instead, there arose two contending schools, the ovists and the spermists, each arguing that the material of heredity lay in its own favored type of germ cell; the other agent, the spermatic "vapour" or the egg albumen, as the case might be, merely providing the physical stimulus or the chemical pabulum.[4] According to the one theory, the ovum (which had not actually been perceived under the microscope) contained a minute model of the parent; according to the other, the model was the homunculus inside the

[4] See the entertaining history of genetics in C. D. Darlington: *The Facts of Life* (London, 1953), particularly at 32ff.

sperm head. These theories were followed by another. It was imagined that the microscopic replica of a man contained in the germ must have, packed within his or her generative organs, the germs of another generation.

If the germinal particles, whether male or female, were to be supposed to contain within them the preformed homunculi of the next generation merely waiting the call to grow, develop, or unfold, it was only too easy to go a step further. It was only natural to suppose that these germs themselves, or those at least of the favoured progenitive sex, should contain the germs of another generation within them, and so on *ad infinitum*. Adam—or Eve, as the case might be—would contain, packed within his or her generative organs, the whole of the future human race like boxes within boxes. At one stroke the Creator had done it all. Such was the theory put forward by Jan Swammerdam of Leyden.

This highly predestinate view of human history put the doctrine of original sin on an apparently scientific basis, a basis that anybody might apprehend. And, when Leibnitz took the matter up and pointed out that souls as well as bodies might be packed, the Box Theory began to contribute to the theological fervour with which, in that very theological age, preformation was sustained by some sects, and opposed by others. The smallnesses involved were inconceivable but no more so than the largenesses revealed at the same time by astronomy. And there was (so some said) a spiritual satisfaction to be obtained from stretching the organs of credulity and conceiving what others found to be inconceivable.[5]

It is evident that this scientific and theological climate was favourable to the assumption that the germ, possessed both of microscopic human likeness and of a soul, needed the protection of the law from the moment when it was planted in the womb in circumstances in which it could develop. What those circumstances were, was only slowly established. It was not until 1854 that a sperm was seen making its way into the egg of a frog. Gradu-

[5] Darlington: op. cit., pp. 37–8. The reader may recall the amusing treatment of this theme in Sterne's *Tristram Shandy*, I. ch. 2.

ally, during the first part of the nineteenth century, the homunculus theory was replaced by the cell theory, which saw living growth as depending on the division and subdivision of a cell. Even Darwin could not decide whether to accept the cell theory or not, though he was one of the last to feel any doubts.

The individual, then, has his origin in the fusion of two cells. Although we may cling to the religious belief in the existence of a soul, we have given up asking when this soul begins, because the question has become evidently insoluble. Clearly the billions of sperm cells that go for naught in a single act of reproduction cannot be conceded to possess souls, and similarly it is impossible to find souls in unfertilized ova. Perhaps the soul is a miraculous addition to the act of fertilization, just as it is a miraculous subtraction from the mortifying body—something coming from and returning along a divine dimension which is outside the ken of a biologist. But in that case, what of the entirely natural phenomenon of spontaneous abortion? It would seem, on this theory, that the naturally aborted embryo perishes possessed of a soul.

There are other difficulties in the orthodox doctrine of the soul which need not detain us. For the legislator, it seems sufficient to say that theological speculations and controversies should have no place in the formation of rules of law, least of all rules of the criminal law which are imposed upon believers and non-believers alike. If we protect the fetus by law, it should be for reasons relating to the well-being of existing human beings. Can it be said, with any degree of reality, that the week- or month-old embryo is an existing human being?

The objection to commencing the legal protection of the embryo at the moment of impregnation is largely met if one commences the protection (as some of the United States still do) at the moment of quickening. The argument in favour of the latter rule is that it permits abortions to be performed by the medical profession instead of by unskilled hands. But the importance attached to quickening rests on what now appears to be a rather obvious superstition, and as a matter of legal administration it causes great evidential difficulties unless some average date is taken.

There is a third possible line in the prenatal period which might be established by the legislature as the beginning of legal protection. This is the time of viability, conveniently fixed at the twenty-eighth week of pregnancy. It may well be that, as a political matter, a radical reform of the present abortion law could best be achieved by fixing this time as the datum. Whatever social arguments may be used, many people will continue to regard abortion as abhorrent because of the sanctity of the young life that is destroyed. That there is weight in this view cannot be denied. The humane, ethical, and parental feeling of the plain man leads him to wish to extend the protection of the criminal law not only to the newly born child but to the viable child before birth. The protection need not, however, be extended beyond viability. As Lord Riddell pointed out, "the destruction of a full-grown child is a revolting affair, whereas the abortion of an early fetus differs but little from the removal of a uterine tumour." [6]

A line drawn at the twenty-eighth week would be socially satisfactory because illegal abortions do not take place after this time: in fact, few occur after the first four months of pregnancy. [7]

[6] *Medico-Legal Problems* (London, 1929), p. 35. Strangely enough, Lord Riddell did not himself draw the obvious conclusion that abortion of an early fetus should be legal.

[7] It was calculated that in the United States only 5 per cent of abortions were performed after the third month of pregnancy, and the danger of the operation to the mother increased greatly after this time: see *Report of the* [English] *Interdepartmental Committee on Abortion,* 1939, p. 95. Cook found that of 350 cases of abortion admitted to hospital, the abortion had generally taken place in the

In between the time of quickening and the time of viability one might take the time at which the fetal brain begins to function. The soul, after all, is frequently associated with the mind, and until the brain is formed there can be no mind. By placing electrodes on the maternal abdomen over the fetal head, electric potentials ("brain waves") are discernible in the seventh month, i.e., shortly before the time of viability.[8] If one were to compromise by taking, say, the beginning of the seventh month as the beginning of legal protection for the fetus,

---

early months; it occurred between 4 and 5 months of pregnancy in 44 cases, and between 5 and 6 months of pregnancy in 10 cases ([1938] 1 *British Medical Journal* 1045). A. Davis reported that in 2,665 illegal abortions, 87 per cent of the women had attained the stage of 12–14 weeks, and usually it took place at the twelfth week ([1950] 2 *British Medical Journal* 123). R. D. Teare put the most usual period at the third and fourth months (19 *Medico-Legal Journal* 81 [London, 1951]). It is understandable that a woman should try to procure her abortion at a time when she knows of the pregancy but others do not as yet do so. Some of the late abortions were perhaps due to the difficulty of finding an abortionist; even if abortions were only legalized during the first three months, one would expect the proportion of abortions after this period to drop. In Russia, when abortion was first legalized, it was prohibited as to pregnancies more than three months in duration, or within six months of a prior operation; also prohibited or strongly discouraged for first pregnancies except on therapeutic grounds: Taussig: op. cit., pp. 406, 442. These restrictions were imposed to minimize the danger of the operation, not for moral reasons or out of regard for the feelings of the surgeon. Since then, methods of abdominal hysterotomy have become safe enough to make the limitations medically unnecessary, except for patients suffering from certain diseases. In the University of Iowa hospitals, for example, between 1926 and 1950, more than half of the interrupted pregnancies were operated upon in the fourth month or later. The death rate, having regard to the general condition of the patients, was not excessive: seven died out of 137 patients, chiefly in the earlier of the years surveyed; and of these seven, five were very seriously ill and would probably have died shortly even if the operation had not been carried out. See Moore and Randall in 63 *American Journal of Obstetrics and Gynecology* 37 (1952). So far as I have been able to discover, now that abortion has been relegalized in the Soviet Union (since 1955), the former restrictions have not been continued.

[8] Gallant in *Therapeutic Abortion,* Harold Rosen, ed. (New York, 1954), p. 177n.

it would practically eliminate the present social problem of abortion.

Finally, it is necessary to insist again on the distinction between morals and law. The Catholic reply to any argument based on social facts is that moral rules cannot be abandoned merely because they are broken, or because their breach causes suffering: to do so is progressively to lower moral standards. This reply, persuasive in the abstract, may be said to be irrelevant in the present context. In the first place, it begs the question whether abortion is in fact immoral. But secondly—and this is much the more important answer, and the one on which there is likely to be a wider measure of agreement—the religious opinion illegitimately assumes that we should always legislate morality. Some moral principles are so infinitely various in their application, or so much the subject of dispute, that they cannot well be cast into the mould of law. The extent to which the application of moral principles must give way to the individual circumstances will always be a matter of disagreement. A realistic humanitarianism—or a true Christianity— might say that it is impossible to judge others, because one cannot live their lives and experience their inner drives and compulsions; and particularly is this true in matters of sex, marriage, and parenthood. But at least we may say this, that if moral rules are to be externalized and enforced by law, they should so far as possible be those that human beings in the mass are able to comply with, without excessive repression and frustration and without overmuch need for the actual working of the legal machine. It is evident that this cannot be said of the present law of abortion.

Moreover, the introduction of criminal sanctions brings in moral problems distinct from the evaluation of the conduct in question. The true issue is not whether abortion is immoral but whether women who procure their own abortion and qualified surgeons who perform it for them should be punished through the instrumentality of the law of the land. This question cannot be answered in abstraction from the consequences of punishment. When these consequences are found to involve social evils greater than the alleged evil of abortion itself, without in fact preventing abortions, the case for continuing the threat of punishment is evidently not made out. On practical grounds, if we have regard to the widespread and strong demand for abortion that in all Western countries has reduced the law to impotence, it would be better to permit abortions conducted by qualified practitioners than to tolerate the activities of the band of abortionists who are now a settled feature of our society.

This, then, seems to be the short and simple solution of the problem of abortion. Let any religious sect characterize abortion as a sin if it sees fit to do so, and punish its members for this sin by censure or other ecclesiastical punishment. But whether abortion should be a crime is to be judged by worldly considerations, and the case against treating it in this way—the case against the rule established in 1803—is, after the experience of one and a half centuries, overwhelming.

Some partial solutions

Those who shrink from a radical solution may at least be prepared to see abortion legalized (within the temporal limit already stated) for a wider class of cases than at present. A partial change could not eliminate secret abortions altogether, but it would at any rate be an improvement upon the existing law. The strongest case is undoubtedly where the child is likely to suffer from a serious defect, either because of inheritance from one or both of his parents or because of some disease contracted by his mother during pregnancy. To allow the breeding of defectives is a horrible evil, far worse than any that may be found in abortion; yet neither church nor law perceives any offence to society in it.[9] Eugenic abortion is resisted on the ground that this work should be done not by abortion but by contraception. Yet contraception is useless for people, such as mental defectives, who are unable or unwilling to practise it. There are many defectives who are not thought to require institutional treatment, who yet are prone to sexual irresponsibility; for these, abortion accompanied by sterilization is a socially desirable operation. Moreover, even for persons of normal intelligence contraceptive efforts always carry some risk of failure.

Yet another clear case for abortion is rape. It is hard to see how any one can support a law that compels a girl to nourish within her body seed violently planted there by a sexual maniac.[1] Other suggested cases concern incest, and women who have borne four children.[2] As will be shown, several countries that generally forbid

[9] Here again Mr. Justice McCardie seems to have been the only English judge to take public notice of the mischief: see his remarks noted in (1932) 51 *Law Notes* (English) 2 (1932). Cf. Claud Mullins: *Marriage, Children and God* (London, 1933), p. 106. Whereas the breeding of degenerates passes unnoticed, it is a heinous crime for brother and sister to sleep together, even though no offspring are born.

[1] So Dr. Eustace Chesser: "There can be few doctors, and even members of the general public, who do not feel it an anomaly that pregnancies, the result of positively illegal acts—e.g., rape or seduction or a girl below the age of consent—cannot be terminated, if the demand is made, *upon that ground alone*" ([1949] 1 *British Medical Journal* 728). Lilian Wyles: *A Woman at Scotland Yard* (London, 1952), pp. 228–9, does not approve complete legalization of abortion, but thinks it should be legalized for rape, even if only for the sake of the unwanted child that would otherwise be born. Dr. M. S. Guttmacher recalls a case where a twelve-year-old child who was impregnated by her father was refused an abortion by a hospital notwithstanding strong efforts made on her behalf. (*Therapeutic Abortion,* Harold Rosen, ed. [New York, 1954], p. 185.)

[2] For all these cases, see Thurtle: op. cit., pp. 57ff., and cf. Taussig: op. cit., p. 448 *fin.*

abortion allow it for rape and incest and on eugenic grounds. Even this list fails to take account of some cases. What of the woman who, already the mother of a considerable family, is deserted by her husband when pregnant? If the state forbids abortion in such circumstances, it must at least assume complete responsibility for the unwanted child. Something could be done to assist these cases by an extension of the medico-social indication for abortion; but the extension would probably need the sanction of the legislature, and would certainly need new hospitals, if it is to be carried out on any considerable scale. As has been remarked, the present medical view is that the strictly medical non-psychiatric grounds for termination of pregnancy are shrinking, with increased knowledge and better forms of treatment; thus, therapeutic abortion, on a narrow interpretation, will do less and less to meet the social need for legalized abortion.

The recognition of an extended list of limited justifications for abortion would raise problems of administration: who is to decide whether the legal conditions are present? For the protection of the surgeon who operates, it would obviously be desirable to have the case passed upon by some official board, as is done in Denmark and Sweden.[3] Apart from the question of legal protection, a surgeon and the nurses who attend at the operation are eased by the knowledge that the case has been considered by an impartial board representing the public, and pronounced fit for the operation. It must not be forgotten that the medical profession, apart from being afraid of legal sanctions, is at the moment affected to some extent by the popular taboo. The operation of abortion, even when performed for therapeutic reasons, is felt by some to be unclean or in some way discreditable. Perhaps this is why many hospitals do not perform it, or severely limit the occasions on which they consent to do so. A

[3] See the excellent discussion by Hermann Mannheim: *Criminal Justice and Social Reconstruction* (London, 1946), pp. 42ff.

change in popular and legal attitude might, however, be expected to reflect itself in medical practice.

The experience of limited legalization

Most countries allow therapeutic abortion, but some have gone further. In Japan, sterilization and abortion were legalized for medical, economic, and eugenic reasons in July 1948, and operations under this law have reached the staggering number of a million a year.[4] This unhealthy use of abortion as a form of population control, which is causing anxiety in Japan, is partly due to the extreme severity of the population problem, which itself is due to the failure over many years to develop a national sense of the importance of contraception.

Apart from the Soviet Union, the other countries to make the most complete break from traditional notions are the Scandinavian. Sweden led the way with a law of 1938; Denmark followed the next year, and Finland in 1950.[5]

The Swedish development (which is paralleled by that in Denmark and Finland) is of great interest. Abortion had been illegal there since the thirteenth century, and during the eighteenth century it was punishable by death. As in other countries, the number of illegal abortions caused concern, one credible estimate being that in

---

[4] The number showed a rapid increase over the years, reaching 1,143,059 in 1954. It is said that an approximately equal number of clandestine abortions is performed. See C. P. Blacker: "Japan's Population Problem," 48 *Eugenics Review* 30 (1956); Thomas K. Burch: "Induced Abortion in Japan," 2 *Eugenics Quarterly* No. 3, September 1955. Many women whose pregancy is terminated are sterilized at the same time.

[5] See Klintskog in 21 *Medico-Legal Journal* 79 (1953).

the year 1930 there were 20 abortions to every 100 infants born alive. Although Swedish law did not at that time contain any exception for therapeutic abortions, the termination of pregnancy on medical indication was considered to be legal where it was necessary in order to save the woman's life or to remove a serious danger to her health. As a result of exhaustive consideration by committees, the law of 1938 extends the grounds of legal abortion to include not only medical but medico-social, humanitarian, and eugenic considerations. As the committee of 1935 pointed out, once abortion is permitted to preserve the mother's health and working capacity, there can be no convincing reason for stopping short at this point, and refusing to take account of wider social grounds.

The Swedish law of 1938 is all the more remarkable because the country was at that time suffering from a fit of alarm over a decline in births to below replacement rate. The way in which the Swedes tackled this problem was the reverse of the usual one. They not only legalized abortion but set up contraceptive clinics all over the country in order that children should only be born when really wanted. At the same time, however, state help was provided for parenthood, by way of tax reliefs, maternal welfare centers, attendance at delivery, free school meals, and subsidized housing. This enlightened approach did not at first hinder the success of the policy for improving the replacement rate, which was pushed up to above parity in the 1940's.[6] Since 1945, however, the birth rate has been falling again. In 1945 there were 135,000 live births; in 1951, only 110,000. Whatever the reasons for this fall, the abortion law cannot account for

[6] Robert C. Cook: *Human Fertility: The Modern Dilemma* (New York, 1951), pp. 284ff.; cf. Frederick Osborn: *Preface to Eugenics* (New York, 1940), pp. 174ff.; Hermann Mannheim: *Criminal Justice and Social Reconstruction* (London, 1946), p. 41.

more than a quarter of it. Also, notwithstanding the fall, births substantially outnumber deaths.[7]

The working of the abortion law has been excellently studied from a medical point of view by Professor Martin Ekblad in his book *Induced Abortion on Psychiatric Grounds,* which deserves to be widely known for the misconceptions about abortion that it manages to dispel. The following short account of the Swedish experience is based upon this book.

The grounds for abortion under the law of 1938 are as follows:

(1) Medical, where on account of illness or physical defect in the woman the advent of the child would entail serious danger to her life or health. This was declaratory of the previous law as generally understood.

(2) Medico-social, where on account of "weakness" in the woman the advent of the child would entail such danger.

(3) Humanitarian, where the woman has become pregnant through a coitus which has involved a criminal act and flagrant infringement of the woman's freedom of action, e.g., rape or unlawful coercion, or coitus with an insane or mentally deficient person or person under the age of consent.

(4) Eugenic, where it may with reason be presumed that the woman or the father of the expected child will transmit to the offspring through hereditary channels of insanity, mental deficiency, or serious phyiscal disease. Where a pregnancy is terminated on account of such heredity in the woman, sterilization must be performed as well (in order to obviate the repeated inducing of abortion on eugenic grounds), unless for special reasons this measure is considered unsuitable. Simultaneous sterilization is considered unsuitable in cases in which the state of the woman's health is very poor, or in cases in which

[7] See the rates given in *World Population and Resources* (P.E.P.: London, 1955), p. 238.

238

a sterilization is unnecessary, e.g., because the woman is near her climacteric or because she is to become a permanent inmate in an institution.

All these proposals had been approved, before being passed into law, by a majority of the reports received from various authorities and societies whose views had been sought by the Government. The Government rejected a social indication for abortion proposed by the committee of 1935, namely where the woman's position was so desperate that she could not reasonably be required to go on with the pregnancy—where, in other words, the advent of a child might inflict upon the woman lasting misery or distress that it was found could not otherwise be averted. This proposal had had a very mixed reception by public opinion, and is not embodied in the Act of 1938. The only social indication permitted under the Act is the mixed medico-social indication of "weakness," which was intended to provide for "worn-out mothers" and similar cases.

The administration of the Act is entrusted to medical boards who are empowered to authorize the termination of pregnancy on the indications stated in the Act. It was hoped that the new system would reduce illegal abortions by providing an opportunity for women desiring an abortion to discuss their problems with responsible persons who might find a solution without resorting to abortion. In the larger cities special advice centers have been set up, in which the applicant for abortion is carefully examined by a specially trained social worker collaborating with a gynæcologist and psychiatrist, or with some other specialist where it is not a matter of psychiatric indications. In this way the abortion problem is brought into the light of day and dealt with as a social problem. Women who are able to pay for private care can have their case brought before the medical board by a consulting physician in private practice, thus avoiding the need to apply to the center.

The working of the new law was studied by a committee which reported in 1944. Since 1935 it had been incumbent upon doctors who had performed abortion on medical indication to submit a report to the Royal Medical Board. After the coming into force of the Abortion Act legal abortions had increased from 439 in the year 1939 to 703 in 1943. The increase was ascribed chiefly to eugenic abortion, and the committee expressed dissatisfaction with the small number of cases in which the operation had been performed on medico-social grounds. Consequently, an Act of 1946 amended the earlier measure in certain ways, the most important being that the previous ground of "weakness" was amplified by a heading of "foreseen weakness." Under this, a pregnancy may be terminated where in view of the woman's conditions of life and her circumstances in other respects it may be presumed that her physical or mental forces would be seriously impaired by the advent of the child and the care of the child. It was not intended to allow purely social considerations to enter, but only to formulate more clearly the medico-social consideration. The point of advance was that illness, physical defect, or weakness no longer had to be manifested in the woman at the time of the operation; attention could now be directed towards the future development. As a result of the new attitude shown by the report of the committee and the consequent legislation, the number of legal abortions in Sweden rose steeply, from 703 in 1943 to 6,328 in 1951, falling to 5,322 in 1952. In 1950 there were 5,889 legal abortions, or 51 for each 1,000 parturients; of these legal abortions 30.2 per cent were for illness or physical defect, 50.7 for weakness, 9.6 for foreseen weakness, 9.2 on eugenic grounds, and 0.3 on humanitarian grounds. The division between "weakness" and "foreseen weakness" is probably somewhat arbitrary, and the weakness indication as a whole acquired a steadily increasing importance, especially after 1946 when the Act was amended. Professor

Ekblad's summary of the situation is that "the most important cause of the marked increase in the number of legal abortions at the end of the 1940's is due to the progressively greater attention paid to social factors and the future health of the woman." [8] This change of attitude on the part of both doctors and administrators is linked with increased emphasis upon psychiatric considerations. "Women who are psychasthenic or neurotic, or who have a tendency to reactive psychic insufficiencies and who are living at the limit of their resources, are now granted legal abortion more easily than formerly. Similarly, a severe reactive depression with suicidal thoughts is regarded as an indication for abortion even if the woman was mentally well-balanced before the unwelcome pregnancy."

The general acceptance of the legislation has not silenced a certain body of opinion that objects to it on medical and social grounds. It is pointed out, with perfect truth, that although there may be the risk of suicide in connection with an unwelcome pregnancy, this is in general slight. An examination of autopsy records for female suicides in Sweden showed that 8 per cent of these women were pregnant and the pregnancy was probably the releasing factor in the suicide. When investigations were made among women who had threatened to commit suicide and who had had their application for legal abortion refused, it was found that none had in fact committed suicide in the years surveyed. However, it is known that this had actually occurred in other years. The risk of suicide is greatest with the deserted woman who is alone. [9]

Another factual ground of criticism of the legislation both in Sweden and in Denmark is that it has not sub-

---

[8] Ekblad: *Induced Abortion on Psychiatric Grounds* (published in the *Acta Psychiatrica et Neurologica Scandinavica*: Stockholm, 1955), p. 19.
[9] Ekblad: op. cit., pp. 94–5.

stantially reduced the number of illegal abortions; according to one opinion, these have actually become more numerous because the legislation has helped to remove the feeling that abortion is wrong, and indeed promotes an abortion mentality which extends to all women who have become unintentionally pregnant. Whether it is true to say that illegal abortions have increased or somewhat diminished is controversial, but investigation has shown that a proportion (ranging from 15 to 33 per cent) of the women refused legal abortion have afterwards had their pregnancy ended by abortion, whether natural or illegal. Some such result is to be expected, because it cannot be hoped that legislation which restricts the grounds for legal abortion will entirely displace the illegal operator. There is convincing evidence that it is to a large extent an entirely new clientele that is now granted legal abortion, that is to say women who would not have had an illegal abortion if they had been refused the legal one. Although the social result is rather to add the total of legal abortions to the total of illegal abortions than to reduce the number of illegal abortions, a body of medical opinion refuses to regret the legal abortions on this account. As Ekblad points out, the women in question are to be found chiefly among the married women living in a harmonious marriage. "Previously, and as a rule thanks to their personal disposition, these women had taken an unwelcome pregnancy with resignation, submissively accepting it without protest. The Abortion Act now gives possibilities of helping them. The service implied in a legal abortion is in these cases extremely difficult to judge, but may frequently be of very great value. As it is in this group that the highest frequency of recidivations is met with, i.e. the greatest number of new unintentional pregnancies, and as it is, moreover, by the same man, perhaps the legal abortion should be reserved chiefly for those amongst them who are so worn out that this constitutes an indication for simultaneous sterilization. If the woman herself urgently desires sterilization there is in general no need to fear that she will regret the measure." [1] The author proceeds to say that a reduction in the number of illegal abortions could be expected if extended indications for legal abortion were recognized for women who find themselves in a severe conventional conflict in connection with the unwelcome pregnancy, particularly those who have been deserted by the male partner. He adds that "in our present community these deserted women probably find it very difficult to take care of a child and at the same time keep their psychic health intact, and this in its turn has repercussions on their working capacity and on their care of the child."

A third line of attack upon the new law is the allegedly undesirable nature of the operation. This, as said previously in this study, is a purely medical question, and really has nothing to do with the question whether the operation should be forbidden by law. However, opponents of the legalization of abortion naturally try to reinforce their case by bringing in the medical issue. In order to examine the argument that the operation involved an undue risk of impairing the woman's mental health, Dr. Ekblad undertook a careful follow-up examination of a large number of patients who had had legal abortion in Sweden. The survey covered 500 women, who were psychiatrically examined after the operation and before discharge from hospital, and then given (as to 479 of the women) another examination between 22 and 54 months afterwards; both examinations were carried out by Dr. Ekblad personally. His report, which is of great human interest and medical value, can only be presented here in the briefest form. It will, no doubt, sound bald and unconvincing to say that in the substantial majority of cases no undesirable sequelæ were found, and

[1] Ekblad: op. cit., pp. 97–8; cf. on sterilization ibid., Chap. 15.

that the operation was pronounced wholly beneficial. The doubting reader should, however, study for himself the full case-histories given by the author, in order to realize how, on numerous occasions, an induction was able to save a marriage, or to prevent a mental or physical break-down on the part of the woman, or even perhaps a suicide.

In the greater number of cases the woman expressed no self-reproach for the operation afterwards. In some, however, she did; and in all the cases where there were unfavourable psychic sequelæ (in the form of depression or other psychogenous insufficiency reactions) these were combined with self-reproaches for the abortion. Of the women studied, 14 per cent expressed mild self-reproach for the operation, and 11 per cent serious self-reproach. This was at the follow-up examination; in the examination some days after the operation only 2 per cent had serious self-reproaches or regretted it. Those who expressed mild self-reproach may well have been affected by the prevailing attitude which tends to condemn abortion; and the desire to present themselves in a favourable light may have led some of them to assert self-reproaches that they had not felt. A close study of the case-histories of the patients with serious self-reproaches showed that even if their subjective sufferings due to the abortion were severe, their depression must from the psychiatric point of view be designated as in general mild. These women seldom needed to consult a doctor on account of these mental troubles.

There were, undoubtedly, a few cases where the operation might seem in retrospect to have been a mistake, or no improvement. The existence of these cases must not, however, be taken as condemning the practice of induction altogether. (1) In five cases (one per cent) where the woman's psychic state after the operation was such that her working capacity suffered, she had manifested severe neurotic symptoms even before the operation. Professor Ekblad thinks it probable that the women would have developed equally severe symptoms even if they had not been granted legal abortion. Nor is there any certainty that the abortion must be debited with the unfavourable symptoms: in four of the five cases it was probably a break with the male partner and the disappointment caused by it, and not the abortion, that constituted the most essential cause of the subsequent depression, and in the fifth case it was a protracted conflict with an alcoholic and violent husband. Speaking generally of the cases where there were unfavourable mental sequelæ, Dr. Ekblad thinks that in some of them the mental instability might not only have existed but been aggravated if the pregnancy had been allowed to continue, for then the woman would have been subjected to the strain of giving birth and bringing up the child—the latter rendered more difficult than usual if the child is illegitimate. If, on the other hand, she were obliged to have the child adopted, this might give rise to even worse repercussions upon the woman's mental health. (2) In some cases the woman, if refused the legal abortion, might have resorted to an illegal one, or committed suicide—it must be remembered that we are here considering especially cases of mental instability. (3) In diagnosis, the best that can be done is to compare the risk of damaging the woman's future physical and mental health through the operation with the risk of such damage being incurred if the pregnancy is not terminated legally. Professor Ekblad's work shows how unscientific it would be to be so swayed by the small percentage of cases with unfavourable outcomes as to give up the performance of the operation altogether.

The position is much the same in Denmark as in Sweden. Before 1939, termination of pregnancy was allowed only to avoid danger to the life or health of the woman. Legislation of 1939 extended the medical indication to cases where the danger to health arose from social circumstances, and also allowed the operation after certain sexual crimes and in cases of severe hereditary taint. Two physicians had to agree on the indication, and the case had to be reported to the public health service. It has been the practice under this law to take into account the general social condition and psychiatric state of the woman; and, under the latter head, attention is paid not only to depressions and suicidal tendencies but also nervous exhaustion and psychasthenia, especially where there are already many children.

The working of the law has naturally led to a considerable increase in legal abortions, from 500 to 5,000 yearly. The increase is almost entirely among married women, and is especially in psychiatric cases. It is difficult to estimate if the number of illegal abortions during the same period has decreased or increased, but in any case the number is very high, perhaps 12,000 yearly, in a population of over four million.

At the time of writing, a law is passing through Parliament to clarify the indications and elaborate the procedure. The new wording of the medical indication is: "A woman is allowed to have her pregnancy interrupted when it is needed to prevent serious danger to the life or health of the woman. The judgment of this depends on (1) present physical or mental illness; (2) threatening physical or mental weakness; (3) the social circumstances under which the woman has to live."

The new procedure is that a woman seeking an interruption of pregnancy must (unless already ill) first see a "mother's help," who prepares the case for the medical board from both the medical and the social points of view. Boards are regional in character, and consist of two physicians (one of whom is a psychiatrist) and a member of the maternity welfare organization. The working policy of the regional boards is co-ordinated by a central advisory standing committee. Where the indication is disease in the narrow sense, the chief physician of a public hospital department may take the affirmative decision.

Medical opinion on the working of the law is thus summarized by Dr. Carl Clemmesen.[2]

> An increased desire for induced abortions seems to have arisen in the population, a desire not based on social necessity but more likely on a rising demand for better living conditions for the women, and the existence of the law has without doubt in a number of cases caused women to consider induced abortion as an obvious way out of an unwanted pregnancy.
>
> Perhaps the law has thus indirectly resulted in more cases of illegal abortions than it has directly prevented, but on the whole most of the physicians in Denmark would certainly not like to do without this liberalized legislation.

In Finland abortion is decided upon by two specialists, one of whom actually induces it.[3] The law appears to be interpreted as liberally as in other Scandinavian countries.

---

[2] 112 *American Journal of Psychiatry* 662–3 (1956). My account of Danish law is taken from this article.

[3] (1953) 151 *Journal of the American Medical Association* 574.

VII

THE PROHIBITION OF SUICIDE

The normal person instinctively rejects the idea of suicide in ordinary circumstances, and this makes the subject a displeasing one to discuss. There is, however, one fact that compels its discussion. When we send people to prison for attempting suicide, or for aiding suicide, or otherwise penalize its commission, it is morally imperative to inquire into the ethical basis of our social attitude. The subject has, indeed, been argued about for more than two thousand years, and, as Albert Bayet observed in his classical *Le suicide et la morale,* it is now in pretty much the same state as when it began. This is largely because it raises the marital disputes of order and freedom, effort and indulgence, holiness and happiness, authority and conscience, which have vexed philosophy for as long as these problems have been thought of, and are unable to achieve any permanent solution. Thus, there is little hope of obtaining an agreed opinion on the ethics of suicide itself. One can, however, detect an unmistakable trend of opinion against attaching penal sanctions to the act of suicide. Substantial progress has been achieved in making the law more humane, and this may give sufficient encouragement to tread once again the old disputed ground.

Two historical questions call for preliminary discussion: how did Western communities come by their notion that self-destruction is wrong, and how did this idea make its way into the law?

The non-Christian attitude

It seems to be impossible to generalize about the attitude of primitive peoples towards this deed. Some thought of it with superstitious horror; others, like the Germanic tribes before the Christian era, accepted it calmly.[1] The suicide of the impotent aged was sometimes regarded as the natural complement of the infanticide of unwanted children. It seems to be true to say, however, that most primitive peoples of different times and places have felt a superstitious fear of the body that has met a violent death, whether by murder or suicide. The elaborate rituals that were performed to prevent its ghost vexing the living may have been the origin of the idea that suicide was itself, like murder, a wrongful act.

Religious philosophies are also lacking in complete accord. Eastern systems (Hinduism and Buddhism) do not pronounce unequivocally and absolutely against suicide. It came, however, to be forbidden by Jewish thought, which was adopted in this respect, probably for certain reasons of its own, by the Christian Church; and the attitude of the latter in turn influenced Islam.

Although the prohibition of suicide is usually referred to the Bible, it is easy to show the unauthenticity of this. The Old Testament records four cases of suicide (Samson, Saul, Abimelech, and Ahitophel), and gives no indication that they were frowned upon. The last, Ahitophel, is recorded to have received due burial in the sepulchre of his father (II Sam. xvii, 23). Later, both Orthodox Jewish and Christian interpreters had to resort

[1] For a review of the literature see Louis I. Dublin and Bessie Bunzel: *To Be or Not to Be* (New York, 1933)., pp. 138ff.

249

to a strained interpretation of the Sixth Commandment in order to stigmatize suicide as a sin.

The first Jewish writer to express the later view was Josephus. He was the commander of an army which was conquered by the Romans. His soldiers wished to kill themselves to avoid surrender, whereas he himself wished to live. It was on this occasion, in an address to his troops, that Josephus expressed his philosophy of the matter.[2] He employed two main arguments: (1) Suicide is a crime remote from the common nature of all animals. (2) The soul is, in the language of Roman law, a *depositum* received from God, and a man therefore acts wickedly in casting it from his body. The reasoning on (2) is confused. One objection to it is that if the soul is a *depositum,* the depositee can in accordance with ordinary legal principles hand it back when he tires of his trust. Yet does it make sense to speak of a man dealing with his own soul? Also, we are told that the soul is immortal, and yet the implication is that this immortal soul is somehow injured by being cast out of the body. The first argument, that suicide is contrary to the nature of animals, is also open to criticism. It is broadly true that suicide is unknown among the lower animals, but the reason obviously is that animals lack the mental ability to argue with themselves that death may be preferable to continued existence. It so happens that man is gifted with this ability. Exceptionally, self-destruction has been observed even in dogs, who may commit suicide, usually by drowning or by refusing food, for a number of reasons—generally when the animal is cast out from the household, but also from regret or remorse or even from sheer ennui.[3] Animal suicide of these kinds is capable of being regarded as a manifestation of intelligence.

[2] Josephus, *BJ* iii. 8, s. 5.
[3] Perlson and Karpman: "Psychopathologic and Psychopathetic Reaction in Dogs," 4 *Journal of Criminal Pyschopathology* 504, at 514–15 (1943). For this reference I am indebted to Mr. Joseph Wallfield, of Co-

After Josephus, the condemnation of suicide is frequently found in Rabbinic writings, and the part of the Talmud known as the Mishnah provides that the person who dies by his own hand is to be given no funeral rites.[4]

It is convenient, before considering the Christian view, to turn from the ancient Jews to the Greeks and Romans.[5] There are traces of suicide-horror in the laws of ancient Greece. In Athenian law the hand that committed the suicide was cut off and buried apart from the rest of the body, which was denied the usual solemnities. In Thebes, too, the bodies of those who killed themselves were deprived of the accustomed funeral rites. These laws probably fell into disuse; at any rate, the balance of Greek intellectual thought was not against suicide. Socrates, who drank poison by judgment of the court, thought that it did not become any one to end his own life before God had imposed some necessity of doing it upon him. "Man," he said, "is situated in this life, as it were on a post or station, which he must not quit without leave; because the gods exert a providential care over us, on which account we are a part (as it were) of their property and possessions; and because, we should think it unjust and punishable (if it were in our power to punish) in any slave of our own, to kill himself without our leave." However, the leave of the Deity can be made manifest by a "visible necessity of dying," as had been by the judgment imposed upon himself. Plato, in the ninth book of his *Laws,* reported these views of Socrates, and maintained the general condemnation of suicide; but he largely destroyed its significance by admitting exceptions

---

lumbia University. See also W. Wynn Westcott: *Suicide* (London, 1885), Chap. 22.

[4] Dublin and Bunzel: op. cit., p. 176.

[5] See Charles Moore: *A Full Inquiry into the Subject of Suicide* (London, 1790), Vol. 1; Manson in 1 *Journal of Comparative Legislation* (New Series) 311 (1899).

of the most elastic character. A man may quit life not only when compelled to it by the judgment of the state, but when afflicted by any extraordinary sorrow or inevitable turn of fortune, or any shame of extreme distress and poverty.

Aristotle, by specious reasoning, concluded that suicide was an offence against the state; he made no mention of divine prohibition. His argument was that law never commands a person to kill himself; but what it does not command, it forbids; therefore, suicide is wrong. The reasoning is demonstrably false, for there are liberties which the law neither commands nor forbids. Another reason given by Aristotle for condemning suicide was that it was an act of cowardice.

Other philosophers admitted a large place for suicide in their scheme of things. Epicurus, who thought that man should live for pleasure alone, and denied the interference of the gods in human affairs, naturally drew the conclusion that the free man was the arbiter of his own life and death. If life ceased to be a pleasure, the remedy was to make an exit. The Stoics, who professed themselves indifferent to pain, yet admitted self-destruction whenever the circumstances might point to it, as in the case of pain or disease. They regarded it as an essential part of human freedom that we continue here by our own consent.

Roman philosophy on the whole adopted the Stoic view that suicide [6] was justified by circumstances. Seneca (in his *Epistles,* and *De Ira*) has many striking passages to the effect that suicide is a last defence against intolerable suffering. "To death alone it is due that life is not a punishment, that, erect beneath the frowns of

[6] The word is not classical: someone remarked that if Cicero had been confronted with such a formation as *suicida* he would presumably have thought it meant a pork butcher. "Suicide" first appeared in 1671, but more than a century later Johnson denied it admission to his dictionary. See Dublin and Bunzel: op. cit., p. 250; H. Romilly Fedden: *Suicide* (London, 1938), p. 29.

fortune, I can preserve my mind unshaken and master of itself. . . . Slavery loses its bitterness when by a step I can pass to liberty. Against all the injuries of life, I have the refuge of death." "Wherever you look, there is the end of evils. You see that yawning precipice—there you may descend to liberty. You see that sea, that river, that well—liberty sits at the bottom. . . . Do you seek the way to freedom?—you may find it in every vein of your body." "If I can choose between a death of torture, and one that is simple and easy, why should I not select the latter? . . . Man should seek the approbation of others in his life; his death concerns himself alone." Seneca's argument was partly founded on a neat reversal of the usual argument from nature: "The eternal law has done nothing better than this, that it has given us only one entrance into life, but a thousand ways of escape out of it. Excellent is the condition of human life, since nobody can be miserable, but by his own fault. Does life please you? Live on. Does it not? Go from whence you came." In particular, Seneca argued for suicide in old age, when the body could not discharge its offices. "When age once begins to shatter my understanding and to impair my faculties, when it leaves me not life, but breath only, I will leap in haste from the rotten and tottering structure." Yet Seneca admitted the duty to live for others, such as parent or wife.

Other writers, such as Cato, Epictetus, and Marcus Aurelius might be cited for the same toleration of suicide. Epictetus used the philosophy as a condemnation of complaints. "Live as long as is agreeable; if the game does not please you, go; if you stay, do not complain." [7]

Partly as a result of these philosophies, suicide was a frequent practice under the first Roman emperors. Persons who were ill starved themselves to death; others, for various reasons, serious or trivial, opened their veins

[7] See generally Charles Moore: *A Full Inquiry into the Subject of Suicide* (London, 1790), I. Chap. 4.

or stabbed themselves; and this was frequently in public, and by whole families at once. In the reigns of the Cæsars, numbers of noble families under threat of prosecution for treason committed suicide in order to forestall condemnation; the advantage of this course being that they avoided forfeiture of property and obtained customary burial, which would have been withheld from those executed for crime.

Notwithstanding these practices, Roman law never came to include any general prohibition of suicide. However, in the particular case of those who committed suicide in order to avoid forfeiture of property for crime it was ordained that the property should be forfeit. In order to prevent any possible injustice to the heirs, they were enabled to try the guilt of the deceased, and if his innocence of the crime charged could be proved, they were entitled to his effects.[8] Thus there was no general forfeiture of property for suicide. Another special provision was made for the soldier, who was punishable for attempted suicide on the ground that this was a kind of attempted desertion from his post, which was of value to the state.[9]

The origin of the Christian attitude

There is no condemnation of suicide in the New Testament, and little to be found among the early Christians, who were, indeed, morbidly obsessed with death. Those were the days when, instead of learning how to live, men studied how to die. The Christian belief was that life on earth was important only as a preparation for the hereafter; the supreme duty was to avoid sin,

[8] *Digest of Justinian* 48.21.3.
[9] *Digest of Justinian* 48.19.38 and 49.16.6.

which would result in perpetual punishment. Since all natural desires tended towards sin, the risk of failure was great. Many Christians, therefore, committed suicide for fear of falling before temptation. It was especially good if the believer could commit suicide by provoking infidels to martyr him, or by austerities so severe that they undermined the constitution, but in the last resort he might do away with himself directly.[1] The sect whom St. Augustine particularly noted for this practice was the Circumcelliones; these people not only sought out martyrdom, profaning the temples of paganism in order to be executed, but, when all other expedients failed, cast themselves by the hundreds in ecstasy from lofty cliffs "till the rocks below were reddened with their blood." "To kill themselves," said Augustine, "out of respect for martyrdom is their daily sport."

There seems to be little need to doubt that it was by way of reaction from these religious excesses that Augustine was led to condemn suicide in forthright terms, and so to become the chief architect of the later Christian view. In the first book of his *City of God,* written in the first quarter of the fifth century, Augustine came out strongly for the view that "suicide is a detestable and damnable wickedness." He argued that suicide was a sin greater than any that could be avoided by its commission; it was "an escape from the ills of time by plunging into those of eternity." His chief difficulty in supporting this conclusion was the precedent of the biblical characters and the embarrassing number of saints who had put an end to their own lives without previous disapprobation. Augustine disposed of the case of Samson by saying that he had acted under secret instructions from God; and he speculated that the same might be true of the other instances.

Augustine derived his own attitude in part from the

[1] See generally W.E.H. Lecky: *History of European Morals,* 3rd ed. (London, 1911), II, 43ff.

Sixth Commandment. To kill oneself is to kill a man; therefore, suicide is homicide, and inexcusable. But this is sophistry, for there are obvious differences between an act of violent hostility to another and the act of a man in voluntarily putting an end to his own life. For example, it becomes a man to leave his life voluntarily for a noble cause, when he would have no right to kill others for that same cause. Thus the moral question of suicide cannot be settled by simple logical deduction from the prohibition of murder. The argument has, however, strongly influenced the legal view.

A second argument employed by Augustine was that the suicide deprives himself of the opportunity for a healing penitence—referring to Judas. Yet Judas' suicide was itself the expression of remorse.

Augustine's third argument was stoical in conception, though he rejected the Stoics. The truly great mind, said Augustine, will bear the ills of life. The argument reappears from time to time in the proposition that suicide is an act of cowardice. Now, the only line between cowardice and caution (or wise retreat) is that the coward does not do what he ought to do. To brand the suicide as a coward is, therefore, to beg the question whether there is a duty to go on living.

The true reason for Augustine's stand against suicide appears plainly enough from the historical events of his age. These indicated that a prohibition of suicide was a necessary corollary of the church's other teaching, which would, without this corollary, have operated, and did in fact operate, as an incitement to suicide. If death means annihilation, there can be no point in suicide except as an escape from suffering. But if man's life on earth is merely a period of waiting for a divine glory to be revealed, the true believer is naturally subject to the temptation to accelerate his eternal bliss, unless a new religious rule is devised to forbid it. Augustine himself pointed this out when he said that if suicide were permissible to avoid sin, then suicide would become the logical course for all those who were fresh from baptism. It is not surprising that Augustine recoiled from this result, but he could deny it, within the framework of his own beliefs, only by postulating a divine prohibition of suicide.

The interdiction of suicide, as an inflexible principle, is, then, part of a particular system of religious belief, and need not be accepted by the positivist, or indeed by anyone who does not accept the traditional eschatology.

The dishonouring of the corpse

The first Christian prohibition of suicide is sometimes attributed to the Council of Arles, A.D. 452. In fact, however, this measure was directed only against the suicide of servants (*famuli*). "Not the act, but dislike of its repercussions as they affect the master and landowner, provides the motive which makes the act criminal in certain cases and envisages the suicide as *diabolicus repletus furore*." [2] The earliest disapproval was expressed by the second Council of Orleans, A.D. 533, which allowed churches to receive the oblations (offerings) even of those who were killed in the commission of a crime, provided that they did not lay violent hands on themselves. This indicates that suicide was regarded as worse than any other crime. The fifteenth canon of the Council of Braga, A.D. 563, denied to suicides the usual funeral rites with the eucharist and the singing of psalms. Canon law was adopted into England by the Council of Hereford in 673, and the denial of burial rites was distinctly reaffirmed by a canon of King Edgar in the year 967. [3]

[2] Fedden: op. cit., p. 115, following Bayet: *Le Suicide et la morale* (Paris, 1922), pp. 373ff.

[3] James O'Dea: *The Philosophy of Suicide* (New York, 1882), p. 183.

The Synod of Nîmes, 1284, refused suicides even the right of quiet interment in holy ground.

This canonical development was undoubtedly influenced in part by the writings of St. Augustine; but he had not demanded any punishment for the deed. In fact, as has been seen, Augustine was prepared to justify some historic suicides as specially commanded by God, and, consistently with this theory, he felt himself constrained to admit that even in his own day a person might rightly make away with himself by special command of God: "only let him be very sure that the divine command has been signified." Such a theory is obviously inconsistent with the anathematizing of the suicide's corpse by way of punishment, for what ecclesiastic can say, after the event, whether the divine command was signified or not? There is another reason for absolving Augustine from sole responsibility for these laws. The severe penalty of depriving burial rites smacks of the pagan practice of dishonouring the corpse, and Bayet consequently maintains, with much force, that it represents an irruption into the church of the pre-Christian popular horror of suicide. Like so much else in ecclesiastical practice and belief, it is a pagan intrusion upon the simple philosophy of the Gospels.

On this last point one can go much further. There is nothing in the original Christian doctrine to justify worldly punishment for any sin whatever. The teaching of the New Testament is the other way. The Christian is to judge not, to turn the other cheek, and to refuse to defend even an unjust action at law. This may be an impracticable ethic, but at least the opposite philosophy of life cannot well be justified in the name of the Founder of Christianity.

It will be convenient to continue the later history of the question of burial. By the custom of many countries the burial of a suicide was not only devoid of Christian rites but accompanied by singular marks of ignominy.

Fulbecke, writing in England in 1601, says that the suicide "is drawn by a horse to the place of punishment and shame, where he is hanged on a gibbet, and none may take the body down but by the authority of a magistrate." Blackstone records that burial was "in the highway, with a stake driven through the body"; in practice it was at the cross-roads, and a stone was placed over the face of the suicide. Stake and stone were intended to prevent the body from rising as a ghost or vampire. (Even today this primitive superstition survives in the many ghost stories which assume that the ghost belongs to a person who has either been murdered or committed suicide.) An obvious explanation of the choice of cross-roads is that they also helped to lay the ghost by making the sign of the cross; but though this may have contributed to the survival of the custom into the Christian era, it has a much earlier ancestry. In early times and among primitive peoples even honourable burial was frequently performed at cross-roads, but this spot was also chosen specifically for murderers and suicides. Among the reasons that have been suggested for the practice are that the constant traffic over the grave would help to keep the ghost down; or that the number of roads would confuse it and so prevent its finding its way home; or that the cross would act as the disperser of the evil energy concentrated in the body or the ghost; or that sacrificial victims (these being frequently criminals) were formerly slain on the altars at cross-roads, which were therefore regarded as fitting places for the execution and burial of criminals, after the introduction of Christianity.[4] The last person treated to cross-road burial in England was the suicide Griffith, who was buried in 1823 at the cross-road formed by Eaton Street, Grosvenor Place, and King's

[4] J. A. MacCulloch in *Encyclopedia of Religion and Ethics*, IV, 33; cf. Dublin and Bunzel: op. cit., pp. 205–6; Radzinowicz: *History of the English Criminal Law* (London, 1948), I, 196–7; Stephen: *History of the Criminal Law* (London, 1883), III, 105.

Road, London. This appears to have been a sporadic revival of a custom that had already lapsed,[5] and the following month a statute was passed to abolish it. In its place, burial was to be privately in a churchyard, at night,[6] and without religious rites. In 1882 suicides were allowed to be buried at normal hours. There is a relic of the earlier religious terrorism in that the service of the Church of England still cannot be used for a *felo de se*,[7] but the burial service of any other Protestant denomination (not, of course, the Roman Church) is available. A verdict of mental unbalance by the coroner's jury displaces the legal consequence, because it is accepted by the clergy as enabling them to officiate.[8]

It seems that the only importation of the practice of unholy interment into the United States was in Massachusetts. In that state, in 1660, the legislature announced that it "judgeth that God calls them to bear testimony against such wicked and unnatural practices, that others may be deterred therefrom," and, therefore, enacted that every self-murderer "shall be denied the privilege of being buried in the common burying place of Christians, but shall be buried in some common highway where the

[5] Horace Walpole, writing in 1788 to Hannah More on the subject of suicide, referred to "the absurd stake and highway of our ancestors" (Fedden: op. cit., p. 227).

[6] Burial of suicides at night was also an ancient Jewish custom mentioned by Josephus.

[7] Halsbury: *Laws of England*, 2nd ed., III, 475; Cripps on *Church and Clergy*, 8th ed., pp. 576–7.

[8] According to statements made in the House of Laity on February 6, 1956, the question of Christian burial for repentant murderers and persons who have committed suicide is to be reconsidered by the steering committees of the Church Assembly. Cf. the opinion of Lord Dawson of Penn: "Not so long ago a suicide was made outcast in this world and the next. Now opinion would wish to treat him with consideration, but the law has unfortunately laid it down that his body cannot have a burial service within the Church of England; and so humanity compels a dispensation, and the verdict avers 'temporary insanity' by way of escape. Such matters would have been far better settled within the Church itself." *Parliamentary Debates* (*House of Lords*), vol. 103, col. 484.

selectmen of the town where such person did inhabit shall appoint, and a cartload of stones laid upon the grave, as a brand of infamy, and as a warning to others to beware of the like damnable practices." [9] Although the statute fell into disuse, and was repealed in 1823, it helped to shape a judicial attitude towards suicide which will be studied later.

The forfeiture of property for suicide

Ecclesiastical censures and contemptuous burial were in due course followed, in the various countries of Europe, by secular laws enforcing the forfeiture of the property of suicides. When this forfeiture was first introduced into England is not precisely known. The practice of forfeiture of the goods of a suicide to his lord was already known to the Danes before they came to England, and would naturally have been brought with them.[1] The canon of King Edgar, already referred to, provides that the self-murderer is to be fined in all his goods to his lord; already an exception is made for those whom ill health and madness drove to the perpetration. Bracton repeats the rule of forfeiture of movables, without saying who takes them; the suicide's land, however, is preserved to his heir. Where the reason for the act of suicide is to avoid forfeiture for conviction of capital crime, the suicide, says Bracton, shall have no heir (i.e., there is forfeiture even of land) because the killing of himself is equivalent to a confession of guilt of the crime of which he has been accused.[2] It is not clear whether,

[9] Quoted in Commonwealth v. Mink, below, p. 289. For an instance of such burial in 1707 see John Noble: *A Glance at Suicide* (Cambridge, Mass., 1903), reprinted from Proc. Mass. Hist. Soc., December 1902.
[1] Wilkins: *Leges Saxonicæ*, f. 90.
[2] Bracton: f. 150a.

in stating the latter rule, Bracton is not simply Romanizing; at any rate, this rule is not stated by Britton, who gives only the rule that the chattels of the suicide "shall be adjudged ours, as the chattels of a felon," [3] and no rule of forfeiture of land is found in later practice. [4] Britton's phrase shows that suicide was in his day regarded as a felony, and it also implies that the forfeiture of goods was not to the lord but to the Crown, a fact which is confirmed by Cowell [5] and later authorities. [6]

During the eighteenth century it became the practice for the Crown to waive the forfeiture in cases where the suicide was not committed to avoid conviction of felony, [7] and later the forfeiture was waived even in this case. Thus the provision in the Forfeiture Act, 1870, which abolished forfeiture for suicide or other felony, did no more than give legal effect to the established practice.

When forfeiture was enforced, it was common for coroners' juries to avoid it by returning a verdict of insanity instead of one of *felo de se;* this also had the effect of entitling the deceased to a Christian burial. The indulgence appears to have grown up during the eighteenth

[3] Book 1, Chapter 8.

[4] Coke, *Institutes,* III, Chap. 8. Suicide did not entail escheat because that occurred only after conviction for felony, which *ex hypothesi* was impossible in the case of suicide: Hales v. Petit, 1 Plowd., at 260, 261, 75 E.R., at 398, 400 (1562). Hales v. Petit arose out of the (supposed) suicide by drowning of Mr. Justice Hales, and the arguments relating to forfeiture that were advanced in that case have become almost the *locus classicus* of sophistry. As is well known, they inspired the colloquy of the gravediggers in *Hamlet.* See Wallace: *The Reporters,* 4th ed., pp. 147ff.

[5] Cowell (*Institutiones Juris Anglicani* [1630], Bk. 4, Tit. 18, s. 16; cf. Bk. 2, Tit. 12, s. 4) says that the king distributes the suicide's goods to pious uses, and that according to one opinion there is no forfeiture if the deceased took his life through the weariness of any disease.

[6] See generally Charles Moore: op. cit.; Stephen: *History of the Criminal Law,* III, 104; Pollock and Maitland: II, 488; Holdsworth: III, 315–16.

[7] Umfreville: *Les Coronatoria* (1761). Before that, waiver of forfeiture might depend upon influence: see Fedden, op. cit., p. 193.

century, and was criticized by writers of the period.[8] It survived the abolition of forfeiture, and an investigation of 4,846 inquests on suicide in the year 1928 showed that the verdict of *felo de se* was returned in only 88.[9] At that date the customary verdict was "suicide while temporarily insane," but in the years following, out of consideration for the relatives, this was changed to "suicide while the balance of his mind was disturbed." The frequency of the verdict prompted Joad's aphorism that in England you must not commit suicide, on pain of being regarded as a criminal if you fail and a lunatic if you succeed. But in truth the coroner's jury has an unhappy choice. Either it must return a verdict of mental unbalance, which casts what may be an unmerited aspersion upon the deceased's kindred, and perhaps lowers their stock in the marriage market, or it must return a verdict of *felo de se,* thus depriving the deceased of a Prayer Book burial and helping to render his life-insurance policy void—which will mean that his family will have no right to the return even of the premiums paid.

In order to end the fictitious verdict, the Committee on Coroners [1] recommended that the verdict of *felo de se* should be abolished, and instead there should be the non-committal statement that the deceased died by his own hand. This has not been generally acted upon, and if it were adopted into law it would create difficulty for the clergy, who would have themselves to decide upon the state of mind of the deceased, in allowing or withholding burial according to Anglican rites. Recently, however, some coroners have taken to adopting the new verdict of their own authority, leaving the clergy to settle their problem as best they can.

[8] Hawkins: *Pleas of the Crown* (1724), Book I, Chap. 27; Blackstone: *Commentaries,* IV, 189; Luke Owen Pike: *A History of Crime in England* (London, 1876), II, 197; Fedden: op. cit., p. 227.
[9] W. Norwood East: *Medical Aspects of Crime* (London, 1936), p. 276.
[1] *Cmd 5070 of 1935,* paras. 82–3.

Although, in theory, all civil penalties for successful suicide have now been removed, there remains as a reminder of former ideas the coroner's inquest with its distressing publicity for the sorrowing relatives.

Discussion of the ethics of suicide

To take up again the ethical problem, the next Christian writer of outstanding importance after Augustine was St. Thomas Aquinas. He adduced three further arguments against suicide, two of them of a secular character:[2] (1) Self-destruction is contrary to man's natural inclinations, natural law, and charity—the charity a man owes to himself. (2) Following Aristotle, St. Thomas argued that a man has no right to deprive society of his presence and activity by suicide. (3) Since we are God's property, it is for God to decide on our life and death.

The first argument is reminiscent of Josephus, and is still sometimes heard. It is, in fact, an application of the usual Catholic method of arguing from an assumed "nature" to morals. Actually, the assumption here is wrong; if suicide were always contrary to man's inclinations, it would not occur. The moral question arises because the individual is, in some circumstances, tempted to suicide. It is true that the majority of mankind prefers to be alive than dead; but this is a simple preference which cannot be associated with morals. Not every disregard of a fundamental instinct is wrong; otherwise, as Fedden points out, a monk would be a sinner, for he denies the fundamental instinct of sex.[3]

[2] *Summa Theologica,* Part II, Second Number, Question 59, Art. 3; Question 64, Art. 5; cf. Edward Westermarck: *Origin and Development of the Moral Ideas* (London, 1908), II, 252–4.

[3] H. Romilly Fedden, *Suicide* (London, 1938), p. 282.

Aquinas's second argument, the social one, will be considered later. His third argument is again, in essence, an illegitimate deduction of an "ought" from an assumed "is." God has given us life, therefore we ought not to commit suicide. A neat reply, certainly no less cogent, was that of the elder Pliny: the existence of poisonous herbs with which one may so easily kill oneself is a benevolent gift from God.

The earliest full-scale attack upon the patristic attitude came from the pen of John Donne, Dean of St. Paul's. His *Biathanatos,* published posthumously in 1646, was directed to the thesis "that self-murder is not so naturally sin that it may never be otherwise." Donne went so far as to express the opinion that the practical basis of the law was to frighten the labouring man from suicide, it being "thought necessary by lawes and by opinion of Religion to take from those weary and macerated wretches, their ordinary and open escape and ease, voluntary death." The work was not convincingly reasoned, and did not have so much influence as the much stronger attack made by Hume in his *Essay on Suicide* (also posthumous). Hume thought that man's life was of no more importance to the universe than that of an oyster. If the disposal of human life were reserved to the Almighty, almost any action would become an encroachment on his privilege. "If I turn aside a stone which is falling on my head, I disturb the course of nature and I invade the peculiar province of the Almighty by lengthening out my life beyond the period, which, by the general laws of matter and motion, He has assigned to it." As to the social argument, Hume said: "A man who retires from life does no harm to society; he only ceases to do good; which, if it is an injury, is of the lowest kind." Moral duties imply reciprocity; when I withdraw myself altogether from society, I am no longer bound. And where my life is a positive burden to society, my withdrawal from it is not only innocent but laudable.

These views found little echo in other writers of the time, and they were combated by Charles Moore in the second volume of his monumental work on suicide, published in 1790. The thesis of Moore's argument was that man does not know the importance of his life; even if his life appears to be useless so far, he can never be certain that his life will always continue so, and he may be "counteracting by his abrupt departure some design of Providence." [4] This is, of course, an argument for never taking any decision.

Before Donne, Montaigne had questioned the prevailing attitude, but it was chiefly under the influence of Montesquieu, Diderot, and Voltaire that France took the lead in legalizing suicide by a statute of 1790. This repealed all sanctions against the body and property of the suicide. The French example was later copied by other European countries.

No appreciable volume of opinion against the traditional attitude to suicide appeared in England or America until the present century. It might have been thought that the utilitarian philosophy of the Victorian era would have resulted in a change of opinion, but even utilitarians failed, in the matter of suicide, to face the logic of their own beliefs. Thus Hastings Rashdall, in his exposition of utilitarianism from the Christian angle, refused to absolve the suicide from moral guilt. [5] More recently, however, a growing number of English and American writers challenge the old theology. Most of them, such as the advocates of voluntary euthanasia, which is discussed in the next chapter, are content to argue that suicide is justifiable in some circumstances. But others, such as Harry Roberts and Romilly Fedden, seem to go back to the Epicurean view that suicide is almost if not entirely a matter of individual discretion. Dr. Roberts, after quoting

[4] Charles Moore: *A Full Inquiry into the Subject of Suicide* (London, 1790), I, 38.
[5] *The Theory of Good and Evil* (Oxford, 1907), I, 207–13.

admiringly from Seneca and Epictetus, wrote: "Than these utterances, I know none more noble in the history of philosophy or in that of religion." He went on:

Of how many of us is it true that the world or any part of it would be the loser were we to end our citizenship of it? In my opinion, of very few. Anyway, it seems to me a problem for each person to decide for himself, if any problem is to be left for individual solution. It is well that we should look upon other people's lives as their most sacred and their most personal possession; but I doubt if it is nobility of mind that drives us to attach some cosmic and sacred significance to our own.[6]

Fedden, too, adopts the individualist approach, arguing that suicide is not wrong in the abstract though it may be irresponsible in particular circumstances. He has his own explanation of why suicide is condemned, namely that it is a form of *lèse-majesté*.

Suicide shows a contempt for society. It is rude. As Kant says, it is an insult to humanity in oneself. This most individualistic of all actions disturbs society profoundly. Seeing a man who appears not to care for the things which it prizes, society is compelled to question all it has thought desirable. The things which makes its own life worth living, the suicide boldly jettisons. Society is troubled, and its natural and nervous reaction is to condemn the suicide. Thus it bolsters up again its own values.[7]

If suicide is capable of being morally rightful or at least colourless, it may seem to follow that the provision of agreeable means of suicide is a necessary social service. A French writer, Binet-Sangle, actually goes as far as this.[8] He proceeds from a suggestion in More's *Utopia* to advocate the foundation of a euthanasia institute for completely voluntary state-assisted suicide. Few would

[6] Harry Roberts: *Euthanasia and Other Aspects of Life and Death.* (London, 1936), pp. 31–2.

[7] H. Romilly Feeden: *Suicide* (London, 1938), p. 42.

[8] *L'art de mourir* (Paris, 1919).

be prepared to travel this distance with him, though, as will be shown in the next chapter, there is much support for voluntary euthanasia in the specific case of painful illness. Ruth Cavan, in her study of suicide, discovered that most people have a suicidal impulse at some time. In reply to a questionnaire answered by 201 American students under 30 years of age (i.e., before the really suicidal period of life had set in), fully four fifths said that they had at some time wished for death.[9] Common sense suggests the unwisdom of having an institutionalized means of gratifying such a passing fancy promptly and painlessly. On the other hand, it might be found that such a scientifically certain method of achieving self-annihilation was not popular even among would-be suicides, for complicated psychological reasons which will be mentioned later.

The religious condemnation of suicide is, of course, still maintained. Thus Paul-Louis Landsberg, a religious writer with leanings towards Catholicism, after a full study of the question, solved it to his own satisfaction by saying that suicide as an escape from suffering is wrong because it is God who makes us suffer for our own salvation.[1] But may not even the most sadistic god be satisfied if he has succeeded in driving a man to suicide?

The social argument and the definition of suicide

The present common sense of the suicide problem is that its rightfulness depends upon circumstances. Aquinas's argument that suicide is antisocial is easily refuted in the absolute form in which it is stated. One

[9] Ruth Cavan: *Suicide* (Chicago, 1928), p. 189.
[1] *The Experience of Death. The Moral Problem of Suicide,* trans. by C. Rowland (London, 1953).

need only point to those instances where dying for fellow men becomes, if not a moral duty, at least a superbly honourable act, as in the classic case of Captain Oates, who, with the words "I am just going outside; I may be some time," walked into the Antarctic snow to die, because his illness made him a hindrance to Scott's party and so a danger to his comrades' lives. Scott's comment— "It was the act of a brave man and of an English gentleman"—is a just appraisal of conduct of which we would all like to feel ourselves capable if faced with the agonizing challenge to such decision. No one can imagine that it falls within any moral condemnation of suicide. In general terms, as Sidney Hook expressed the matter:

Far from being a crime against society, suicide may actually further the welfare of society. The logic of utilitarian ethics leads inevitable to this position, to the surprise of a number of its professed adherents. The greatest good or happiness of the greatest number may sometimes be attained by personal sacrifice, as the annals of heroism and martyrdom well attest.[2]

This reply is countered by some writers who escape from the difficulty by defining suicide in such a way as to exclude meritorious self-removal from the meaning of the term. In Catholic doctrine this is achieved by the principle of double effect.[3] Captain Oates, it is said, did not commit "direct" suicide, because he did not wish to die; he merely wished to disembarrass his comrades of his presence. It may be doubted, however, whether Oates, brave man that he was, would have welcomed a protracted existence alone and unprotected in the polar snow, even if this had been possible. Given the choice that he made, death was a merciful release that he might well have welcomed. It is only the emotive effect of the

[2] "The Ethics of Suicide," 37 International Journal of Ethics 173, at 178 (1927).

[3] Cf. Joseph B. McAllister: *Ethics with Special Application to the Medical and Nursing Professions,* 2nd ed. (Philadelphia, 1955), p. 173.

word "suicide" that leads one to wish to withhold it from situations of this type, where man, faced with the challenge to greatness, deliberately chooses to make the sacrifice of life.[4]

Aquinas's social argument was also rejected, for a different reason, by Landsberg, whose work has already been mentioned. He commented that the argument "would perhaps, have a certain value in an ideal society; but, in reality, people often kill themselves because the very imperfect societies in which they are condemned to live prevent them from leading any form of creative life. . . . The argument may be valid in certain cases, where someone may in fact be abandoning an important social duty, but it is clearly inadequate as a general argument against suicide as such."

The issue becomes more concrete when one thinks of the emotional impact of a suicide upon those who come to know of it. A suicide is nearly always a shocking event, since it suddenly reveals to the rest of us the utter despair of one of our fellows. The shock is greatest of all for the immediate family. Landsberg belittled this consideration, but in this I think he showed (if the criticism may be allowed with profound respect) a certain lack of imagination and limitation of experience. He wrote: "As a general argument, this also fails to convince. First of all, a lot of people have no families, or a shattered or detestable family, and secondly, the question is really

---

[4] It may be mentioned that Durkheim, the leading sociological writer on the subject, defined suicide as "any cause of death which results directly or indirectly from the positive or negative act of the victim who knew that it was bound to produce this result" (Emile Durkheim: *Le Suicide* [Paris, 1897], p. 5). This definition would cover altruistic suicides. It would also cover those early Christian martyrs who offered themselves up to a violent death, as Bayet points out.

In old English law, a person charged with felony who, refusing to accept jury trial, was pressed to death (*peine forte et dure*), was not regarded as committing suicide, so that he did not forfeit his property. Here, however, the death was occasioned by the positive act of others; and this act, being authorized by law, did not inculpate the accused who suffered it.

far too personal to be decided by such arguments. Everyone dies sooner or later, and society and the family get over it." On the concluding words, one may say that it is probably true that children will in large degree get over the suicide of a parent; but the suicide of an only son or daughter will almost infallibly destroy the mother's happiness for the rest of her life. If a young person who has parents living commits suicide, he does so either when he is not morally responsible for his act, or from the most utter selfishness and indifference to his obligations to others.[5] Landsberg is, however, right in saying that the family argument does not show all suicide to be wrong, and, therefore, does not support the peremptory religious condemnation. Fedden's views are similar.

In practice the abstract entity "society" is nothing but the striving individuals which compose it. When such of these individuals as are misfits voluntarily remove themselves and their misery by suicide, society directly benefits by their actions. Suicide thus appears as a process by which society rids itself of elements of misery and dissatisfaction. . . .

That suicide may be harmful to a certain section of society, the friends and relatives of the dead man, is sometimes true. As often as not, however, the suicide of the businessman saves his family, and that of the melancholy neurotic comes as a secret relief to those around him. Moreover, those who have others dependent on them do not often kill themselves. Responsibility interposes. Suicide is the act of the solitary. . . .

In all cases where suicide merely forestalls the processes of disease and old age, to speak of society's loss or gain is beside the point. A man has done his work, and reason simply anticipates death. . . . We cannot, in fact, say that suicide is a danger to society, we can only say that sometimes (like mar-

---

[5] To characterize the conduct as (objectively) selfish is not necessarily to subscribe to a philosophy of moral responsibility. Moral judgment is particularly difficult in this instance. It is found that psychopathic adolescents may at times kill themselves, out of spite against their parents, on the most trivial pretexts. See Zilboorg in 92 *American Journal of Psychiatry,* at 1356 (1936).

riage, or anything else) it may be irresponsible, ill-timed, and thus anti-social.[6]

The strongest argument in favour of the popular condemnation of suicide is that it strengthens the will to live. This was the contention of Wilbur Larremore, who, however, rejected the attempt to control suicide by means of the criminal law.

In the vast majority of instances the apparent mountain of anguish would seem but a molehill of temporary embarrassment in the perspective of a long life. If the momentary impulse be resisted, the unfortunate or discouraged one will have many years of average felicity in which to congratulate himself on his self-control. To the end of helping him to bear the ills he has, a strong popular sentiment is of great efficacy. It is of public as well as personal advantage to have suicide in general regarded as immoral, cowardly, and disgraceful.[7]

However, in view of the very large number of suicides and suicidal acts that occur each year, the efficacy of the popular sentiment may be doubted. There are more than 18,000 suicides a year in the United States, and probably an additional 100,000 make unsuccessful attempts to kill themselves.[8] In England, in the year 1955, there were 4,982 suicides and 5,220 attempted suicides known to the police. The official number of attempted suicides, in the sense of suicidal acts, certainly underestimates the actual position. According to a guess of the Statistical Department of the Metropolitan Insurance Company of New York, the number of "attempted suicides" (i.e., suicidal acts) is about six or seven times as great as that of suicides; Professor Stengel thinks that it

[6] Fedden: op. cit., p. 283.
[7] Larremore in 17 *Harvard Law Review* 331 (1904).
[8] 41 *New York State Journal of Medicine* 1720 (1941). See also Frederick L. Hoffman: *Suicide* (Prudential Press, 1927); Harry Alpert: "Suicides and Homicides," 15 *American Sociological Review* 673 (1950).

is probably much larger even than that. One reason why so many suicidal attempts fail to reach the ears of the English police is that it is against medical ethics for a physician to report them.[9] Were he to do so, persons who had unsuccessfully attempted suicide would be discouraged from seeking medical advice and treatment, and the only result would be an increase in the actual number of suicides.

The punishment of attempted suicide in England

The long-vanished history recounted on previous pages is of some legal interest because it helps to explain how England obtained its law of attempted suicide. The English courts punish this act on the reasoning that every attempt to commit a crime is punishable; suicide is a crime; therefore, attempted suicide is punishable. How did the notion originate that suicide is a crime? Although no written memorial now remains, it is fairly easy to recapture the mental processes involved. It will be remembered that the rule in Edgar's canon was that forfeiture of goods was to the lord, whereas according to the later rule it was to the king. The object of the king's judges was to enrich their master, and their readiest argument to this purpose was that suicide was a felony. Since every felon forfeited his goods to the king, it had only to be decided that suicide was a felony to divert the forfeiture from the suicide's immediate lord to the royal coffers. This step had been taken at least by Britton's day. It was, of course, facilitated by the ecclesiastical view of suicide as mortal sin.

The general law of attempts to commit crime is of somewhat late development, and its particular applica-

[9] See (1952) 1 *British Medical Journal* 339.

tion to suicide did not occur until 1854.[1] The criminality of attempted suicide was then ruled as a self-evident truth, and it became firmly established by later decisions.[2] There can be no doubt that incitement and conspiracy to commit suicide are to be treated in the same way.[3]

If we are to find a substantial reason for the punishment of attempted suicide, we must look back into the old authorities which treated suicide as a felony in order to work a forfeiture and for other incidental legal purposes. The reasoning of these authorities naturally reflected the sentiments of their time. In *Hales v. Petit* (1562),[4] when the question of forfeiture was in issue, Mr. Justice Brown said that suicide was criminal as "an offence against nature: because to destroy oneself is contrary to nature, and a thing most horrible. Also against God, because a breach of the commandment; and against the king, in that thereby he has lost one of his mystical members." The concluding reference is to the anthropomorphic theory of the state, with the king as head and the subjects as limbs.

Blackstone, who always excelled himself at finding reasons for legal rules, said that "the suicide is guilty of a double offence: one spiritual, in evading the prerogative of the Almighty, and rushing into his immediate presence uncalled for: the other temporal, against the

[1] Regina v. Doody, 23 L.T.O.S. 12, 6 Cox 463.

[2] Regina v. Burgess, L. & C. 258, 169 E.R. 1387 (1862); Regina v. Mann [1914] 2 K.B. 107 (C.C.A.) For the armed forces, the offence was put on a statutory footing by the Army Act, 1881, s. 38.

Several legal problems remain undecided, and it is to be hoped that they will continue so. Is it criminal for a person wishing to die (1) to refuse to undergo a necessary operation; (2) to refrain from self-preservation when her husband, having proposed a suicide pact, turns on the gas; (3) to go on hunger-strike in prison? The sociological definition of suicide as including omissions (above, p. 270, n. 4) may not apply in law.

[3] Regina v. Leddington, 9 C. & P. 79, 173 E.R. 749 (1839), is frequently misunderstood on this; it turned not on inchoate incitement but on the law of accessories before the fact.

[4] Above, p. 262, n. 4.

king, who hath an interest in the preservation of all his subjects." [5] Commenting upon the first of these reasons, Sir Ernest Barker said:

So far as that great and grave offence is concerned, it would seem to rest between man and his Maker; nor is there any obvious reason in the nature of things, why English law should show a peculiar solicitude in vindicating the prerogative of God. It ceased to burn heretics when the writ *de hæretico comburendo* was abolished in the reign of Charles II; and is not the punishing of suicide, if suicide be regarded as a spiritual offence, on a par with the burning of heretics? [6]

Blackstone's theological justification of the law of suicide becomes all the quainter when it is recollected that English law has always assumed the right to send persons convicted of murder to a premature and unnatural death. If, as is sometimes supposed, suicide is a form of self-murder, then, but for the accident that the culprit is beyond the jurisdiction, he would be punished for his wicked self-destruction by being destroyed.[7] One writer poses this question: suppose the survivor of a suicide pact is sentenced to death for murder in the usual way, and then granted a pardon in the usual way on condition that he submits to life imprisonment: could he refuse the pardon, thus compelling the Crown to enable him to commit suicide *rite ac sollenniter* under the authority of law and by its officers? [8]

Blackstone's second and secular reason was a less metaphysical form of Brown's remark, and meant in effect that society is impoverished by being reduced in numbers. There may well have been a time, in the Middle Ages and afterwards, when this was true. When the lord

---

[5] Blackstone: *Commentaries*, IV, 189.

[6] *The Times* (London), December 24, 1932.

[7] Hawkins saw the difficulty: see his *Pleas of the Crown*, ii, Chap. 37 s. 9.

[8] G. S. Wilkinson in 14 *Modern Law Review*, at 442.

had an interest in his man, and when plagues and wars depopulated the country, the social importance of the individual was manifest. But it was not manifest during the Malthusian scare, and its validity must depend upon the state of population at the time, as well as upon the value of the particular individual to society. A man does not attempt suicide unless he has lost a sense of purpose in life, and feels himself unable to recapture it. Mercier put the position thus:

> Whether the presence in the community of a person whose circumstances are such, or whose mental attitude is such, that he contemplates suicide, is a source of strength or weakness to the community, is arguable; and does not seem so certainly determinable in the former sense, as to justify any very serious attempt, on the ground of the welfare of society, to prevent him, or to deter others, from accomplishing this purpose.[9]

Quite apart from the general debate on the ethics of suicide, the punishment of attempted suicide has to meet the twin objections that it is cruel and inefficacious. The prime fact about suicide is that legal sanctions cannot stop it. No country has ever succeeded in repressing suicide by this method; the threat of punishment for attempted suicide can only make the offender more likely, if anything, to make sure of succeeding at the first attempt. But for most persons the threat will have no effect one way or the other, because people who are bent on throwing their lives away are not likely to consider the possibility of punishment on failure. These simple and obvious truths have often been pointed out. Dr. Harry Roberts wrote:

> It is hard to believe that anyone intent on suicide and with resolution and means to carry it out is ever dissuaded from his purpose by reason of its illegality. It is not unilluminating

[9] Charles Mercier: *Crime and Insanity* (Home University Library, n.d.), p. 127.

that in England the annual number of suicides is seventy-nine per million of the population, whereas in Scotland [where the attempt is not an offence] the figure is forty-five per million.[1]

The argument from humanitarianism is equally strong. The girl stricken with infantile paralysis; the bachelor living alone who suffers from periodic bouts of depression; the woman who has lost her husband and her children in tragic circumstances; the business man overburdened with responsibilities who suddenly feels that life is too much for him—the humanitarian will wish to comfort and relieve them and persuade them that their life still has value for others; but it is not for the criminal law to stand in judgment if they seek to put an end to their misery. To quote Fedden again:

It seems a monstrous procedure to inflict further suffering on even a single individual who has already found life so unbearable, his chances of happiness so slender, that he has been willing to face pain and death in order to cease living. That those for whom life is altogether bitter, should be subjected to further bitterness and degradation seems perverse legislation.[2]

In England, as has just been pointed out, the law of attempted suicide is the result not of deliberate penal policy but of a mechanical legal logic working from a premise developed by mediæval judges for the purposes of enriching the royal treasury. Similar forces were at work in other European countries, but a reform movement arose which scored its earliest success in France. As a result of the critical comments of Beccaria[3] and other writers of the Age of Enlightenment, the crime of attempted suicide was abolished in France after the Revo-

[1] *Euthanasia and Other Aspects of Life and Death* (London, 1936), pp. 15–17. Similar observations are made by Louis I. Dublin and Bessie Bunzel: *To Be or Not to Be* (New York, 1933). Cf. Pike: *A History of Crime in England* (London, 1876), II, 197; 36 *Journal of Criminal Law and Criminology* 441.

[2] Fedden; op. cit., p. 263.

[3] *On Crimes and Punishments,* Chap. 32.

lution. Other European countries, such as Germany, Italy, Switzerland, and the Scandinavian countries, followed suit. Even when Germany and Italy fell under totalitarian governments, pursuing vigorous population policies, they did not reintroduce an offence of attempted suicide; and the same is true of the Soviet Union. Two civil-law countries of the British Commonwealth, Scotland and South Africa, also refrain from punishing this act.[4]

Although English law on the subject has not been altered, the new attitude towards suicide has brought about a considerable change in practice. Before the First World War, imprisonment was quite a regular punishment for attempted suicide,[5] and for a second or subsequent attempt it might be as long as six months.[6] This was sometimes rationalized as a measure "in the interests of the defendant's health,"[7] the theory perhaps being that in prison he would be prevented from repeating the attempt. The change of approach was expressed in 1921, when a Home Office circular to all police forces called attention to the practice of the Metropolitan Police in prosecuting for attempted suicide only where there was some definite circumstance calling for punishment or the order of the court constituted the only chance of refuge and asylum for one too weak to stand alone. This formula was commended for general adoption.[8] Undoubtedly it now represents the general practice of the police, but its interpretation, particularly the interpretation of "some definite circumstance calling for punishment," varies. Some Forces exclude the question of punishment altogether, the Chief Constable refraining from prosecution

---

[4] Some writers make it at any rate a police offence in Scots law (Erskine: *Principles,* 20th ed., p. 612; Anderson: *Criminal Law of Scotland,* p. 148), but prosecutions are unknown. See below, p. 303.

[5] E.g., six weeks in Rex v. Crisp 7 C.A.R. 173 (1912).

[6] Rex v. Mann [1914] 2 K.B. 107.

[7] Rex v. Sanders 9 C.A.R. 119 (1913).

[8] Sir Leonard Dunning in 1 *Police Journal* 46 (1928).

if the culprit has parents or friends or even the Salvation Army to go to and is willing to be looked after; on the other hand there will be prosecution if the culprit declares that he is going to do it again. In the latter event, the magistrate after hearing the case will usually put the defendant on probation, and the probation officer will often succeed in changing his outlook.

Two other statements of police practice are worth quoting for the sake of the limitations expressed in them.

It is seldom that police take action in cases of attempted suicide unless there is some outstanding feature only a prosecution might cure, or if there have been repeated attempts at self-destruction. A severe lecture on their stupidity is mostly delivered to the offenders by a senior officer who has already satisfied himself he can hand over their future well-being to relatives or friends willing to look after them. Lilian Wyles: *A Woman at Scotland Yard* (London, 1952), p. 81.

Attempted suicide is a matter of which the police take cognisance, but once the patient is in medical hands the case, with rare exceptions, is dropped. One of these exceptions is where the patient is not certifiable and refuses voluntary treatment. Another instance is where repeated attempts have been made, and it is evident that these are not genuine, but due to sensation mongering: e.g. a girl several times threw herself down into shallow water where she could not possibly drown, but caused the authorities a lot of trouble by her acts. W. Lindsey Neustatter: *Psychological Disorder and Crime* (London, 1953), p. 68.

There is a legal misconception in the latter passage. If an attempt is not seriously intended, it is not, in law, an attempt, and neither a prosecution nor a conviction is justified. There is no crime of attempted self-manslaughter by knowingly running a risk of death. Annoyance to the authorities is not in itself a reason for convicting of attempted suicide. It is by no means unlikely, however, that a number of convictions for attempted suicide take place where there is no legal foundation for them in the evidence, properly considered. This will be considered again in a moment.

The change of attitude towards attempted suicide is further shown by a number of procedural rules. The charge can be tried summarily by magistrates,[9] and the accused may, on a finding of guilt, be discharged absolutely, or conditionally upon his mere promise not to do it again. Alternatively—and this is a frequent course —he may be put on probation with a condition to submit to mental treatment.[1]

These improvements in practice do not remove some undesirable features. The would-be suicide, if charged, is charged as for a crime.[2] He may be remanded in custody, that is to say, to prison, "for further inquiries," and this is frequently ordered for the deliberate purpose of "calming him down," or to teach him not to make a nuisance of himself—the latter reason is, of course, not a legal justification for remanding in custody before trial. Even those offenders who are ultimately put on probation may have spent some weeks in prison in this way, and the imprisonment will not appear in the criminal statistics.[3] A kinder course is to remand the accused on bail and allow him to become a voluntary patient in a mental hospital during the period of his bail. The worst feature of the present law, however, is the possibility that the defendant may be sentenced upon conviction to a term of imprisonment. This possibility still becomes an actuality in a small proportion of cases. On page 272 the

[9] This now rests on the Magistrates' Courts Act, 1952, s. 19.

[1] Criminal Justice Act, 1948, s. 4.

[2] A recent case was reported in the English press under the heading "Clergyman is accused." The report, after giving the defendant's name and address, stated that the charge was of attempting to commit suicide.

[3] Cf. Cecil Chapman: *From the Bench* (London, 1932), p. 38: "At Wormwood Scrubbs, which is a prison used for first offenders, all prisoners have meals together, and a poor fellow who is remanded for attempted suicide may find himself sitting next to a foul-mouthed criminal who is not likely to do him any good."

figures were given of attempted suicides known to the police in 1955. The following is the record of the proceedings taken. Six persons were tried on indictment for attempted suicide. Four were placed on probation; one was sentenced to imprisonment for eighteen months or two years (the statistics do not make it clear which), and one sentenced to imprisonment for four years. Five hundred and thirty-five persons aged 21 and over were tried summarily. Two were fined, four detained in a police cell (probably for a day only), 41 imprisoned for periods no higher than 6 months (17 were imprisoned for between 3 and 6 months); the rest were treated in the usual ways by being discharged, bound over, placed on probation, or having a reception order made in respect of them; only 28 charges were withdrawn or dismissed. No information is available on what happened to the offenders who were not charged.

It would be interesting to know on what principle of selection a small minority (43 out of 5,220) were selected for incarceration in prison. Can it be that there was no other principle than the idiosyncrasy of the judge or magistrate?

Three illustrations may be given of actual cases, of various dates, where a sentence of imprisonment was imposed.

In 1938 a woman attempted to commit suicide by swallowing spoons, and from that date until 1940, when she was prosecuted, she was in hospital. The magistrates' court sentenced her to six months' imprisonment, but fortunately this sentence was reversed on appeal, the Recorder saying:

"When this woman left hospital she had rid herself of her mental instability and was recovered. I cannot imagine a more certain way of bringing about a return of her mental condition than sentencing her to prison for six months." [4]

[4] 5 *Howard Journal* 228 (1940).

In 1950 the Rochester Bench sent a woman to Holloway for six months for a second attempt at suicide. Her mother had died in a mental home, and she herself had shown other symptoms of being unbalanced. In announcing the sentence the Chairman said: "You have been here before and we gave you every opportunity to go straight." No appeal was taken.[5]

In 1955 a man, after arrest on a charge of larceny, attempted to commit suicide in his cell (or, at least, gave the appearance of such an attempt, by cutting his neck with glass, though as he then proceeded to call the gaoler the seriousness of his intention was open to doubt). The Recorder sentenced him to two years' imprisonment for the larceny and two years for the attempted suicide, the two sentences to run consecutively. On appeal the sentence for attempted suicide was reduced to what was called the "nominal" one of one month. The Lord Chief Justice expressly disagreed with the opinion expressed by the Recorder that "self-murder is one of the most serious crimes on our calendar."[6]

These illustrations show how the law of attempted suicide creates a standing danger of maladministration of justice, especially when individual judges and magistrates may base their decisions upon religious opinions that are no longer held by what may be called enlightened opinion. They disprove the theory, advanced by some apologists for the present law,[7] that people are

[5] *Chatham Observer,* Sept. 16, 1949; Jan. 20, 27, 1950.

[6] Regina v. French, *The Times* (London), December 13, 1955.

[7] Sir W. Norwood East: *Medical Aspects of Crime* (London, 1936), p. 142; Cecil Binney: *Crime and Abnormality* (London, 1949), pp. 132–3. The former says of imprisonment for attempted suicide: "The patients have an opportunity to recover their normal emotional level with the assistance of the rest, good food, quiet and medical attention in the prison hospital." It would be interesting to know whether the author would have liked, say, his wife or mother to have this good treatment, made available to the "patient" as a sentence upon conviction of crime. Contrast the comment of Dr. Hermann Mannheim upon the criminal statistics of attempted suicide: "What a waste of time and labour must have been involved even in this mod-

never sent to prison for attempted suicide except in the fulness of Christian love.

The nature of attempted suicide

It was pointed out on a previous page that a suicidal act is not punishable as an attempt unless it was intended to result in suicide.

Much light has been shed upon this matter, which is of great potential importance in the administration of the criminal law, by a recent medical study made by Professor E. Stengel and Miss Nancy Cook.[8] This study, the result of work carried out at the Institute of Psychiatry in London, indicates that the great majority of so-called attempted suicides are not in fact single-minded efforts at self-destruction. Most persons who commit suicide do it at the first attempt; only about 13 per cent have made a previous suicidal attempt. On the other hand, the persons who unsuccessfully attempt suicide rather seldom achieve it afterwards. Professor Stengel[9] says: "In recent years, several follow-up studies of groups of people who attempted suicide have been carried out, some covering a period of up to ten years. In none of the groups studied more than one in ten committed suicide." Of 138 persons admitted to a London mental observation ward because of so-called attempted suicide, 35 died

erate proportion of prosecutions! Any kind of social, psychological, or psychiatric diagnosis and treatment which was necessary might have been much more effectively carried out without all the stigmatizing paraphernalia of criminal procedure." See his *Criminal Justice and Social Reconstruction* (London, 1946), p. 11; the whole discussion deserves study.

[8] "Recent Research into Suicide and Attempted Suicide," 1 *Journal of Forensic Medicine* 252 (1954); cf. Stengel: "The Reactions of Society to Attempted Suicide," 9 *Howard Journal* 199 (1956).

[9] 9 *Howard Journal* 199.

within the next five years; but of these 35 only one had killed himself. It would seem reasonable to suppose that this result cannot wholly be explained by reference to the mental treatment given in hospital. Thus, there are two populations which only rather slightly overlap each other: the persons who actually commit suicide, and the persons who demonstrate an unsuccessful attempt. The conclusion is supported by various differences between the two populations, e.g., that women are in the majority among those who are said to attempt suicide, while men prevail among the actual suicides.

What, then, is the precise character of the so-called suicidal attempt? Stengel and Cook analyse it in the following words:

If one views suicidal attempt as a behaviour pattern and considers its social aspects, several interesting features emerge. Firstly, in the majority of cases a warning of the suicidal intention, which usually takes the form of an expressed threat or a casual reference to suicide, had been given but had gone unheeded. In many instances this could be established only through careful enquiry. This observation proves that the widely held belief that people who threaten suicide do not attempt it, is erroneous. Secondly, in the suicidal attempt, by which we always mean the unsuccessful one, the contact with fellow beings is as a rule not given up, with the result that they are in a position to intervene. There is reason for assuming that most attempts have a hidden appeal character, i.e. in the constellation of the patient's behaviour a call for help can be discerned. But most attempts have the character of a gamble, the outcome of which depends on chance. They seem unwittingly arranged in such a way that the prospects of survival are not inconsiderable. Such an outcome is almost invariably accepted for the time being and further attempts are rarely made immediately, even if there is no lack of opportunity. The outcome of the attempt is accepted like that of a trial by ordeal in mediæval times. . . .

One of the functions of the suicidal attempt is that of an appeal to society. If that appeal, which is usually unconscious, is heard and understood, the suicidal attempt has fulfilled one of its functions. This appeal character has hitherto been regarded as a feature in the suicidal attempts of hysterical individuals only. Our investigations have demonstrated beyond doubt that it is inherent in most suicidal attempts irrespective of the mental state and the personality of the person carrying it out.

It seems from this that what may be generically called "suicidal acts" are of three kinds. First there are the genuine attempts at suicide, which may or may not succeed, but usually—if they are genuine—do succeed. Secondly, there are the suicidal demonstrations, where what is superficially an attempt at suicide is not seriously meant, but is merely, in Dr. Neustatter's words, "a gesture by a patient suffering from a bad depression, calling upon the world to take notice of his misery." Thirdly, and intermediate between the other two, are suicidal acts that are consciously an attempt at suicide, but unconsciously a gesture. It is in these that the patient gambles his life, running perhaps grave risk of death but unconsciously hoping that it will turn out to be merely a successful gesture, resulting in an improvement of his situation.

The three kinds of suicidal acts call for separate consideration from a legal point of view. Genuine attempts at suicide are offences under present English law. Suicidal demonstrations are not, as such, offences. The legal status of the third group is undetermined; indeed, no court has yet had to pronounce upon unconscious motivation in the criminal law. It seems probable, however, that such motivations, even if proved to the satisfaction of the court, will be ignored, on the ground that legal sanctions can deal only with the conscious mind. If this is so, then the third group will be treated as suicidal attempts.

There is a grave evidential difficulty in distinguishing between the second and third groups. The distinction lies in the conscious purpose of the accused, but this may well be impossible to determine. Generally, in law, intention is inferred from conduct, and so in the present context the court would perhaps incline to go upon the apparent seriousness of the attempt, i.e., upon the degree of risk of death into which the defendant placed himself. Thus, superficial cuts on the neck or wrist might be taken as a demonstration, and deep slashes as an attempt. This criterion is, however, rejected by the medical study just referred to. The authors say:

It is often believed that suicidal acts carried out by patients with a genuine, non-hysterical mental disorder are as a rule more dangerous than those undertaken by hysterical individuals and others. Our investigation did not bear this out. Frequently suicidal attempts made by patients suffering from severe psychotic depression were of such a nature that, had they been carried out by notorious hysterics, they might have been regarded as typical examples of insincere demonstrations. The apparent degree of seriousness of a suicidal attempt cannot, therefore, be taken as a diagnostic aid.

Suicide and transferred malice in England

The punishment for what is essentially an attempted suicide is increased if the would-be suicide accidentially kills another—the commonest case being an attempt to commit suicide with a gun where the shot kills a person who is endeavouring to interpose. Here, by the legal fiction of "transferred malice," it is pretended that the person attempting suicide intended to kill his rescuer, and the killing technically becomes murder.[1] This rule may have harsh consequences, which we are

[1] Rex v. Hopwood, 8 C.A.R. 143 (1913), where, however, the evidence pointed to ordinary murder; Blackstone: *Commentaries,* IV, 189.

no longer ready to tolerate. Thus when a woman jumped from a window, and accidentally killed another in her fall, and also killed herself, the coroner refused to direct the jury to return a verdict of murder against the deceased woman.[2] When a woman struggling to shoot herself shot her lover instead, the judge allowed the jury to bring in a verdict of manslaughter.[3]

It is convenient to mention here two other minor results of the common-law attitude towards suicide. Since suicide is a felony, the conclusion was drawn by an American judge that "everyone has the right and duty to interpose" to prevent it.[4] It is a freak result of present legal principles if there is a duty to save a would-be suicide from drowning, when there would be no such duty if he did not wish to drown. In fact, however, the validity of the rule is doubtful. An English judge said: "If I saw a man, who was not under my charge, taking up a tumbler of poison, I should not become guilty of any crime by not stopping him."[5] In any case the duty to prevent felony, if it ever existed, is no longer enforced.

There is a presumption against suicide (as against any other crime) where such an issue arises in a civil case. If, however, the fact of suicide and sanity is proved, no recovery can be had in England under a life policy. This rule applies, with remorseless logic, whatever the particular circumstances, as where a cancer patient commits suicide to avoid a horrible end. If the coroner's jury returns a verdict of "suicide while the balance of his mind was disturbed," instead of a verdict of *felo de se,* the policy moneys are in practice recoverable, for then it must be taken that there is no crime.[6] Since juries proceed on no ascertainable principles in the form of their

[2] Quoted by Fedden: op. cit., p. 263.
[3] Rex v. Barney, *The Times* (London), July 7, 1932.
[4] Per Gray C.J. in Commonwealth v. Mink, 123 Mass. 422 (1877).
[5] Per Hawkins J. in Regina v. Paine, *The Times* (London), February 25, 1880.
[6] Cf. Hale, *Pleas of the Crown,* I, 412.

verdicts, the right of recovery of insurance moneys depends on a fortuitous circumstance.

Attempted suicide and transferred malice in the United States

In America the question of suicide first came before the courts of Massachusetts, and it seemed in early years that the English view would be fully adopted. Although the English law of forfeiture had not been imported into Massachusetts, the disapproval of suicide was expressed in the law of burial (above, p. 260), and this had an effect on the earlier decisions. In a case of 1816 suicide was pronounced a felony, so that a successful counselling of suicide was murder.[7] However, in 1870 it was held that attempted suicide was no offence, because the statute law on the subject of attempt did not provide for attempted suicide, and had to be taken as exhaustive.[8] This was merely a decision on statutory construction, and no pronouncement was made on the general attitude towards suicide. Hence in 1877 the court felt itself able to attach a partial sanction to attempted suicide. It was held that a person who attempted suicide, and who accidentally killed another in the attempt, was guilty at the least of manslaughter if not murder. "Since it has been provided by statute that 'any crime punishable by death or imprisonment in a state prison is a felony, and no other crime shall be so considered,' it may well be that suicide is not technically a felony in this Commonwealth. . . . But being unlawful and criminal as *malum in se,* any attempt to commit it is likewise un-

[7] Commonwealth v. Bowen, 13 Mass. 356, 7 Am. Dec. 154.
[8] Commonwealth v. Dennis, 105 Mass. 162.

lawful and criminal."⁹ This decision rests not on the law of transferred malice, but on the law of constructive homicide, though the result is much the same either way.

A few states still approximate to the English position on suicide. In South Carolina the court was prepared to hold that suicide retained its character as a common-law felony, and accordingly that the law of transferred malice applied.¹ It is not clear whether attempted suicide is a crime in that state. It is, however, a crime in New Jersey.² This is distinctly a minority position. In New York the Penal Code of 1882 (s. 178) punished attempted suicide, and this was incorporated also into the law of North and South Dakota. But the provision fell into disuse in New York,³ and was repealed in 1919. Attempted suicide is not an offence in Indiana,⁴ Iowa,⁵ Maine,⁶ or Pennsylvania,⁷ and the decisions make it plain that it is also unpunishable in Ohio, Illinois, and Texas (below, pp. 300–1).

The English rule that suicide prevents recovery under a life policy is followed in the United States as a matter

⁹ Commonwealth v. Mink, 123 Mass. 422, 25 Am. Rep. 109.

¹ State v. Lovelle, 13 S.E. 319 (1891).

² State v. Carney, 55 Atl. 44 (1903). The reason given was that state legislation punished all offences of an indictable nature at common law, if not otherwise provided for by act of the legislature.

³ See May v. Pennell, n. 6, below.

⁴ Prudential Ins. Co. of America v. Rice, 52 N.E. (2d) 624 (1944). Held that there were no common-law crimes in Indiana, and attempted suicide was not made a crime by statute. The court saw nothing against public policy in enforcing a policy of insurance where the injury occurred through an attempted suicide.

⁵ State v. Campbell, 251 N.W. 717 (1933). Held that there were no common-law crimes in Iowa, and attempted suicide was not made unlawful by statute. If the accused shot the deceased while attempting suicide, he was not doing an unlawful act, and hence was not guilty of murder under the doctrine of killing in the course of an unlawful act. It was left open whether he could be convicted of either murder or manslaughter by the reckless use of deadly weapon.

⁶ May v. Pennell, 64 Atl. 885 (1906).

⁷ Commonwealth v. Wright, 26 Pa. Co. Ct. 666 (1902).

of common law, but several states have statutes providing that suicide is no defence to the company if it occurs after a specified period, unless the assured intended to take his own life when he effected the insurance. Canada also has certain legislation modifying the common law on this subject.[8]

Legislative proposals for the treatment of attempted suicide

Proposals for a change in the English law of attempted suicide are sometimes resisted on the ground that the police must have power to prevent a person laying violent hands on himself. Even granted the condemnation of suicide implied in this argument, the experience of many countries, and indeed English experience itself, shows that the use of the criminal law is unnecessary. When a case of attempted suicide comes to the notice of an English physician, his professional code forbids him to inform the police; but he has adequate means of dealing with the situation without their aid. He may send the patient into a general hospital, or persuade him to become a voluntary patient in a mental hospital. If the patient refuses both courses and appears to be still suicidal, there will often be sufficient indication of mental unbalance to warrant certification in order to give the patient care and protection for his own safety. If, however, the person attempting suicide is of sound mind in every way, no case for interference, otherwise than by persuasion, exists.

In some instances, the legal powers possessed by the police are a positive hindrance to medical treatment.

[8] See Dublin and Bunzell: op. cit., Chap. 19; 17 *Canadian Bar Review* 508 (1939).

Professor Stengel's comments upon the situation, based on his medical experience, are as follows:

The fear that a suicidal attempt may lead to prosecution tends to make some people lie to the doctor about it and maintain that it was an accident, thus making psychiatric treatment impossible and a repetition more likely. . . .

Who decides whether or not a charge should be brought? The local police officer, probably acting according to directions from his superiors. Those directions vary from place to place, and from time to time, and so do their interpretations. Often the police officer informs the doctors in hospital that unless the patient is sent to a mental hospital, even against his will, he will bring a charge for the purpose of having the patient put on probation under the condition that he consents to hospital treatment. I do not know of a case in which the police officer had consulted the medical expert about the treatment required, which, of course, he is not obliged to do under the law. Some weeks ago I was called into a general hospital to see a woman who had made a suicidal attempt following the discovery of her husband's infidelity. I found her quite calm and formed the opinion that there was no need for her to enter a psychiatric hospital as an in-patient. She was willing to attend an out-patient department. I then learned that the local police inspector had sent a message asking to let him know when the patient was going to be discharged as he intended to bring a charge against her so that she would be bound over under the condition that she would undergo hospital treatment. But there was no need for this pressure at all. I wrote a letter to the police officer stating the facts and pointing to the harmful effect which appearance in court might have on the patient. No proceedings were taken, but the case illustrates how the law is applied. Had I not intervened, the poor woman, who had been punished enough, might have had to suffer further humiliation. That her husband would have suffered, too, would have been small comfort, and the chances of reconciliation would not have been improved by court proceedings. In some areas, people who are known to have made their second suicidal attempt are charged indiscriminately. Sometimes the only way of protecting one's patients against this traumatic experience is to keep them in hospital for a time.[9]

Even if some official powers are thought desirable in the case of attempted suicide, this does not require the use of the criminal law. Wilbur Larremore suggested that one who attempts suicide should be classed not as a criminal but as an unfortunate person amenable to temporary deprivation of liberty. He should be made subject to restraint in the discretion of the magistrate not exceeding a brief, definite period.[1] This suggestion has not been adopted by any legislature, and, so far as is known, no inconvenience has been felt to arise from the absence of specific powers in those American jurisdictions that do not punish attempted suicide. Theoretically, however, the law should allow some right of interposition to prevent a suicide. Self-destruction is frequently the outcome not of the settled philosophical determination of a balanced mind but of a passing impulse or temporary depression. The natural and human thing to do with a person who is suddenly discovered attempting suicide is to interpose to prevent it. This interposition, where only mild force is used, cannot be accounted a battery upon the would-be suicide. Following the frustration of the attempt, there may have to be some temporary restraint or surveillance while it is considered whether the attempter can be medically treated or dissuaded from the attempt. To justify this interference with liberty, it may well be thought that there should be the ultimate safeguard of a magistrate's order—which leads back to Larremore's suggestion. However, even if this suggestion is thought to have sufficient in its

---

[9] 9 *Howard Journal* 199 (1956).

[1] 17 *Harvard Law Review* 331, at 340 (1904). An approach to the idea is seen in the legislation of six states (Montana, New York, North and South Dakota, Oklahoma, and Washington) allowing any person to restrain another person who is deprived of reason (even though temporarily) from committing an act dangerous to himself or to another.

favour to justify its enactment, there would be no need for the hearing by the magistrate to take place in public; and to allow the proceedings to be reported would be a gratuitous invasion of the patient's privacy at a time when he needs to be protected from unnecessary strain. Further, there would be no need for a magistrate's order unless the patient positively requires it. The magistrate should presumably have a wide discretion as to the place and conditions of detention and the person under whose surveillance the patient is to be placed. It is probable that legal provisions along these lines would in practice remain in the background; it would probably be rare for the machinery actually to be invoked.

A very short time limit should be placed on the detention order, unless the patient is certified, and it should be provided that no second detention order should be made unless quite a substantial period has elapsed in the meantime. Ultimately, society cannot stop a free man from committing suicide, nor should it try. What can be done is to make sure that the determination upon self-destruction is fixed and unalterable.

It may be expected that a proposal along these lines would enjoy a large measure of support. It could be supported by those who regard suicide as indifferent to morals, and it could also be supported by those who regard suicide as wrong but legal attempts at repression as useless. In 1947 a special committee set up by the Council of the British Medical Association contemplated a scheme very much on these lines, recommending that attempted suicide should cease to be a legal offence, but tentatively suggesting that a guardianship procedure might be devised for adults in need of care or protection.[2] The committee pointed out, however, that legal machinery was hardly ever required for making a patient accept treatment. This authoritative statement raises once again the doubt whether special legal provision of any kind is worth while.

[2] *British Medical Journal,* Supplement, May 17, 1947, p. 103.

Men who repeatedly attempt suicide when under the influence of drink present a special problem, which is, however, an aspect of the general problem of the treatment of drunkenness rather than one calling for a law of suicide.

Suicide is sometimes attempted in ways constituting what is in fact, whether or not it is in law, a public nuisance—for example, when a man repeatedly steps in front of oncoming traffic and invites the drivers to run him down. Often the circumstances of such conduct will indicate that there was not a genuine attempt at suicide, so that even the present law, if honestly and properly applied, provides no solution. There is, however, no penological reason for not punishing demonstrations of this kind. To do so would require a specially devised law, aimed not against attempted suicide but against deliberate self-endangerment to the nuisance, annoyance, or danger of others. Whether such self-endangerment should be made a special offence depends upon how frequent and serious a cause of annoyance it is found to be. The guardianship procedure previously suggested would certainly be preferable to the creation of a new offence.

Studies of the causation of suicide

The statistics of suicide and attempted suicide quoted previously indicate a social and medical problem of large importance. Since the law of attempted suicide purports to be a method of controlling suicide, it is of some interest to consider the causes of suicide in order to discover whether there are any other or more effective methods of control. This subject can, however, be mentioned only briefly in the present work.

Many sociological studies have been made attempting

to correlate suicide with other social facts, such as economic depression, murder rates, social status, insanity, and the degree of integration of society. There are also psychological studies of suicide as a release of aggression. Among the leading writers in the field are Durkheim in France, Masaryk in Austria, Morselli in Italy, and Ruth Cavan and Messrs. Andrew F. Henry and James F. Short in the United States. Gregory Zilboorg, in a study of suicide among civilized and primitive races, has exploded the notion that the suicide rate increases with the development of civilization, and that it is necessarily connected with mental disease.[3] Certainly the correlation with insanity is much below that suggested by coroners' verdicts. East's finding has already been reported that out of 4,846 inquests on suicides in England in the year 1928, the verdict of *felo de se* was returned in only 88, the rest being attributed to temporary insanity. His own opinion, based on an examination of 3,000 cases of attempted suicide, was that only a fifth of all suicides were insane in fact.[4] This proposition obviously depends upon a particular definition of insanity, and if one were to look for mental abnormality instead of insanity in the narrow sense the proportion would become higher—amounting to a hundred per cent if suicide were itself taken as a conclusive symptom of derangement. Between these extremes, Sainsbury found that of the cases that he studied, mental disorder appeared to be the principal factor in 37 per cent, and in an additional 17 per cent the personality appeared to have been abnormal.[5] Tredgold expressed the opinion that "compulsive obsessions are a much more frequent cause of suicide, and perhaps even of homicide, than is generally thought." [6]

[3] 92 *American Journal of Psychiatry* 1347 (1936).

[4] W. Norwood East: *Medical Aspects of Crime* (London, 1936), p. 276; same in (1931) 2 *British Medical Journal* 242.

[5] P. Sainsbury: *The Ecology of Suicide in London* (London, 1954).

[6] *Mental Deficiency,* 8th ed. (London, 1952), pp. 327–8.

Many economic, social, and individual factors have been found to be statistically associated with the suicide rate; but according to Sainsbury's recent English study, the most significant correlations are in respect of social isolation (persons living alone and in boarding-houses and hotels), social mobility (immigrants, etc.), and social disorganization (divorce, illegitimacy). The investigation is of value in indicating the type of social remedy that may usefully be tried.

The punishment of secondary parties in England

In the Middle Ages forfeiture was the only legal consequence of suicide, apart from the special feature of burial; but the development of the law of secondary parties to a crime enabled an important step to be taken. It came to be held by the English courts that the survivor of a suicide pact was guilty of murder by construction of law, because he was a principal in the second degree to the self-murder of the other. Thus if a man and woman agreed to commit suicide together, and the woman died but the man survived, he could (and can) be charged with the murder of the woman. But if the survivor were a wife, it seems that she could not at common law be successfully charged with the murder of her husband, because she was shielded by the presumption of coercion.[7] The presumption was abolished by Parliament in 1925. Although it was hardly the intention of Parliament at that date to extend the harsh rule relating to suicide pacts, such was the effect, and the wife thenceforth became subject to the law.

[7] But the only case in point is imperfectly reported: *Anon.* (1604), Moo. K.B. 754, 72 Eng. Rep. 884; Wallace: *The Reporters,* 4th ed. (Boston, 1882), p. 123.

There was formerly another beneficent technicality to protect the accessory before the fact. If one man incited another to commit suicide, and was absent when he did it, the inciter was technically an accessory before the fact to the other's self-murder, and so himself guilty of murder; but he could not be convicted, because of the rule that an accessory could not be convicted before the conviction of the principal. Since, here, the principal never could be convicted, the accessory was safe. The general rule for accessories was altered by Parliament in 1861, but without accessories to suicide specially in mind; and it was at first held that the statute did not intend to alter the law for the particular case of the accessory before to suicide, who thus remained unpunishable as such.[8] Later, for no very clear reason, and indeed without any discussion of the question, this view was reversed;[9] and the accessory before is now punishable as for murder.

These developments are good examples of the purely mechanical manufacture of criminal law, with no reference to penal policy. No judge has ever considered whether a secondary party to suicide ought to be treated in the same way as a secondary party to the murder of another. Policy is considered only in exercising executive clemency, and here the Home Secretary has to work with the legal presupposition that suicide pacts are in principle punishable. The practical result is a compromise between the postulate of punishment and considerations of humanity. It has long been the custom to commute the death sentence if the suicide pact was genuine, and

---

[8] Rex v. Russell, 1 Mood. 356, 168 Eng. Rep. 1302 (C.C.R. 1832); Regina v. Leddington, 9 C. & P. 79, 173 Eng. Rep. 749 (1839).
[9] Regina v. Gaylor, D. & B. 288, 169 Eng. Rep. 1011 (C.C.R. 1857); Rex v. Croft [1944] K.B. 295 (C.C.A.). In the latter case, counsel for the defence did not cite Rex v. Russell, last note; counsel for the prosecution cited it, but only in a misleading quotation from Russell on *Crimes,* which did not state the decision fully; apparently no one engaged in the case looked up the report, and the court acted in ignorance of it.

not a mere device to get rid of an unwanted companion. In such cases the period of detention varies; it may be very short. If, however, it is doubtful whether there was a genuine attempt or intention by the survivor to commit suicide on his own part, it has sometimes been thought right to let the law take its course.[1]

It was said before that the secondary party is held guilty of murder because he is a party to the self-murder of the other. Although suicide was regarded as self-murder by the older authorities, and is still self-murder for this particular purpose, a contradictory conclusion on the point of principle was reached in one case,[2] which decided that an incitement to suicide is not an incitement to murder within the meaning of a statute attaching an increased penalty to this particular offence. Consequently, English law says that suicide both is and is not self-murder for different purposes.

There is a difference of legal analysis between what may be called respectively the double-suicide pact and the murder-suicide pact. In the first, each party agrees to commit suicide, as by drinking poison. Here the survivor is, as already stated, a principal in the second degree to the self-murder of the other. In the murder-suicide pact, one party kills the other with the latter's consent, under an agreement or understanding that he is then to commit suicide. An example is where a husband, by agreement, shoots his wife and then turns the gun upon himself. If he kills his wife but survives himself, he is guilty of ordinary murder as principal in the first degree, since it was by his own hand that his wife met her death, and her consent to be killed was neither an excuse nor, in law, a circumstance of mitigation. This consent may, however, result in the exercise of executive

---

[1] *Royal Commission on Capital Punishment, Report, Cmd 8932 of 1953*, para. 165; same: *Minutes of Evidence* (1949), 3–4.

[2] Regina v. Burgess, L. & C. 258, 169 Eng. Rep. 1387 (1862); see Mikell in 3 *Columbia Law Review* 379 (1903).

clemency, just as in the case of the double-suicide pact. The purely technical nature of the distinction between the two kinds of pacts may be illustrated by an agreement between spouses to "commit suicide" by gassing themselves in a closed room. Let us suppose that after all preparations have been made the husband turns on the gas. If he survives, he is guilty of murdering his wife as principal in the first degree, since it is his hand that has killed her, and the case is one of a murder-suicide pact. If the wife survives and the husband dies, she is guilty as principal in the second degree to the suicide of her husband, the case from her point of view being the same as in the double-suicide pact. It would be discreditable if any actual legal consequence were made to hinge upon such distinctions.

The excessive severity of the common law in treating homicide upon request or with consent as ordinary murder has sometimes been remarked upon, and under Macaulay's influence the Indian Penal Code adopted a mitigated penalty for this crime.[3] The same is true of the penal codes of several European countries.

The punishment of secondary parties in the United States

American jurisdictions treat the instigator or conspirator in suicide in one or other of three ways. Some punish him as a party to the suicide, or as a murderer on his own account. Some regard him as not guilty of crime. And some make him guilty of a special offence.

In those few states, such as South Carolina, which appear to adopt the English rules on suicide, the instigator

[3] See Macaulay: *Works* (Lady Trevelyan, ed., 1866), *Notes on the Indian Penal Code*, 1837, pp. 503–4.

or conspirator is presumably punishable as a principal or accessory in murder.[4] With these states may be grouped Ohio and Illinois, which furnish examples of how the English doctrine may be rejected in words but accepted in its practical consequences. It was held in 1872[5] that suicide was not a crime in Ohio, and therefore there could be no accessories or principals in the second degree to suicide. However, the court proceeded to say that administering poison to another was a crime, irrespective of the consent of the other; and moreover that it was an administering of poison (within the meaning of a statute) merely to furnish poison to the other with intent that he should with it commit suicide. This seems to be a strained construction of the statute, and it goes far to nullify the previous proposition that there can be no accessory to suicide. The court further held that it was a crime if the accused, without furnishing any poison, was merely "present at the taking thereof by the deceased, participating, by persuasion, force, threats, or otherwise, in the taking thereof." In view of this extended notion of killing, the participant in a suicide pact seems to be just as punishable as if suicide itself were deemed criminal. It is not clear whether one who counsels suicide but is absent from the event is punishable.

The Ohio decision was cited with approval by an Illinois court in 1903.[6] This court disapproved the early Massachusetts view that suicide was a felony, explaining the non-adoption of the English view by saying that "as we have never had forfeiture of goods, or seen fit to define what character of burial our citizens shall enjoy, we have never regarded English law as to suicide as applicable to the spirit of our institutions." But it was held to be murder either to administer poison to another

---

[4] Cf. McMahan v. State, 53 So. 89 (1910); People v. Roberts, 178 N.W. 690 (1920).

[5] Blackburn v. State (1872) 230 Oh. St. 146.

[6] Burnett v. People, 68 N.E. 505.

(who intended to commit suicide) or to persuade or procure another to take poison for that purpose; and such a
person could be indicted for murder upon the death of
the victim. The court referred to the rule that it is a
crime to persuade a lunatic to commit a criminal act,
and seems, therefore, to have intended to base its decision on the opinion that one who procures another to
commit suicide commits murder through an innocent
agent. This opinion, however, involves some rather subtle
metaphysics, for not only is the person who commits suicide an innocent agent according to the law of the state,
but the consequence (viz., his own death) is, on the
reasoning of the court, legally innocent; hence it is difficult to see how the doctrine of innocent agency can inculpate the procurer.

Texas is a representative of the most lenient attitude
towards suicide found in the United States. In 1902,
Justice Davidson declared: "It is not a violation of any
law of Texas for a person to take his own life. Whatever may have been the law of England . . . it does not
obtain in Texas. So far as the law is concerned, the
suicide is innocent; therefore the party who furnishes
the means to the suicide must also be innocent of violat-
ing the law." Consequently he held that where the accused merely prepared poison, and the deceased took it
freely with intent to commit suicide, this was not murder.[7] The case was followed in 1908, the same judge
saying: "It may be a violation of morals, and reprehen-
sible, that a party may furnish another poison or pistols,
or any other means or agency for the purpose of the
suicide to take his own life, yet our law has not seen
proper to punish such persons or such acts."[8] However,
a distinction was drawn between the mere supply of the
materials of suicide and a direct killing. If the accused
went so far in assisting the deceased as to shoot him,

[7] Grace v. State, 69 S.W. 529.
[8] Sanders v. State, 112 S.W. 68.

or by his own hand to administer the poison, placing it in the mouth of the deceased, this was murder, the consent of the deceased being no defence.[9] Although this is a distinction that occurs naturally to the legal mind, it is too technical to be satisfactory.

Intermediate between the states that punish the instigator as a murderer and those that acquit him are those that convict him of another offence. Thus Missouri treats the case as one of manslaughter.[1] New York, too, when it did away with the offence of attempted suicide in 1919, retained the punishment of manslaughter for those who assisted or encouraged another to take his life or to attempt to do so.[2]

The punishment of secondary parties in other countries

Critics of the laws of suicide who argue that suicide should not as such be regarded as a crime are generally content to allow instigators and conspirators to be punished as for a special offence—the solution adopted, as has been seen, in states like New York. This was proposed by the Draft Code of the English Criminal Law Commissioners of 1879, s. 183, and again by the Royal Commission on Capital Punishment in 1953, the proposed punishment being imprisonment for life. From the severity of the proposed maximum punishment it will be seen that the offence was regarded by both Commissions as potentially a serious one, though

[9] Sanders v. State, last note; Aven v. State, 277 S.W. 1080 (1925).
[1] R.S. Mo. 1939 s. 4383.
[2] Penal Law, ss. 2304, 2305. See also Cal. Penal Code s. 401 (Deering, 1949); Minn. Stat. Ann. (1945) s. 619.03; Wisc. Crim. Code s. 940.12.

not heinous enough to justify the automatic death-penalty carried by the conviction for murder. The suggestion of 1879 has been generally adopted in the codes of different parts of the Commonwealth.[3] The Indian Penal Code, s. 306, is more lenient, reducing the punishment of the abettor to ten years' imprisonment if the person who committed suicide was eighteen years of age and of sound mind; if these conditions are not satisfied the abettor is punishable with imprisonment for life. This section applies also in Pakistan and Ceylon. The survivor of a suicide pact seems not to be guilty of any offence in these countries, provided that he did not instigate the suicide or kill with his own hand.

Almost all countries outside the influence of the common law have legal rules or practices for according leniency to suicide pacts, without having to invoke executive clemency after conviction for murder. In Scotland, prosecutions are unknown, and some deny that suicide pacts are even technically punishable. Mr. Norman D. Macdonald, joint author of Macdonald's *Criminal Law of Scotland,* wrote:

If two agree to commit suicide together and jump into the Tweed hand in hand from the south bank the survivor has the terrible ordeal of a trial on the capital charge and may be hanged. To do likewise from the north bank would not bring him even to police-court, nor would he be arrested, for it is not even a misdemeanour to attempt suicide in Scotland. He has taken no life, not even his own, and would seem more a subject for pity or for mental care than a hanging or even prison.[4]

---

[3] *Report of the Royal Commission on Capital Punishment, Cmd 8932 of 1953,* pp. 447–8.

[4] Letter to *The Times* (London), December 24, 1932. In the absence of precise authority, however, there is always the possibility of the survivor being held punishable. Cf. *Royal Commission on Capital Punishment, Minutes of Evidence, Memorandum by the Faculty of Advocates of Scotland; Report, Cmd 8932 of 1953,* paras. 44, 167.

Similarly, in South Africa suicide is not regarded as a crime and a suicide pact is not punished.[5] In countries of the European continent the general solution is to punish instigation to suicide and abetment of suicide but to make special provision for suicide pacts. French law attempts to settle the problem by distinguishing between suicide proper and homicide in pursuance of an agreement. In the case of suicide proper, all the participants are guiltless. In the case of homicide in pursuance of an agreement, the survivor incurs the penalties of murder, because the consent of the victim is no justification for the killing. The choice between the two descriptions will depend upon the facts, and particularly upon the degree of initiative which can be imputed to the survivor. In practice the difficulty is nearly always surmounted by the constant indulgence of the jury.[6]

Switzerland has a more precise provision. According to the federal criminal code of 1937, which came into force in 1942, killing another with his consent is punishable, but inciting to suicide or lending assistance with a view to suicide is punishable only if the inciter is impelled by selfish motives; hence a physician who provides poison for a patient suffering from fatal illness is free from responsibility (Arts. 111—15). In the Soviet Union suicide and attempted suicide are not crimes; but for a person to influence another, who is in a position of dependency upon him, to commit or attempt to commit suicide is punishable by deprivation of liberty for five years. "Influencing" includes criminal conduct driving the other to suicide. The relation of dependency may be between master and servant, official and subordinate, husband and wife, and parent and child. Instigating the suicide of a person in a dependent position is

---

[5] Gardiner and Landsdown: *South African Criminal Law and Procedure,* 5th ed., II, 1408.

[6] Professor Donnedieu de Vabres in *Royal Commission on Capital Punishment, Minutes of Evidence* (1949), 816.

also punishable if that person is a minor or an adult known to be incapable of understanding the nature or significance of his acts.[7]

Legislative proposals for the treatment of secondary parties

A discussion of legislative policy on the subject of abettors in suicide may start from the proposition, now generally agreed by all save one or two writers who defend the English practice, that attempted suicide should not be punishable, if only because the punishment of a genuine attempt can have no other effect than to make the individual particularly careful to succeed. If this is agreed, it seems necessarily to follow that the survivor of a genuine suicide pact should not be punished. Suicides in pursuance of a pact are merely cases of double or multiple suicides. There can be no more justification for punishing an attempted double suicide than for punishing an attempted individual suicide. As in the case of an attempt at individual suicide, punishing the survivor of a genuine pact can serve no deterrent purpose, may hinder medical treatment, and is merely useless cruelty. It can do no more than strengthen the will to succeed in the act of self-destruction.

The only trouble is in distinguishing the genuine suicide pact from the case where the survivor pretended to agree for the purpose of getting rid of his companion and without any real intention to commit suicide himself. Perhaps it was this that weighed with the Royal Commission on Capital Punishment, which refrained

[7] See Harold J. Berman: "Principles of Soviet Criminal Law," 56 *Yale Law Journal* 803, at 828 (1947). See generally also, on comparative law, Yosef Nedova: "A Comparative Study of Suicide" (unpublished thesis for the degree of Ph.D. in the University of London, 1955).

from recommending that the survivor should be exempt from punishment.[8] Yet the Commission admitted that no difficulty was shown to have been experienced in Scotland, which does not punish suicide pacts, and that the majority of English witnesses, including Judges, the Director of Public Prosecutions, and several former Home Secretaries, considered that it would be possible to frame an amendment of the law which would not open the door to abuse.[9] Difficulties of fact-finding must always be faced in the application of legal rules, and they must be faced at present in determining upon executive clemency.

If the reader has travelled so far in accord with these proposals, he may be invited to take one additional step. This is to assimilate the murder-suicide pact with the double-suicide pact. Failure to make such an assimilation is a point of criticism of those countries, such as Switzerland, which generally refrain from punishing the survivor of the suicide pact proper, but punish "homicide upon request." The artificiality of this line has already been indicated by the illustration of a couple's agreement to commit suicide by gassing themselves. The most that Continental countries do is to provide a reduced punishment for homicide upon the request of the victim;[1] this is an improvement on the English position, where no reduction is provided by law, but does not meet the objection to providing any punishment at all in murder-suicide cases.

Here, again, the present law is defended by those who argue that the risk of fraud presents an insuperable obstacle to change. The Royal Commission on Capital Punishment thought that this risk was inevitably greater for the murder-suicide pact than for the double-suicide

[8] See the *Report, Cmd 8932 of 1953*, para. 168.
[9] Ibid., para. 169.
[1] See the same *Report*, pp. 449–51.

pact.[2] However, the Commission proceeded to forget this objection when it recommended that the situation should be left to the discretion of the Home Secretary in the exercise of the prerogative of mercy. Evidently fraud, if it exists, may impose upon the Home Secretary just as it may upon a judge and jury. It is submitted that the only question relates to the framing of the rule of exemption; once this is done, there is no reason for preferring the fact-finding ability of the executive to that of the ordinary courts of law, at any rate for the decision in the first instance. In order to show that a workable rule can be framed, and if so desired can be framed in narrow terms, it might be provided that it shall be a defence to a charge of murder to prove that the murder was committed upon the request of the victim and in pursuance of an agreement that the defendant should afterwards commit suicide himself, the defendant having at the time a genuine intention to carry out his promise. This rule would place the burden of proof upon the defendant, who would always be subject to the risk of failing to discharge the burden and so being convicted. It is hard to imagine that a rule framed in these terms would be of interest to the calculating murderer. Such possibility of abuse as it affords exists also at present in the appeal for executive clemency.

If so much be conceded with regard to the suicide pact in its two forms, the next question is the proper treatment of the abettor to suicide where there is no suicide pact—i.e., where he does not agree to commit the deed upon himself. At first sight an argument can be constructed, from the material already proposed, for making even such an abettor dispunishable. If X, under the new rule for attempted suicide, commits no crime in swallowing poison, it would seem to follow that Y should commit no crime in furnishing the poison to X at his

[2] *Cmd 8932*, para. 176.

request.[3] This should equally be so even though Y originally suggested the suicide to X. Y is not furnishing the
tools of crime, because X's act is not a crime. The case
would be precisely the same as supplying X with peroxide
to bleach his hair; it would be a crime for Y forcibly
to bleach X's hair, but not a crime for him to supply
X with the peroxide to do the bleaching himself, or
to suggest to X that X do it.

The conclusion is also supported by what has been
said on suicide pacts. If Y, by agreement, kills X and
then, in pursuance of the same agreement, attempts to
commit suicide himself, he is immune from punishment
under the rule suggested for the murder-suicide pact. But
why should it be essential to Y's immunity that he has
agreed to commit suicide himself, and tried to do so?
Is not the essential factor that X consented to be killed?

It may be argued to the contrary that suicide is against
public policy, but that the person who attempts suicide
is exempt from punishment for a particular reason,
namely that the threat of punishment can only stiffen
his will to succeed at the first attempt. This reason, it
may be said, does not operate in favour of one who did
not himself intend to commit suicide, so that the instigator to suicide may properly be punished in this case.

Between the extremes of these two views various intermediate positions may be taken. It will be universally
conceded that one who incites a young person to suicide,
for example, is properly punishable: while on the other
hand a physician who give his dying patient the opportunity of a merciful release may well be regarded as
outside the scope of any intelligently conceived prohibition. These sensible results could be achieved by a law

---

[3] This was held to be the case in Texas, where suicide is innocent at
common law: above, p. 301. It is not clear in present English law
whether the act described in the text involves the guilt of participation in the suicide, but apparently it does: see Williams: *Criminal
Law: The General Part,* p. 191.

framed on the lines of that adopted in Switzerland or the Soviet Union (p. 304). Although the Swiss concept of "selfish motives" has not hitherto found expression in Anglo-American law, it seems to be a very good one for the purpose. However, a situation of this kind seems logically to require a further step which has not yet been taken in any country. This is the assimilation of abetment of suicide with homicide by consent. The previous arguments against distinguishing between these two situations apply with equal force here. Suppose that a physician supplies his dying cancer patient with a poison, and watches him take it. According to the Swiss and Soviet rule, the physician is not guilty of a crime in thus abetting the suicide of a non-dependent person for unselfish reasons. Now suppose that the physician raises the poison to the patient's lips so that he may voluntarily make the motion of swallowing. Is this an abetment of suicide, or a killing by consent? It would be absurd to distinguish it from the first case. Finally, suppose that the physician pours the poison down the patient's throat, or injects it into his veins. Again there is no reason of penal policy for distinguishing the case: either the physician should be punishable in all cases, or he should be immune in all.

Here again there is a danger of false evidence. If a husband is charged with the murder of his wife, it may in some circumstances be temptingly easy for him to say that his wife, being tired of life, asked to be put out of the way. In the nature of things this is not an issue that can easily be tried after the death of the alleged consenting party. The defence will be all the more likely to succeed if the circumstances lend colour to it, as if the wife is painfully ill at the time of her alleged request. Thus the proposed law, if it were passed, might enable the relatives of invalids to dispatch them and then plead their consent, safe in the knowledge that their victims cannot give evidence on the subject.

This objection will seem to many to be an insuperable

one. But the same reply may be made as before—the danger of false evidence is one that the law has to meet in almost all situations, and it is not in itself a sufficient reason for opposing a change that is otherwise desirable. Moreover, the danger can easily be exaggerated. If voluntary euthanasia were legalized, a person who proposed to perform it upon another would have no reason for secrecy, but rather the reverse. Thus if a sufferer demanded to be painlessly killed, the person carrying out the order would obviously, for his own protection, call witnesses to hear the request. If he did not, he would often place himself under grave suspicion, and would have himself to thank if he were subsequently the victim of a miscarriage of justice. There are many situations in criminal law in which the *bona fides* of an act is tested by whether it is done furtively or in the open.

On the whole, then, it is submitted that the law might well exempt from punishment the unselfish abetment of suicide and the unselfish homicide upon request. This rule would solve at a stroke the problem of voluntary euthanasia in cases of fatal illness.[4] It would, of course, go much beyond the legal change usually advocated by supporters of euthanasia, because it would not be limited to persons suffering from an incurable and painful illness. Since it is probably too radical a change in the law for present public opinion in the English-speaking countries, more limited proposals for the legalization of euthanasia will be canvassed in the next chapter.

It need hardly be added that whatever solution is found for the problem of abetment to suicide should be applied also to the inchoate crime of incitement to suicide where the act of suicide is not carried out. This application of the crime of incitement is such a rare one that there appears to be no reported instance of it.

[4] It would also reach a satisfactory result for the suicide pact and murder-suicide pact, except that it might be argued, for instance, that a young man who persuades his girl-friend to commit suicide with him does so from selfish motives. Hence a special exemption for the suicide pact seems to be desirable.

VIII

EUTHANASIA

The morality of voluntary euthanasia

Whatever opinion may be taken on the general subject of suicide, it has long seemed to some people that euthanasia, the merciful extinction of life, is morally permissible and indeed mandatory where it is performed upon a dying patient with his consent and is the only way of relieving his suffering. According to this view, which will be accepted in the present chapter, a man is entitled to demand the release of death from hopeless and helpless pain, and a physician who gives this release is entitled to moral and legal absolution for his act.

One of the earliest expressions of the opinion in England came from no less a Catholic than Sir Thomas More, who, in the second book of his *Utopia,* wrote that in his imaginary community "when any is taken with a torturing and lingering pain, so that there is no hope either of cure or ease, the priests and magistrates come and exhort them, that, since they are now unable to go on with the business of life, are become a burden to themselves and all about them, and they have really outlived themselves, they should no longer nourish such a rooted distemper, but choose rather to die since they cannot live but in much misery."

Perhaps an opinion to the same effect, though not couched in the same forthright terms, can be seen in Francis Bacon's *New Atlantis.* "I esteem it," he wrote, "the office of a physician not only to restore the health, but to mitigate pain and dolours; and not only when such mitigation may conduce to recovery, but when it may serve to make a fair and easy passage."

A hundred years later the Reverend Charles Moore, in his monumental treatise designed to condemn suicide, conceded that "the most excusable cause seems to be an emaciated body; when a man labours under the tortures of an incurable disorder, and seems to live only to be a burden to himself and his friends. This was thought to be a sufficient apology for the action in ancient days and can only be combated in modern ones by the force and energy of that true religion, which both points out the duty and reward of implicit resignation." [1]

This writer's opinion that euthanasia as a form of suicide can be condemned only according to a religious hope of immortality was supported by Hastings Rashdall, who approached the subject, like Charles Moore, as a Christian moralist. Rashdall wrote:

It does not seem possible to decide whether the continuance of moral discipline is worth the prolongation of an existence from which all else that gives value to life has departed without asking what are to be the fruits of this moral discipline, whether it is rational to hope for another state in which the character thus formed may have further opportunities of expressing itself in moral activity. . . . I may add that this is almost the only case (unless we include also the somewhat parallel question of infanticide) in which the answer to any detailed question of ethics can rationally be affected by the answer that is given to a purely theological problem. [2]

If it is true that euthanasia can be condemned only according to a religious opinion, this should be sufficient at the present day to remove the prohibition from the criminal law. The prohibition imposed by a religious belief should not be applied by law to those who do not share the belief, where this is not required for the worldly welfare of society generally. But, further, the ancient

[1] *A Full Inquiry into the Subject of Suicide* (London, 1790), I, 270.
[2] *The Theory of Good and Evil* (Oxford, 1907), I, 209.

opinion that religion requires resignation, that the more unpleasant of two alternatives has some intrinsic moral superiority, has lost nearly all its support. At the present day it seems self-evident to most of us that laughter is better than sorrow, oblivion better than the endurance of purposeless pain. It was previously shown that the former religious objections to anæsthetics in surgery and childbirth have been given up, even by Catholics who were the last to express them. Yet Catholics, and a considerable number of members of other religious communions, still object to euthanasia. They allow the medical use of narcotics to annihilate the senses, provided that life is not destroyed. Thus one writer on Catholic medical ethics declares that "it is not euthanasia to give a dying person sedatives merely for the alleviation of pain, even to the extent of depriving the patient of the use of sense and reason, when this extreme measure is judged necessary." [3] In practice, however, this permission does not solve the whole problem: even the latest advances in medical science have not enabled pain to be eliminated from the terminal stages of certain diseases; and the question remains whether the physician can rightfully accelerate the release of death.

The religious objection is principally the familiar one that killing falls under the ban of the Sixth Commandment. This theocratic morality is, however, no more successful in the present application than in those previously considered. The true translation of the Sixth Command-

[3] "Code of Ethical and Religious Directives for Catholic Hospitals," printed in Joseph B. McAllister: *Ethics with Special Application to the Medical and Nursing Professions*, 2nd. ed. (Philadelphia, 1955), p. 396. The permission is not unanimously accorded in Catholic circles: Joseph Fletcher: *Morals and Medicine* (Princeton, N.J., 1954), p. 182, quotes the Catholic authority Koch-Preuss as requiring that drugs should not deprive the sufferer of consciousness, but as allowing even the artificial hastening of death if this condition is observed. In neither respect does Koch-Preuss state the predominant Catholic opinion. The desire to preserve consciousness while dying is due to the importance attached to the ceremony of extreme unction.

ment is not "Thou shalt not kill" but "Thou shalt do no murder," as the Book of Common Prayer has it;[4] and it is only by a stretch of words that a killing with the patient's consent, to relieve him of inexpressible suffering, can morally be described as murder. If wholesale killing in war and the punitive killing of criminals are not "murder," surely a killing done with the patient's consent and for his benefit as an act of mercy can claim to be excluded from this ugly word. Moreover, if the act is regarded as a type of assisted suicide, it falls outside the moral arguments against suicide studied in the previous chapter. Even on the religious hypothesis of a soul, to release the soul from the tortured body and set it at liberty is surely to confer a benefit upon it and not an injury.

The most thorough presentation of the Catholic case against euthanasia is that by the Reverend Joseph V. Sullivan, published in the *Studies in Sacred Theology* of the Catholic University of America. The argument is that supreme dominion over life belongs to God alone, and it is never lawful for man on his own authority to kill the innocent directly. The author explains that God may authorize man to kill, as in the mass killing reported in Deuteronomy iii, 2–6; but he adds that "today there is no indication that God is giving anyone orders to kill the innocent." "Innocent" in the thesis means a person who has not been adjudged worthy of death by lawful authority, and who is not a combatant opposing a nation that is fighting a just war, or an unjust aggressor. In addition to the argument from biblical revelation, the author refers for support to Western tradition on the subject of killing; and he brings in the usual religious masochism—the mental agony of approaching death, he says, is "part of the sacrifice that God demands for the sins

---

[4] See Joseph Fletcher: op. cit., p. 196, pointing out that the Hebrew of the Decalogue "clearly means unlawful killing, treacherously, for private vendetta or gain."

and faults of life"—as well as religious fatalism—"some suffering is necessary; God knows how much each man needs." Finally, there is the familiar argument from the "wedge principle," which is used to deny the possibility of looking at particular circumstances in applying moral rules. The author defines it as follows.

The wedge principle means that an act which, if raised to a general line of conduct would injure humanity, is wrong even in an individual case.[5]

This use of the "wedge" objection evidently involves a particular determination as to the meaning of words, namely the words "if raised to a general line of conduct." The author supposes, for the sake of argument, that the merciful extinction of life in a suffering patient is not in itself immoral. Still it is immoral, because if it were permitted this would admit "a most dangerous wedge that might eventually put all life in a precarious condition." It seems a sufficient reply to say that this type of reasoning could be used to condemn any act whatever, because there is no human conduct from which evil cannot be imagined to follow if it is persisted in when some of the circumstances are changed. All moral questions involve the drawing of a line, but the "wedge principle" would make it impossible to draw a line, because the line would have to be pushed farther and farther back until all action became vetoed. Logically, the only "general line of conduct" involved in permitting a particular case of voluntary euthanasia of a suffering patient in a fatal illness is that all suffering patients in fatal illnesses may have voluntary euthanasia. It is illegitimate to ignore these limitations of the principle in pronouncing upon the morality of the act.

The "wedge" objection is sometimes stated more persuasively as a matter of psychology. It is said that a person who has taken life lawfully will then have his

[5] Joseph V. Sullivan: *Catholic Teaching on the Morality of Euthanasia* (Washington, D.C., 1949), p. 54.

inhibitions so far removed that he is likely to take life unlawfully. This may be true in some applications, but it is ridiculous as applied to the physician who gently and humanely extinguishes his patient's life as the last service that he can perform for him. If the argument has any validity, it is valid for the executioner and above all for the soldier; yet the "wedge" principle is not invoked against them. It is common knowledge that crimes of violence increase after a war, because the practice of violence in war does tend to remove inhibitions. Yet we continue to regard peace-time violence as wrong, thus showing that even the cataclysmic reversal of moral standards involved in war can be compartmentalized in the mind.[6]

The manifold arguments against euthanasia contrast with the simple humanitarian argument for it. This is perhaps an application of C. M. Cornford's observation that "there is only one argument for doing something; all the others are for doing nothing." Yet behind the simple humanitarianism of the affirmative argument there lies a somewhat profound question of philosophy. It is good that men should feel a horror of taking human life, but in a rational judgment the quality of the life must be considered. The absolute interdiction of suicide and euthanasia involves the impossible assertion that every life, no matter what its quality or circumstances, is worth living and obligatory to be lived. This assertion of the value of mere existence, in the absence of all the activities that give meaning to life, and in face of the disintegration of personality that so often follows from prolonged agony, will not stand scrutiny. On any ration-

[6] Cf. Wechsler and Michael: "A Rationale of the Law of Homicide," 37 *Columbia Law Review*, at 740 (1937): "The point that officially sanctioned killing tends to some extent to promote disrespect for the value of life has force in general but seems to us of slight weight in this instance considering the purposes of voluntary euthanasia and the circumstances surrounding it in practice." See ibid., p. 739 for literature.

ally acceptable philosophy there is no ethical value in living any sort of life: the only life that is worth living is the good life. Sidney Hook, after quoting Aristotle to this effect, continued:

> We may define the good life differently, but no matter what our conception of the good life is, it presupposes a physical basis—a certain indispensable minimum of physical and social well-being—necessary for even a limited realization of that good life. Where that minimum is failing together with all rational probability of attaining it, to avoid a life that at its best can be only vegetative and at its worst run the entire gamut of degradation and obloquy, what high-minded person would refuse the call of the poet *"mourir entre les bras du sommeil"*? We must recognize no categorical imperative "to live," but "to live well." [7]

From a religious point of view, the most conspicuous omission from the Catholic consideration of euthanasia is the teaching of the New Testament. "How these Christians love one another!" exclaimed Shylock, and his words might have been uttered about any of the religious objections to the liberalization of the penal law. According to the usual view of the Christian religion, however little it may be applied in practice, the greatest of all commandments is to love, and this surely means that euthanasia is permissible if performed truly and honestly to spare the patient and not merely for the convenience of the living.

Finally, on this side of the question, the pretension of the moral theologian, sitting in the calm of his study, to dictatorial powers of moral interpretation must be rejected. This question, at least, is one for the patient himself, or else for the practical judgment of the medical practitioner, for these two alone know the hard and terrible facts of the last stages of malignant disease.

It has been noticed before in this work that writers

[7] "The Ethics of Suicide," 37 *International Journal of Ethics,* at 186 (1927).

who object to a practice for theological reasons frequently try to support their condemnation on medical grounds. With euthanasia this is difficult, but the effort is made. One of the standard arguments is that no sufferer from an apparently fatal illness should be deprived of his life because there is always the possibility that the diagnosis is wrong, or else that some remarkable cure will be discovered in time. In support of the former of these possibilities, instances are quoted of patients who have been given little time to live by their medical advisers and who yet have in fact survived happily for many years. However, it does not follow that in the cases so cited the physician who took this pessimistic view of his patient's prospects would have felt the case to be sufficiently clear for euthanasia. It may be allowed that mistakes are always possible, but this is so in any of the affairs of life. And it is just as possible to make a mistake by doing nothing as by acting. All that can be expected of any moral agent is that he should do his best on the facts as they appear to him.

The present law

Under the present law, voluntary euthanasia would, except in certain narrow circumstances, be regarded as suicide in the patient who consents and murder in the doctor who administers; even on a lenient view, most lawyers would say that it could not be less than manslaughter in the doctor, the punishment for which, according to the jurisdiction and the degree of manslaughter, can be anything up to imprisonment for life.

More specifically, the following principles may be stated:

(1) If the doctor gives the patient a fatal injection with the intention of killing him, and the patient dies in consequence, the doctor is a common murderer because it is his hand that has caused the death. Neither the consent of the patient, nor the extremity of his suffering,[8] nor the imminence of death by natural causes, nor all these factors taken together is a defence. This, at any rate, is always assumed by lawyers, though there is no case in which the argument that the concurrence of all three factors may present a defence has been actually advanced and decided. It is by no means beyond the bounds of imagination that a bold and humane judge might direct the jury, if the question were presented, that voluntary euthanasia may in extreme circumstances be justified under the general doctrine of necessity. Just as, in the case of *Rex v. Bourne,* the jury were directed that the unborn child may be destroyed for the purpose of preserving the yet more precious life of the mother, so, in the case of voluntary euthanasia, it is possible to imagine the jury being directed that the sanctity of life may be submerged by the overwhelming necessity of relieving unbearable suffering in the last extremity, where the patient consents to what is done and where in any event no span of useful life is left to him. Although a persuasive argument can be advanced in support of such a direction, it must be emphasized that no hint of it appears in the existing legal authorities. On the contrary, the authorities precisely exclude, on a charge of murder, any defence that the deceased consented to the extinction of his life, any defence of good motive, and any defence that the deceased would shortly have died in any event. The question of legal necessity will be resumed later.

(2) If the doctor furnishes poison (for example, an overdose of sleeping tablets) for the purpose of enabling the patient to commit suicide, and the patient takes it accordingly and dies, this is suicide and a kind of self-

[8] See Rex v. Simpson, 11 C.A.R. 218 (1915).

murder in the patient, and the doctor, as an abettor, again becomes guilty of murder. So, at any rate, is it in strict legal theory. One can, however, conceive an indulgent judge ruling the case to be manslaughter merely, if indeed he does not accept the argument from necessity already mentioned; and of course there is always the possibility or indeed probability that, whatever direction the judge gives, the jury may take the law into its own hands and acquit.

An illustration both of the legal mind and of the jury's good sense is afforded by the Massachusetts case of *Commonwealth v. Bowen* (1816),[9] which, though not a case of euthanasia, is the authority usually cited for the rule that wilfully accelerating death, by however short a space of time, involves the full guilt of murder.[1] The facts were that the accused was in a prison cell situated next to the condemned cell; he, being able to converse with a fellow prisoner in the next cell who was under sentence of death, urged him to destroy himself, and thus disappoint the sheriff and the people who might assemble to see him executed. After receiving this advice, the fellow prisoner hanged himself in his cell during the night before the day fixed for his execution. The authorities saw fit to charge the accused with the murder of the other, and the judge directed the jury that on the facts given in evidence he was guilty. The atrocity of the offence, said the learned judge, was not in the least diminished by the consideration that justice was thirsting for a sacrifice, and that but a small portion of the deceased's earthly existence could in any event remain to him. Happily, the jury acquitted the accused notwithstanding the judge's direction; but it is the judge's direction, not the jury's disobedience, that is taken as representing the law.

[9] 13 Mass. 356.
[1] Other authorities for this rule are Hale, *P.C.,* 428; Regina v. Murton, 3 F. & F. 492, 176 Eng. Rep. 221 (1862). Cf. Earengey: "Voluntary Euthanasia," 8 *Medico-Legal Review* 91, at 111 (1940).

(3) A case that may be thought to be distinguishable from both of those already considered is that of the administration of a fatal dose of a drug where this dose is in fact the minimum necessary to deaden pain. Where a patient is suffering from an incurable and agonizing disease, and ordinary quantities of a drug fail to render the pain tolerable, many doctors will give the minimum dose necessary to kill the pain, knowing that this minimum is at the same time an amount that is likely to kill the patient. In other words, faced with the choice of either doing nothing, or killing both the pain and the patient, the doctor chooses the latter course, knowing that in any event the patient has not long to live.

Some Roman Catholics, who as a religious group form the strongest opposition to voluntary euthanasia, are nevertheless prepared to accept this situation, on their principle of double effect. The will of the doctor is directed to the relief of suffering, an effect which he achieves; it is merely a secondary effect that the patient is killed. In just the same way St. Alphonsus Liguori, a Catholic theologian of the nineteenth century, thought a man justified in committing suicide by leaping from a window to get out of a blazing building, because the mode of death chosen is adapted to escape even though it will not succeed.[2]

One may welcome the principle of double effect as an alleviation of the orthodox attitude towards suicide, while at the same time regretting, as in the case of abortion, the casuistical nature of the exception. It is altogether too artificial to say that a doctor who gives an overdose of a narcotic having in the forefront of his mind the aim of ending his patient's existence is guilty of sin, while a doctor who gives the same overdose in the same circumstances in order to relieve pain is not guilty of sin, provided that he keeps his mind steadily off the

[2] *Theologia Moralis,* III, n. 367, quoted by Joseph Fletcher: op. cit., p. 182.

consequence which his professional training teaches him is inevitable, namely the death of his patient. When you know that your conduct will have two consequences, one in itself good and one in itself evil, you are compelled as a moral agent to choose between acting and not acting by making a judgment of value, that is to say by deciding whether the good is more to be desired than the evil is to be avoided. If this is what the principle of double effect means, well and good; but if it means that the necessity of making a choice of values can be avoided merely by keeping your mind off one of the consequences, it can only encourage a hypocritical attitude towards moral problems.

What is true of morals is true of the law. There is no legal difference between desiring or intending a consequence as following from your conduct, and persisting in your conduct with a knowledge that the consequence will inevitably follow from it, though not desiring that consequence. When a result is foreseen as certain, it is the same as if it were desired or intended. It would be an undue refinement to distinguish between the two.

A much better line of reasoning would be to say that the act, in the circumstances supposed, is justified by necessity. The doctrine of necessity in the common law refers to a choice between competing values, where the ordinary rule has to be departed from in order to avert some great evil. The theoretical argument for the recognition of necessity as justifying euthanasia may be presented as follows.

When a patient is suffering from a painful and incurable disease it is established practice to administer a narcotic, but with the tolerance resulting from habituation this must be given in constantly increasing doses in order to relieve pain. To take an illustration, a grain of morphine might for ordinary persons be a fatal dose; but it has been found that a patient who is in pain and treated with injections of morphine may develop resistence to it so rapidly that at the end of only a month he is taking as much as eighteen grains a day in order to obtain relief. With a progression of this kind, there must come a time, if the patient does not die from other causes, when the dose administered is of a fatal character. (In the case of morphine, an excessive dose depresses the respiratory centre and causes death either directly or through the intervention of bronchial pneumonia.) Thus it will be seen that the logic of morphine and other like drugs is sooner or later to present a choice between administering what is likely to be a fatal dose and leaving the patient without relief. The question is whether it is lawful in such circumstances to administer the fatal dose.

It must be realized that even under the existing law the physician is not required to treat life as an absolute value. For example, every surgical operation involves some risk that the patient may die under the anæsthetic, but this does not make the operation unlawful. Risk to life may properly be undertaken if the chance of improving the patient's health is sufficiently great to counterbalance it. In other words, the greatly increased prospect of better health counterbalances the slightly increased prospect of immediate death. It is capable even of counterbalancing the *greatly* increased prospect of immediate death, as in a difficult operation upon the heart where the alternative is for the patient to be an invalid for the rest of his life.

In the same way, when a patient is suffering from a painful illness the doctor may lawfully administer a narcotic to relieve pain even though he knows that the drug, used in quantity as it sooner or later has to be, is likely to prove fatal if not anticipated by the disease. The immediate relief of pain counterbalances the risk of accelerated death. If so much be admitted, it obviously becomes very difficult to determine when, if ever, there is an unlawful act of euthanasia in the progressive administration of the drug. The more violent and protracted the pain to be relieved, the greater the dose of the drug required to be administered, and the more the doctor is justified in ignoring the risk that this drug will immediately or indirectly bring about a curtailment of life. As the fatal illness draws to a close, with less and less life remaining to the patient, risk increases, and the curtailment of life comes to be not a speculation for the future but a matter of immediate choice—a choice, perhaps, between death today and death next week or tomorrow. Thus a point is reached at which, proceeding upon the same principles as he has followed heretofore, and which have so far been lawful, the doctor is led to give what he knows is likely to be an immediately fatal dose. It would be extremely artificial to say that this last dose, which is administered upon the same principle as all the previous ones, is alone unlawful.

The fact is that there is no logical or moral chasm between what may be called shortening life and accelerating death. Once admit the principle that a physician may knowingly, for sufficient reason, shorten a patient's expectation of life—which cannot be denied—and one is compelled to admit that he may knowingly, for sufficient reason put an end to his patient's life immediately. If you may curtail a probable span of five years by one year, you may curtail a probable span of five days by one day, and of five minutes by one minute.

This line of argument tends to show that a physician may give any amount of drug necessary to deaden pain, even though he knows that that amount will bring about speedy or indeed immediate death. His legal excuse does not rest upon the Roman Church's doctrine of "double effect," for it would be both human and right for him in these circumstances to welcome his patient's death as a merciful release. The excuse rests upon the doctrine of necessity, there being at this juncture no way of relieving pain without ending life.

In this limited form the excuse of necessity would be

likely to be accepted by a judge, and to this extent it may be held that euthanasia is permitted under the existing law. It is, however, most doubtful whether a judge would go any further, and permit a physician to anticipate matters by administering a fatal dose—say, doubling the previous dose of morphine—in order to save the patient from dragging out a numbed, miserable, and hopeless existence. In other words, although death may legally be preferred to great pain, it probably may not, under the existing law, be preferred to existence in a state of drugged torpor. This is the field in which the possibility of a change in the law has to be considered. It is, perhaps, not quite so good a debating-ground for the advocates of change as the other. Any one can see the great strength of the case for saving a patient from intolerable pain. There is likely to be more disagreement on whether a patient, provided he is saved from the extreme of pain, is to be required to continue an artificial, twilight existence, in a state of terrible weakness, and subject perhaps to nausea, giddiness, and extreme restlessness, as well as the long hours of consciousness of a hopeless condition. Most people, however, especially those who have seen a friend or relative in this desperate plight, will think that such an existence is not to be imposed on a person who wishes to end it.

The law is also probably adverse where the physician in order to put an end to his patient's suffering departs altogether outside any treatment that has previously been given. Medical men who are moved by compassion to administer euthanasia are well acquainted with methods of killing that leave no trace and so are practically impossible to prove. Provided that the act is expertly done and no unwise admissions made, the question of legal responsibility remains academic. On the other hand the physician may deliberately bring about death in a way that can be proved. For example, one of the most merciful ways of doing so is by the intravenous injection of a barbiturate—an act that could have no explanation except on the supposition that the physician wished to bring about painless death. Although there may be no logical difference between this mode of ending a patient's existence and the act of administering narcotics in increasing doses until they become fatal, it is for psychological reasons somewhat less favourable to defend in a law court.

(4) We come, finally, to the problem of killing by inaction. "Mercy-killing" by omission to use medical means to prolong life is probably lawful. Although a physician is normally under a duty to use reasonable care to conserve his patient's life, he is probably exempted from that duty if life has become a burden to the patient. The morality of an omission in these circumstances is conceded even by Catholics.[3]

The administration of the law

The theoretical statement of the law on the subject of euthanasia is misleading unless one bears in mind four practical factors relating to its administration.

In the first place, a charge against a physician of murdering through the administration of a humane overdose is inherently difficult to establish because of the nature of the evidence required. When the patient is gravely ill and has been receiving large doses of a drug over a considerable period, it may be difficult to determine the amount of the final dose, if that is disputed, or whether death was due to it. Again, the line between a lawful though large dose of drug, and one so large as to be unlawful, may be a narrow one; so also is the line between curtailing life and bringing about death. Even if the law

[3] Joseph V. Sullivan: op. cit., p. 64.

requires the line to be drawn, it is one of such inherent difficulty as to give much scope to the defence.

Secondly, prosecuting authorities are naturally reluctant to take criminal proceedings against a doctor of repute for an act done in good faith in a situation of great difficulty, particularly when the evidence is such that the charge is unlikely to succeed.

Thirdly, a jury will be reluctant to convict a doctor in these circumstances, and may not only seize upon any defect in the evidence as a reason for acquitting, but may even acquit when the evidence and the judge's direction leaves them with no legal reason for doing so.

Fourthly, assuming that the worst happens and the doctor is convicted of murder, executive clemency will in all probability intervene to prevent the execution of the death penalty; in England it will certainly do so.

These various considerations may give the doctor the assurance that he has little to fear from the present law. However, it cannot be said that there is absolutely no danger. Even though the official policy is not to prosecute for certain classes of acts, prosecutors may feel themselves forced to initiate a charge if an informant presses a case upon their notice. It is not impossible to imagine that in a case of euthanasia a doctor may be imperilled by the indiscretion of a nurse and the malice of a relative of the patient. In England not only may the police in such a case feel in duty bound to prosecute, but the angry relative may himself undertake a prosecution, as every private citizen has the right in that country to do. Thus the law is a sprung trap, and no doctor who practises the "humane overdose" knows when he may fall victim to it. If he is convicted, it is true that he will not be hanged; but he may quite possibly have to serve a sentence of imprisonment, with unpredictable results upon his practice and upon the attitude of the medical disciplinary body. It is small wonder if, with this fear in their minds, many doctors refuse to give their patients relief from suffering upon the scale they need.

There seems to be only one instance of the prosecution of a physician for mercy-killing either in the United States or in England. In 1949 a New Hampshire physician, Dr. Sander, dictated into the hospital record an admission to mercy-killing by the injection of air; on his trial he denied that his act had caused the patient's death, and this defence succeeded before the jury. In some other cases in the United States, where the defendant was a relative of the deceased and not a physician, he was acquitted or otherwise escaped punishment; yet on other occasions there was a conviction and a sentence of imprisonment.[4] Thus the prospect of a sentimental acquittal cannot be reckoned as a certainty.

The English jury is less prone to take the law into its own hands than its counterpart in America. Yet a compassionate acquittal took place in 1927, when a man drowned his incurably ill child, suffering from tuberculosis and gangrene of the face. He had nursed her with devoted care, but one morning, after sitting up with her all night, could no longer bear to see her suffering. The jury returned a verdict of "not guilty" of murder. In the course of his summing-up, Mr. Justice Branson said:

It is a matter which gives food for thought when one comes to consider that, had this poor child been an animal instead of a human being, so far from there being anything blameworthy in the man's action in putting an end to its suffering, he would actually have been liable to punishment if he had not done so.[5]

[4] See Helen Silving: "Euthanasia," 103 *University of Pennsylvania Law Review* 350 (1954).

[5] Quoted by Harry Roberts: *Euthanasia and Other Aspects of Life and Death* (London, 1936), p. 5, and in *Parliamentary Debates* (*House of Lords*), vol. 103, col. 471. In R. v. King, *The Times* (London), October 16, 1953, a woman pleaded guilty to a charge of attempting to suffocate her husband as he lay dying in great pain. She was granted a conditional discharge.

The movement for the legalization of voluntary euthanasia

The medical prolongation of life has resulted in a great increase in the degenerative diseases, particularly cancer, and this fact has naturally attracted more general attention to the case for voluntary euthanasia. The organized movement in England commenced in 1932, but some premonitory shots had already been fired. F. A. W. Gisborne, in his essays entitled *Democracy on Trial,* published in 1928, wrote as follows:

In the case of the victim of incurable physical disease, doctors, not less than two in each case, should be empowered to administer an opiate sufficiently strong to afford lasting relief. . . . The question should be left entirely to medical experts to decide, and there would be no need to consult the sufferer. There would then be no cause for after-regrets, and the survivors of the departed would not be haunted by painful memories. Rather, they would feel comforted by the thought that one who had been dear to them had been spared unnecessary suffering. Consolation might be found in the notable lines of Lucretius addressed to the dying (Dryden's translation):
For thou shalt sleep and never wake again,
And quitting life, shall quit all living pain,
But we, thy friends, shall all those sorrows find,
Which in forgetful death thou leav'st behind.
No time shall dry our tears nor drive thee from our mind.
The worst that can befall thee, measured right,
Is a sound slumber, and a long good night.

Three years later the Reverend Peter Green, Canon of Manchester, argued the same cause but with the addition of safeguards.

Many men every year do commit suicide to escape lingering agony. But they do it in a spirit of angry revolt against God; they die without the consolation of religion; they lose the whole of any insurance they have made for wife and children; they shock their loved ones, and outrage public opinion. In such a case I should myself like my doctor, in conjunction with a specialist, to be allowed to state that the disease was fatal and likely to be slow and painful; and then I might be permitted to end my life at once in some painless manner. This would enable a man to settle his affairs; to say goodbye to his friends; and to receive the last rites of the church. What are the arguments against the granting of such liberty, by church and state, to those who desire it? [6]

In 1932 Dr. Killick Millard introduced the topic into public debate. In his presidential address to the Society of Medical Officers of Health, he advocated that mercy-killing should be legalized. So much support was found that a new society was formed, the Voluntary Euthanasia Legalisation Society, under the presidency of Lord Moynihan, President of the Royal College of Surgeons. It was supported by many physicians, public figures, and ministers of religion of all denominations except Catholic. They included Dr. Julian Huxley, Sir James Jeans, Havelock Ellis, Sir G. M. Trevelyan, H. G. Wells, G. B. Shaw, Mr. (now Sir) Harold Nicolson, Dr. W. R. Matthews (the Dean of St. Paul's),[7] the Chancellor of Leicester, Dean Inge, Dr. Rhondda Williams (Chairman of the Congregational Union), Dr. Norwood (President of the Free Church Council); and amongst doctors, Sir Humphry Rolleston, Sir William Arbuthnot-Lane, Sir Leonard

---

[6] *The Problem of Right Conduct* (London, 1931), p. 283.

[7] Dr. Matthews addressed the Society in 1950, and his remarks were printed (*Voluntary Euthanasia: The Ethical Aspect*). The Primate expressed disagreement in a public announcement the next day. Later in the same year Dr. Barnes, the Bishop of Birmingham, in an address to the British Association advocated both voluntary euthanasia and compulsory sterilization: his opinions were condemned in a leading article in *The Times* (London), September 4, 1950.

Hill, Sir Walter Langton-Brown, Sir James Purves-Stewart, and Sir Frederick Menzies. As a result of the efforts of the society, in 1936 Lord Ponsonby introduced a bill into the House of Lords to legalize voluntary euthanasia. The Bill was lost.[8] In 1950 Lord Chorley moved in the Lords that the matter be inquired into, but his motion was also lost.[9]

The Royal Commission on Capital Punishment, after considering the general problem, refused to recommend any special rule for mercy-killings, preferring to leave them to the discretion of the Home Secretary;[1] but the report of the Commission deals only with the proposal to legalize mercy-killings by any one (e.g., relatives), and does not specifically consider the more limited proposal to legalize voluntary euthanasia administered by physicians.

The example of the English society (now called the Euthanasia Society) inspired the founding of an American counterpart, the Euthanasia Society of America, in 1938. Of 3,272 physicians who replied to a questionnaire in New York State, 80 per cent were favourable to voluntary euthanasia, and 1776 joined a committee of physicians for the legalization of euthanasia. Support was also expressed by 387 Protestant and Jewish ministers of religion of the same state. The society prepared a bill, broadly on the lines of the English bill, and an unsuccessful attempt was made to introduce it in the New York State Assembly. The measure was introduced by Senator John A. Comstock into the Nebraska Assembly in 1938, but failed of acceptance. There is also a Voluntary Euthanasia Society of Connecticut, which has its own proposals to put forward.

An opinion poll taken in 1939 indicated that 46 per cent

---

[8] *Parliamentary Debates (House of Lords)*, vol. 103, col. 466 (December 1, 1936).
[9] Ibid., vol. 169, col. 552 (November 25, 1950).
[1] *Cmd 8932 of 1953*, paras. 177-80.

of people living in the United States were in favour of some kind of legal euthanasia, while a similar poll organized by the British Institute of Public Opinion in the same year showed a British majority of 68 per cent. In 1952 a petition was organized to the United Nations for the legalization of euthanasia for incurable sufferers, as a human right, and this received 2,513 signatures including many well-known names. There is still a great body of opposing opinion in both countries, chiefly from religious quarters. In 1950 the Church of England Hospital Chaplains' Fellowship expressed itself by general agreement as against euthanasia.[2] The general secretary of the American Council of Christian Churches, an organization of fundamentalist Protestants, denounced the 54 clergymen who had supported the euthanasia bill, saying that their action was "an evidence that the modernistic clergy have made further departure from the eternal moral law." And the General Convention of the Protestant Episcopal Church of America in 1952 placed themselves "in opposition to the legalizing of the practice of euthanasia under any circumstances whatsoever."[3]

The difficulty of securing political action on euthanasia is much the same as in the other fields treated in this book. Legislators know that there are no votes in law reform, but only votes to be lost through offending sectarian opinion. Moreover, legislators are themselves strongly affected by the traditional moral generalizations and taboos. Largely, perhaps, because of these facts, no country in the world has yet taken the step of legalizing voluntary euthanasia in fatal illnesses. The nearest approach is that made in Switzerland, which, as already shown (p. 304), allows the physician to put the poison into the patient's hand, though not to administer it himself. Norway, also, provides that the judge may reduce the punishment for

[2] *The Times* (London), May 30, 1950.
[3] Both quoted by Fletcher: op. cit., pp. 183, 195.

mercy-killing below the minimum normally fixed by statute.[4]

The English society's bill of 1936

Mention has been made of the bill sponsored by the English society which was debated in the House of Lords in 1936 and again called to the attention of the House in 1950. It is worth reviewing, briefly, the provisions of the bill, and the principal arguments used against it.

The object of the bill was to legalize voluntary euthanasia. The patient desiring euthanasia must be over twenty-one years of age and suffering from an incurable and fatal disease accompanied by severe pain. The bill excluded any question of compulsory euthanasia, even for hopelessly defective infants. Unfortunately, a legislative proposal is not assured of success merely because it is worded in a studiously moderate and restrictive form. The method of attack, by those who dislike the proposal, is to use the "thin end of the wedge" argument. They say that the proposal as it stands seems innocuous, but if accepted it may lead to further legislative proposals and ultimately to a complete breakdown of accepted standards. This "wedge" argument is one of the favourite objections to legal change; it was used throughout the nineteenth century in opposition to reforms that we now take for granted, and it was used by the Archbishop of Canterbury, the late Lord Lang, in opposition to the bill. There is no need to comment on it further, except to say that there is no proposal for reform on any topic, however con-

[4] Helen Silving in 103 *University of Pennsylvania Law Review,* at 368.

ciliatory and moderate, that cannot be opposed by this
dialectic.

Then there is the very difficult problem of safeguards. The promoters of the bill hoped that they might
be able to mollify the opposition by providing stringent
safeguards. Now, they were right in thinking that if they
had put in no safeguards—if they had merely said that
a doctor could kill his patient whenever he thought it
right—they would have been passionately opposed on
this ground. So they put in the safeguards. Under the proposals of the bill, the patient must sign a statutory form,
in the presence of two witnesses, requesting euthanasia.
The form, accompanied by two medical certificates, goes
up to an official euthanasia referee appointed by the Minister of Health; he interviews the patient to make sure
that he really wants it. Then euthanasia is administered
in the presence of an official witness, who must be a
justice of the peace, barrister, solicitor, doctor, minister
of religion, or registered nurse.

Did the opposition like these elaborate safeguards? On
the contrary, they made them a matter of complaint. The
safeguards would, it was said, bring too much formality
into the sick-room, and destroy the relationship between
doctor and patient. So the safeguards were wrong, but
no one of the opposition speakers said that he would
have voted for the bill without the safeguards.

Much the most important of these opposition speeches
were delivered by two of the acknowledged leaders of
the medical profession, the late Lord Dawson of Penn
and the late Lord Horder. Their speeches were looked
forward to with great interest because it was not known
exactly what line they would take. Although these two
peers rejected the proposals in the bill, the reasons they
gave for doing so deserve careful study.

Lord Dawson for the greater part of his speech seemed
to be in sympathy with the views of the bill. He scouted
the opposition notion that the only duty of the doctor is

to save life. That, he said, was the nineteenth-century view, but medical opinion has changed; we now think that it is also the doctor's duty to relieve pain. Hence anæthesia in childbirth and dentistry, and all the new drugs to assuage pain and bring sleep and forgetfulness to the troubled mind. Lord Dawson proceeded: "I would say that this is a courageous age, but it has a different sense of values from the ages which have gone before. It looks upon life more from the point of view of quality than of quantity. It places less value on life when its usefulness has come to an end." So "there has gradually crept into medical opinion, as it has crept into lay opinion, the feeling that one should make the act of dying more gentle and more peaceful even if it does involve curtailment of the length of life."

Then Lord Dawson went on: "If once you admit that you are going to curtail life by a single day, you are granting the principle that you must look at life from the point of view of its quality rather than from its quantity under these special circumstances. . . . I would give as my deliberate opinion that there is a quiet and cautious but irresistible move to look at life and suffering from the more humane attitude, and in face of a disease which is undoubtedly incurable, and when the patient is carrying a great load of suffering, our first thoughts should be the assuagement of pain even if it does involve the shortening of life." This means that the physician will, at the end, drug the patient even though he knows that this will shorten the patient's life. But what if death is still far off? Lord Dawson said: "When the gap between life burdened by incurable disease and death becomes wider, then greater difficulty presents itself, and greater variety in practice holds among individual doctors and patients. None the less there is in the aggregate an unexpressed growth of feeling that the shortening of the gap should not be denied when the real need is there. This is due, not to a diminution of courage, but rather to a truer conception of what life means and what the end of its usefulness deserves."

This remarkable speech seemed not merely to concede the case for euthanasia but to admit that it was actually practised, consciously or subconsciously, by the medical profession. Moreover, the concluding reference to "shortening the gap" seems to be a cautious admission of the principle that euthanasia is permissible, and is practised, not only where this is the only way of avoiding pain, but also where it is the only way of avoiding the prolongation of a life burdened by an incurable disease and robbed of all the quality that makes life worth while. This is a concession of the first importance to the cause of euthanasia.

Although he went thus far with the promoters of the measure, Lord Dawson opposed the bill on the ground that he preferred the present position under which everything was left to the discretion of the doctor. The Archbishop of Canterbury seized upon this idea with approval and relief; at the end of his speech he guardedly admitted that "cases arise in which some means of shortening life may be justified";[5] but he thought that Parliament should fold its hands because these cases were best left to the medical profession. Apparently the Primate thought that the consent of the patient would not be necessary, for one of his points was that a man racked with pain and full of drugs may be incapable of making a moral judgment. Thus these opponents of the bill, in allowing the doctor to end life without seeking the patient's consent, were in an important way prepared to go further than the proponents of the measure.

Lord Horder's argument was broadly similar to Lord Dawson's, though he did not elaborate it in the same way. He declared that it is outside a doctor's reference to put an end to life; but "the good doctor is aware of

[5] So also the late Archbishop of York in the later debate: *Parliamentary Debates* (*House of Lords*), vol. 169, cols. 562–3.

the difference between prolonging life and prolonging the act of dying." The former comes within his terms of reference, the latter does not. On this it may be commented that there must obviously be room for a good deal of difference of opinion on what is meant by "not prolonging the act of dying." It is not, really, a very satisfactory formula, because it appears, misleadingly, to point to simple inactivity. A doctor who is engaged in giving large doses of a narcotic is not merely "not prolonging the act of dying"; he is doing something positive which may well have the effect of shortening the act of dying. There is, also, vagueness as to the temporal limits of the "act of dying." Notwithstanding these difficulties, Lord Horder's formula has become a cliché in orthodox medical circles, where it is apparently thought to solve the whole problem of euthanasia.[6] There is, however, an opposing body of medical opinion which would welcome change.

Reviewing the outcome of the debate, the laissez-faire solution proposed by the medical opponents of the measure must appear to the lawyer to be indefensible. It leaves the doctor unprotected against the (admittedly remote) possibility of a vindictive prosecution, the result of which, if it takes place, and if the defendant is unlucky in his judge and jury, may be professional ruin—loss of reputation, loss of liberty, loss of livelihood for himself and his dependents. Even if no prosecution is brought, there is the possibility of blackmail. Moreover, the course favoured by the opponents of the bill would leave unsettled the question whether euthanasia as now practised by the profession is lawful or not. There is at present no legal authority for distinguishing between cut-

---

[6] Commenting upon the second debate in the House of Lords, the *British Medical Journal* wrote: "A part of the morale of the sick-room in which a person lies dying resides surely in the general belief that the good doctor will distinguish between prolongation of life and the unnecessary prolongation of the act of dying."

ting short life and cutting short the act of dying. It is not impossible that Lord Dawson and the Archbishop of Canterbury put themselves in the position of encouraging and advocating what is in law the crime of murder. One finds it hard to see how these speakers could have contemplated with such phlegm the responsibility and risks to the medical man in the course they were advocating. It is not fair to the ordinary practitioner to expect him to take them. Nor is it fair to the patient, because a doctor who has to make a decision under the threat of prosecution, even though it may be a remote one, is the less likely to be able to attend solely to the welfare of his patient.

While rejecting these objections to the bill, one may at the same time agree with the opposition view that the bill as drafted was unsuitable for the ordinary case where euthanasia was required. Thus Dr. Harry Roberts, proclaiming himself in sympathy with the aims of the Euthanasia Society, said that he thought that the limitations and conditions of the bill made it of narrow applicability, even if it became law. He added:

"When a good physician can keep life no longer in, he makes a fair and easy passage for it to be out," wrote Thomas Fuller in *The Holy State;* and such should I think be regarded as the bounden duty (whatever the law may say) of every practising doctor. Personally, I would not hesitate painlessly to end the life of an acquiescent patient at an advanced stage of such a painful and incurable disorder as cancer of the larynx or œsophagus—regardless of convention or formal legality. When my sympathy outweighs my fear of, and my respect for, the law, I obey the orders of the former.

So saying, this practising physician went on to suggest that the best solution of the problem was to legalize suicide.[7] However, even if this solution were politically pos-

[7] Harry Roberts: *Euthanasia and Other Aspects of Life and Death* (London, 1936), pp. 15–17. Another admission that he had taken patients' lives in these circumstances was made by Dr. E. A. Barton in

sible, it would not give protection in the common case where the fatal dose is administered by the physician and not taken by the patient's own hand.

A legislative suggestion

It may be suggested that the most hopeful line of advance would be to bring forward a measure that does no more than give legislative blessing to the practice that the great weight of medical opinion approves. In other words, the reformers might be well advised, in their next proposal, to abandon all their cumbrous safeguards and to do as their opponents wish, giving the medical practitioner a wide discretion and trusting to his good sense.

In England, there is a precedent for this line of action in the Infant Life (Preservation) Act, 1929. This statute, which was studied in a previous chapter, made it an offence to destroy a child capable of being born alive, but added an exception: "Provided that no person shall be found guilty of an offence under this section unless it is proved that the act which caused the death of the child was not done in good faith for the purpose only of preserving the life of the mother." The section protects anybody, not merely doctors; there are no "safeguards"—not even a second medical opinion is required; and the burden of proving bad faith is cast on the Crown. A similar formula might be adopted for euthanasia, though restricted to doctors. The essence of the bill would then be

---

an address to the Voluntary Euthanasia Legalization Society on May 21, 1947. The next day a spokesman for the British Medical Association said: "I think a good many doctors feel as Dr. Barton does —that euthanasia ought to be legalized." For similar admissions by American doctors see Fletcher: op. cit., pp. 205–6.

simple. It would provide that no medical practitioner should be guilty of an offence in respect of an act done intentionally to accelerate the death of a patient who is seriously ill, unless it is proved that the act was not done in good faith with the consent of the patient and for the purpose of saving him from severe pain in an illness believed to be of an incurable and fatal character. Under this formula it would be for the physician, if charged, to show that the patient was seriously ill, but for the prosecution to prove that the physician acted from some motive other than the humanitarian one allowed to him by law.[8]

This measure, if it were passed, would accept the view of Lord Dawson that there should be no formalities and that everything should be left to the discretion of the doctor. But it would leave the issue to the discretion of the doctor by law, and so would remove from doctors the fear of the law that now hangs over them. There would be no danger in it, because it would simply legalize a practice that, according to Lord Dawson and many other eminent medical men, is already widespread and beneficial.

The bill would clearly allow the medical practitioner to administer the culminating dose in a series regarded as necessary to deaden pain, and to this extent it would I think be merely declaratory, though useful as clarifying the law. But the wording I have suggested would also permit the practitioner, with the consent of his patient, to anticipate the final and painful stage of the disease, by administering a drug the immediate intention of which

---

[8] I have not followed the English bill of 1936, and the similar measure proposed by the American society, in limiting the formula to patients over 21; this seems to me to be unnecessary in a measure that does not give the patient the right to euthanasia. The use that may be made of my proposed measure in respect of patients who are minors is best left to the good sense of the doctor, taking into account, as he always does, the wishes of the parents as well as those of the child.

is to bring the patient's life to an end. In this respect the measure would confer protection on the doctor for an act that, though motivated by the strongest instincts of humanity, is probably at the moment a serious crime under the law.

The moral issue under this bill would be much clearer than under the bills previously proposed by the English and American societies. Under the latter bills the legislative question is whether you approve of euthanasia, for the setting up of a state euthanasia referee implies a judgment that voluntary euthanasia is right. Under the bill here proposed, the rightness or wrongness of euthanasia would not be directly in issue, for the bill would merely leave this question to the discretion and conscience of the individual medical practitioner. Under this bill, the question for opponents would be not "Do you approve of euthanasia?" but "Do you think euthanasia so clearly wrong that a doctor should be punished for administering euthanasia to end hopeless pain even though he thinks his act to be required by the most solemn duty of his profession?" In other words, the moral question would no longer be whether euthanasia is right, but whether the doctor should be punished. If the law were to remove its ban on euthanasia, the effect would merely be to leave this subject to the individual conscience.

This proposal would not only test the sincerity of those medical opponents who objected to the earlier English measure, but would also be easy to defend, as restoring personal liberty in a field in which men differ on the question of conscience, and as bringing the law into accord with the ethical feeling of most doctors and with the actual practice of many of them. This less formal measure would also create less strain within the family than the rigid legalities of the bills hitherto proposed by the two societies, and this would be a partial answer to one of the objections made to those bills. However, to the extent that strain within the family is a necessary accompaniment of voluntary euthanasia it must be accepted as the lesser evil.

The present position is that the advocate of euthanasia is liable to be outvoted by an alliance between two extremes. There are those who oppose any form of euthanasia on religious principle. And there are those who support the medical practice of euthanasia, but who are afraid that a measure like the English bill of 1936 would restrict rather than facilitate it. The bill here proposed should be much easier of acceptance by advanced medical opinion because, except in its requirement of the patient's consent, it would do nothing more than give formal legislative approval to these advanced practices. Incidentally, it may be observed that the argument that euthanasia is already a general practice is overstated. Inquiry among members of the medical profession seems to show that many doctors still fear to administer the humane overdose even in the last extremity, and it can hardly be said that any will take the risk of acting in the earlier stages of disease. It would be the purpose of the proposed legislation to set doctors free from the fear of the law so that they can think only of the relief of their patients.

One result of the measure that doctors would welcome is that by legalizing euthanasia it would bring the whole subject within ordinary medical practice. For example, a doctor whose patient asks for euthanasia cannot, at present, safely or wisely seek a second opinion: the responsibility for any decision he makes must be his alone. Under the proposed law the doctor could confer with a colleague in the usual way and so obtain help and advice in his onerous duty. It might be wise, out of abundance of caution, to confine the legalization of euthanasia proposed to be conferred by the bill to the case where the defendant practitioner has acted with the concurring opinion of another medical practitioner.

In one respect the suggested bill would fall short of the practice of some doctors. Under the bill as I have pro-

posed to word it, the consent of the patient would be required, whereas it seems that some doctors are now accustomed to give fatal doses without consulting the
patient. I take it to be clear that no legislative sanction
can be accorded to this practice, in so far as the course of
the disease is deliberately anticipated. The essence of the
measures proposed by the two societies is that euthanasia
should be voluntarily accepted by the patient.

The legalization of voluntary euthanasia might require
a change in the present habit of some medical men of
deceiving their patients. They will not admit to the patient suffering from cancer that he is doomed to a pitiful
end; and instances have occurred of doctors proceeding
to remarkable lengths to keep up the deception. For my
part I think that they sometimes go too far in this; and
certainly a system of voluntary euthanasia presupposes
that the patient suffering from a painful and incurable
illness be informed of his plight so that he can make a
choice. When a patient is faced with irremediable agony,
and when he demands to be told the truth for the purpose of requiring euthanasia if he is incurable, the doctor
has no moral right to refuse him the truth, and society
has no right to deny him the only release possible—to
pass upon the midnight without pain.

Of course, in requiring the patient's consent to euthanasia, advocates of the legalization of euthanasia put
themselves in a difficulty of which their critics are not
slow to obtain the advantage. If a person is suffering
from a painful illness, and particularly if he is under the
influence of drugs, his mind may be uncertain and
variable. The patient may, as Lord Horder pointed out,
desire euthanasia during the morning depression, and
later in the day may think quite differently, or forget
all about it. Under a system of voluntary euthanasia this
change of mind may cause the doctor some embarrassment, and it was partly in an attempt to provide for it
that the English bill of 1936 and the corresponding meas-

ure proposed in America required formalities extending over some period of time in order to determine whether the patient had a settled intention. Under the proposal here put forward, this kind of safeguard would disappear. However, the problem can be exaggerated. Every law has to face difficulties in application, and these difficulties are not a conclusive argument against a law if it has a beneficial operation. The measure here proposed is designed to meet the situation where the patient's consent to euthanasia is clear and incontrovertible. The physician, conscious of the need to protect himself against malicious accusations, can devise his own safeguards appropriate to the circumstances; he would normally be well advised to get the patient's consent in writing, just as is now the practice before operations. Sometimes the patient's consent will be particularly clear because he will have expressed a desire for ultimate euthanasia while he is still clear-headed and before he comes to be racked by pain; if the expression of desire is never revoked, but rather is reaffirmed under the pain, there is the best possible proof of full consent. If, on the other hand, there is no such settled frame of mind, and if the physician chooses to administer euthanasia when the patient's mind is in a variable state, he will be walking in the margin of the law and may find himself unprotected. Under the measure as I have worded it the burden of proof would be on the prosecution to prove that the patient did not consent. If desired the burden could, instead, be put on the physician to show that the patient consented.

While confining the new legalization of euthanasia to the case where the patient has consented, there would be no need to upset the present law whereby narcotics may be given to any extent necessary to deaden pain. A patient who accepts the relief afforded by these drugs must be taken to accept also the inevitable effects upon his body of their potent action. It would be inhumane and impracticable to expect the physician, in administering

344

them, to bring to the forefront of the patient's mind their
secondary effects. In order to put the law beyond all possibility of doubt, it might be well to provide for this
situation in a separate clause. It might also be expressly
provided, for the avoidance of doubt, that a physician
should not be legally responsible for failing to prolong
the life of one suffering from an illness involving severe
pain and believed by the physician to be of an incurable
and fatal character.

These various provisions might be worded in the following way:

1. For the avoidance of doubt, it is hereby declared
that it shall be lawful for a physician whose patient is
seriously ill—

(*a*) to administer to the patient drugs lawfully made
and sold for the purpose of keeping patients insensitive
to pain or of inducing sleep or unconsciousness, and to
increase the doses of such drugs to the extent necessary
to compensate for the establishment of the patient's tolerance thereof; and

(*b*) to refrain from taking steps to prolong the patient's life by medical means;

—unless in either case it is proved that the act was not
done, or the omission was not made, in good faith for
the purpose of saving the patient from severe pain in an
illness believed to be of an incurable and fatal character.

2. It shall be lawful for a physician, after consultation
with another physician, to accelerate by any merciful
means the death of a patient who is seriously ill, unless
it is proved that the act was not done in good faith with
the consent of the patient and for the purpose of saving
him from severe pain in an illness believed to be of an
incurable and fatal character.

There should be included a section defining "physician"
as any person licensed (or registered) for the practice of
medicine in the state concerned.

It remains to point out one other difference between

the previous bills, adopted by the English and American societies, and the measure here suggested. The previous bills would have created what may be called a human right to euthanasia. Under the present suggestion, no patient would have a right to euthanasia: it would be in the discretion of his doctor to agree or to decline. This difference is, however, more apparent than real. Even under the previous bills, it was not contemplated that the patient's own doctor should be under a positive duty to do an act that might be against his conscience. In practice, the administration of euthanasia must depend on finding a doctor who is willing to do it. If the measure here proposed became law, a patient would be able to inquire frankly of his doctor whether he is prepared to end life mercifully in case of need. At present, such an inquiry cannot be expected to be truthfully answered. Under the new rule, patients would be able to choose the doctor whom they trust to act as they wish in this important matter. Some may wish to be satisfied that their physician will never in any circumstances administer euthanasia; others may feel that the knowledge that euthanasia is open to them is a reassurance. On a question like this there is surely everything to be said for the liberty of the individual.

Other proposals for euthanasia

The question of legalizing suicide and voluntary euthanasia in specific circumstances does not confine itself to the case of the painful, fatal illness. There is, for example, the incapacitating but non-painful affliction, such as paralysis. Has a man the right to demand to be released from a living death, if he regards his affliction as that? As science produces more remedies to prolong life, without arresting decay of the intellect, the question becomes more acute. Again, a person who knows himself to have contracted a mortal disease may, even in its early stages, wish for euthanasia in order to save himself from total dependence on others.

Persons condemned to long periods of imprisonment, or ordered to be detained in hospitals for the criminally insane, sometimes prefer death. They may succeed in committing suicide, but at present every effort is made to prevent them, partly because such a suicide is bad publicity.[9] There have been many cases where persons charged with capital crime, who wished to die, pleaded guilty as the surest way of effecting their purpose.

If the present attitude towards suicide were reversed, these problems of voluntary euthanasia, where an exercise of volition is possible, would be largely solved. But the argument for a change of attitude becomes far less strong when the attention is turned to involuntary euthanasia, as for example in the case of senile dementia. It may, indeed, be that mankind will one day have to revise its present ethics of keeping people alive. It is increasingly common for men and women to reach an age of "second childishness and mere oblivion," with a loss of almost all adult faculties except that of digestion. When the mind goes, purely animal health seems to improve. These facts are reflected in increasing rates of admission to mental hospitals, increasing numbers in those hospitals, and constant problems of overcrowding.[1] The ultimate logic of preserving the body while the mind decays would be the

[9] See, for example, the moving story told in John Edward Allen: *Inside Broadmoor* (London, 1952), p. 171, and also that related by Sir Winston Churchill in *Parliamentary Debates (House of Commons)*, vol. 453, col. 1440 (July 15, 1948).

[1] According to a report of the British Board of Control published on September 28, 1955 (H.M.S.O.), mental hospitals in England and Wales were overcrowded by as many as 18,932 patients in 1954. Admissions numbered 71,699, compared with 72,069 in 1953 and 55,856 in 1950. About one third of the patients admitted were over 55 years of age and about one fifth were over 65 years or over.

preservation of the physical part of human beings to eternity in some culture-solution, if such a thing were possible.

At present the problem has certainly not reached the degree of seriousness that would warrant an effort being made to change traditional attitudes towards the sanctity of life of the aged. Only the grimmest necessity could bring about a change that, however cautious in its approach, would probably cause apprehension and deep distress to many people, and inflict a traumatic injury upon the accepted code of behaviour built up by two thousand years of the Christian religion. It may be, however, that as the problem becomes more acute it will itself cause a reversal of generally accepted values. Sir George Thomson, in his recent book *The Foreseeable Future,* points out that if all the causes of senility are discovered and found to be curable, all death will be by accident or intent. Such a situation, he says, "will profoundly alter men's attitude to death, and perhaps not for the better. It may make them cowardly, for there will be more to lose. Perhaps, and that is what one would hope, they will become more philosophical, willing to resign their place on earth after a long innings and make way for new life."

To discuss this problem is to anticipate vexations that for one reason or another may never eventuate. Even at present, however, the problem of values is a practical one in two respects. In the first place, it has to be faced by the physician who has to decide whether to continue his exertions to keep alive a senile person or other incurable invalid. Medical science has already reached a stage when life can be prolonged in the face of the most appalling cankers; the physician has to decide how long he will continue the battle he is slowly but inevitably losing. There is almost no discussion of the ethics of this situation in the medical world, notwithstanding that it is now an everyday problem of general practice; obviously it is awkward for practising physicians to make public pronouncements upon their attitude towards it. In the second place, the scale of values generally accepted may guide the path of scientific research. Sir George Thomson, in his discussion of the problem of old age to which reference has already been made, suggested that it might be more profitable to concentrate on the post-ponement of senility rather than to attack the remaining killing diseases. The suggestion evidently derives from current ethical attitudes: there is nothing wrong in a death from natural causes; but if man once becomes able to control the disease, he may not replace the natural death by one of his own contrivance, even though the death he inflicts is painless while nature's way is by vile torture.

The other problem of involuntary euthanasia is in respect of hopelessly defective infants. While the Euthanasia Society of England has never advocated this, the Euthanasia Society of America did include it in its original program. The proposal certainly escapes the chief objection to the similar proposal for senile dementia: it does not create a sense of insecurity in society, because infants cannot, like adults, feel anticipatory dread of being done to death if their condition should worsen. Moreover, the proposal receives some support on eugenic grounds, and more importantly on humanitarian grounds —both on account of the parents, to whom the child will be a burden all their lives, and on account of the handicapped child itself. (It is not, however, proposed that any child should be destroyed against the wishes of its parents.) Finally, the legalization of euthanasia for handicapped children would bring the law into closer relation to its practical administration, because juries do not regard parental mercy-killing as murder. For these various reasons the proposal to legalize humanitarian infanticide is put forward from time to time by individuals.[2] They

---

[2] Millard S. Everett wrote, in his *Ideals of Life* (New York, 1954), p. 347: "My personal feeling—and I don't ask anyone to agree with

remain in a very small minority, and the proposal may at present be dismissed as politically insignificant. However, as was shown in the first chapter (pp. 19–20), even the present law which forbids humanitarian infanticide is capable of being interpreted or applied in a merciful manner.

---

me—is that eventually, when public opinion is prepared for it, no child shall be admitted into the society of the living who would be certain to suffer any social handicap—for example, any physical or mental defect that would prevent marriage or would make others tolerate his company only from a sense of mercy. . . . Life in early infancy is very close to non-existence, and admitting a child into our society is almost like admitting one from potential to actual existence, and viewed in this way only normal life should be accepted." In England the most outspoken exponent of this opinion is Alderman W. L. Dingley: see *The Times* (London), February 16 and June 13, 1955. The question was debated in a B.B.C. broadcast, "Any Questions?", March 1, 1955: only one member of the panel agreed with Alderman Dingley, and the applause showed that the audience agreed with the majority view. One member, who expressed the opinion that every baby had a soul, received loud applause.

TABLE OF CASES

i

INDEX

abortion: among married women, 211*n*, 224–5; biology of pregnancy, 227–9; brain, commencement of, 231; burden of proof of legality, 180–3; Catholic attitude, 190, 192–6; Christian attitude, 148–52, 190–6; dead fetus, 147*n*, 191; definitions, 146–7; in Denmark, 223*n*, 235–6, 241, 245–7; ectopic pregnancy, 201–3; eugenic, 174–6, 233–4, 238; in Finland, 236, 247; in Germany, 223*n*; guilt of mother, 153–5; history of law, 148–52; hospital practice, 168–9; illegal, 206–15, 230–1; for incest, 234; Jewish attitude, 192; medical etiquette, 183–7; medical practice, 187–91; mental grounds for, 166–76, 241; partial solutions, 233–5; present law, England, 152–6, 160–80, 183–6; present law, United States, 156–60, 164–86; problem of ends and means, 198–205; proposals for reform, 216–25; Protestant attitude to, 192; psychiatric grounds, 166–76, 241; quickening, 149, 151–2, 157–9, 229–30; for rape, 161–2, 234, 238; social facts of, 206–15; in Soviet Union, 219–20; spontaneous, 226–7; in Sweden, 235; terminology, 146–7; therapeutic, 160–91; three fears,

abortion (*continued*)
221–5; time of viability, 146–7; tubal pregnancy, 201–3
accessory before the fact, 297
Adam and original sin, 16, 52, 61–2, 150, 194
adultery, 122–5, 129–38
aging, problems of, 347–9
anæsthetics, 61–3
animals, suicide of, 250
Aquinas, 55, 151, 264–5, 268
Aristotle, 148–9, 252
Arles, Council of, 257
artificial insemination: adultery, 122–5, 129–38; definition, 112; divorce and nullity, 118; eugenics of, 116; false declaration, 127–8; history, 112–13; legitimacy of child, 118–21; masturbation, 130, 138–40; medical attitude, 113–14; medical practice, 112–17, 120, 140; New York regulations, 125–6; social issues, 141–5; statutory rape, 127; theological opinions, 129–41
Augustana Lutherans, 56
Augustine, St.: on marriage, baptism, and original sin, 16, 52–3; on pain in childbirth, 61–2; on suicide, 255–8; on the soul, 150–1; on war, 199*n*
Aurelius, Marcus, 253

Bacon, Francis, 311

A NOTE ON THE AUTHOR

GLANVILLE LLEWELYN WILLIAMS was born in Wales in 1911. He was educated at Cowbridge School, Glamorganshire; University College of Wales, Aberystwyth; and St. John's College, Cambridge (B.A., 1933; M.A., Ph.D., 1936; LL.D., 1946). He was called to the Bar at the Middle Temple in 1935. He was Professor of Public Law, and later Quain Professor of Jurisprudence at the University of London from 1945 to 1955. Since then he has been a Fellow of Jesus College, Cambridge and, since 1966, Professor of English Law in the University of Cambridge. He has written eight books for the legal profession and has contributed extensively to legal periodicals, but this is his first book addressed to the general reader. In the spring of 1956, while he was Visiting Professor on the Faculty of Law at Columbia University in New York he delivered the James S. Carpentier Lectures.

A NOTE ON THE TYPE

This book is set on the Linotype in GRANJON, *a type named in compliment to Robert Granjon, who in 1523 began his career as type-cutter and printer, working in Antwerp, in Lyon, at the Vatican and Medici presses in Rome, and in Paris, where he died in 1590. Granjon, the boldest and most original designer of his time, was one of the first to practice the trade of type-founder apart from that of printer.*

Linotype GRANJON *was designed by George W. Jones, who based his drawings upon a face used by Claude Garamond (1510–1561) in his beautiful French books.* GRANJON *more closely resembles Garamond's own type than do any of the various modern faces that bear his name.*

The typography and binding designs are based on originals by W. A. Dwiggins.